TELL FREEDOM

TELL FREEDOM

by

PETER ABRAHAMS

COMPLETE AND UNABRIDGED

faber and faber

LONDON BOSTON

First published in 1954
by Faber and Faber Limited
3 Queen Square, London WC1N 3AU
First published in Faber Paperbacks in 1981
Reprinted 1982, 1985 and 1988
Printed in Great Britain by
Richard Clay Ltd, Bungay, Suffolk

© *1954, 1981 Peter Abrahams*

ISBN 0 571 11777 5 Faber Paperbacks
ISBN 0 571 11778 3 Non-net Paper covers

For
MY MOTHER, MY SISTER, AND ZENA
and all those others who,
in their different ways,
asked me to tell this.

And judgment is turned away backward, and justice standeth afar off: for truth is fallen in the street, and equity cannot enter.

ISAIAH

BOOK ONE

I

I pushed my nose and lips against the pane and tried to lick a raindrop sliding down on the other side. As it slid past my eyes, I saw the many colours in the raindrop. . . . It must be warm in there. Warm and dry. And perhaps the sun would be shining in there. The green must be the trees and the grass; and the brightness, the sun. . . . I was inside the raindrop, away from the misery of the cold damp room. I was in a place of warmth and sunshine, inside my raindrop world.

'Lee.'

The sound jerked me out of my raindrop world. I was at the window, looking out, feeling damp.

'Lee.'

I sensed that that was the sound by which I was identified. I turned and looked at the man who had made it. He was tall, thin and dark. He had a big head, wide forehead, and long face that tapered down to a narrow chin. His eyes were big, round, and hooded. There was a softness in them. He leaned back in a chair, his legs stretched in front of him, the right crossed over the left. He held his right hand out to the fire in the centre of the room. With his left he played with the hair of a girl who sat on the floor beside his chair.

I knew that man. Although I seemed to be seeing him for the first time, he was no stranger to me. He belonged most naturally and intimately to me and my world.

The man said:

'Come, Lee. Tell us what you see and we'll make it into a story.'

The way he looked at me disturbed me. I felt tense and desperate suddenly. I was unsure of this man, unsure of what he wanted from me. I turned my eyes from his face. It was then that I saw the woman on the other side of the fire. The word 'Mother' leaped to my mind. I burst out crying and ran to her. I knew her. She was Mother. She belonged to me. With her I had no doubts, no uncertainties. With her everything was always all right. She folded her arms about me and held me tight. She whispered words of comfort till I stopped crying.

Leaning on her knees, I turned to the man again. And then I knew that he was my father. He was almost as safe as she was. . . . Mother and Father go together. . . . I knew that instinctively. It was silly to have cried.

I looked at the children on the floor. There was a boy and two girls. These were my brother and sisters. These were my people and I was seeing them for the first time in a way that I could remember for the rest of my life. What went before I know only from hearsay. A little of what came after has slipped back into the shadows.

I can build what went before out of hearsay and after-knowledge.

My mother was a member of the Cape Coloured community. Coloured is the South African word for the half-caste community that was a by-product of the early contact between black and white. The first children of Europe who reached the Cape of Storms were men without women. They set up a half-way house to the East there. There was intercourse between white men and black women. The results were neither white nor black. So, the Cape Coloureds began. Later, when white women came to the Cape, the white men were more discreet in their taking. But the coloured community continued to grow. During the days of slavery political prisoners from the Dutch East Indies were brought into the country. They too, went into the racial melting-pot.

In time the coloureds emerged as a distinctive community.

My father came from Ethiopia. He was the son of land-owners and slave-owners. He had seen much of Europe before he came to South Africa. In after years, when my mother talked about him, she told wonderful stories of his adventures in strange parts of the world.

I recall a time when she made me recite, like a catechism, my father's family tree. It went something like this: 'I am Peter Henry Abrahams Deras, son of James Henry Abrahams Deras whose name at home was Karim Abdul, son of In-gedi(e) of Addis who was the son of somebody else who fought in some battle who was the son of somebody else, who was the son of somebody else who was with Menelik when he defeated the Italians. . . .' It went on for a very long time. And the 'Deras' or 'de Ras' was the family title.

My mother was the widow of a Cape Malay (a product of the East Indies' strain of the coloured community) who had died the previous year and left her with two children. She was alone except for an elder sister, Margaret. My mother and her two children were living with her sister Margaret when she met the man from Ethiopia. Margaret was the fairer of the two sisters, fair enough to 'pass'. Her husband was a Scot. He worked on the mines. They had a little girl with blonde hair and blue eyes. They lived in 19th Street, Vrededorp. And there, in the street, the two brown children, my brother and sister, played with their cousin, the little white girl with blonde hair and blue eyes.

To this street and this house came the Ethiopian. There, he wooed my mother. There, he won her. They married from that house. They found a house of their own further down the street. They made of it a home of love and laughter. From there they sent their boy and girl to the Coloured School above Vrededorp. From there the Ethiopian went to work on the mines each morning. To that house he returned at the end of each day. In that house my sister, the third child in the family, was born. And there, early on the morning of 19th March 1919, I was born.

It was there, in that house, one rainy day, that a voice said: 'Lee.'

And I turned from the raindrop world and saw my family; my mother and my father, big brother Harry, big sister Margaret, and not-so-big sister Natalie: that was the beginning of awareness. I do not know exactly how old I was. Three, perhaps; or four; or perhaps a little older.

There are sharp, clear-cut flashes of memory. . . .

I found a stray kitten in the street one day. It had hardly any fur on its body which was dotted with sores. Thick yellow matter oozed from its eyes. Its left front paw was cut and bleeding. I picked it up and took it home. Only my mother and Natalie were at home. The other two were at school, my father was at work. I went through the muddy lane to our back door.

'Look, ma!' Natalie cried.

My mother turned from her washing.

'What *have* you got, Lee?'

A name for the kitten flashed into my mind.

'It is Moe, ma.' He made a sound like that.

'Well, get him out of here at once!'

I stood my ground at the door.

'No. He's mine!'

My mother came nearer and looked at the kitten. She shook her head.

'Where did you find him?'

'The street.'

'Well, take him back there.'

'No.'

'You can't keep him.'

'No.'

'Go on, put him in the street and come back so that I can wash you. The thing may give you some disease.'

12

'No.'

'I said go, Lee!' That was the voice of authority.

I began to whimper. I held the kitten tight. Nobody was going to part me from Moe. He was, quite suddenly, the most important thing in my world. Half-fearful, half-defiant, I screamed:

'I won't! I won't! I won't!'

That was the beginning of a battle that lasted, intermittently, throughout the long day. It flared up again in the afternoon when Harry and Margaret returned from school. It reached new heights when Harry managed to get Moe away from me. I screamed and raved like one gone mad.

In the end it was my father, the law-giver of the family, who solved the problem. He said I could keep Moe provided he was bathed in a strong disinfectant. I wanted to get into the tub with Moe but the family would not allow it. Nor would they permit us to eat out of the same plate. We did, however, have two identical little enamelled plates and ate side by side on the floor. And often, when the others were not looking, we ate out of each other's plates. The food was much more tasty that way.

I had a cat called Moe
My little brother Moe;
He had a bleeding toe,
Poor sickly little Moe.

I loved my sickly Moe,
I nursed his bleeding toe;
We played all day, you know,
And O, we loved it so!

One day death came to Moe,
No blood dripped from his toe;
I lost my brother Moe,
I grieved and grieved him so.

My brother Harry made a coffin out of an old fruit box; my sister Margaret made a little white dress for Moe. One Sunday morning we took him to the Ottoman's Valley above Vrededorp, and buried him. While I prayed with tears streaming down my face, my brother and sisters were in hoots of laughter.

There was a sudden thunderstorm. I had to cut my prayers short, cover Moe quickly, and run for shelter. This amused the others more. I did not forgive them for a long time.

There are flashes of memory.

I remember the family picnics on Sundays. My mother and father would lie on the grass talking. We children would play about on the grass. The grass always seemed very green, the sky was always far away. On Sundays, in the Ottoman's Valley, my mother always had a basket filled with things to eat. And the sun always shone on our picnic Sundays. I remember the cool sweetness of an orange after I had run myself silly.

I remember going to Sunday school with my sisters, and the special kind of quiet the place had, and the special kind of voices in which people spoke and prayed. And I remember the beautiful cards I was given as I went out of the Sunday school.

I remember the stirring music of the Salvation Army Band.

I remember the marching children in the Band of Hope and seeing my brother and sisters marching among them with their broad purple sashes, and crying because I could not wear a sash and march with them.

I remember the peaceful laughter of our house. Everyone in it seemed to be happy.

I remember my first experience of crime and punishment. Fresh milk was unknown in Vrededorp. Those who could afford it, used tins of sweetened condensed milk. Two holes were made in the top of the tin and the milk was poured out. The first time, the tin of milk was left within my reach on the table. There was no one in the room so I tasted it. It was good. After that, I bided my time and stole milk whenever I could. The safest thing was to take the tin under the bed. I could not be surprised there. I was caught by my mother one morning. She pulled me from under the bed and beat me till I could not sit on my seat. And while she beat me she wept. It made the beating all the more painful.

I remember my mother and father merging into each other in my mind. Together, they were my symbol of peace and laughter and security.

Then my father died.

I remember the shadow that was over our house: the solemn faces of my brother and sisters; the new strangeness of my mother. It surprised me to see her crying.

I remember the many people who suddenly invaded the house, making me feel a stranger in my own home. My mother's sister, Aunt Margaret, became a real person for me then. It was she who did the things my mother had always done. She fed and clothed me, and when I wanted a piece of bread I asked her, not my mother.

I remember someone lifted me up and I looked into the coffin where my father lay. Because he did not smile at me, and because my mother cried, I cried too.

Then they took him away. And I never saw him again.

With his going, the order and stability that had been in my life, dissolved. There was no bread-winner so we had to leave the place that had been our home.

[ii]

I walked down Nineteenth Street with the strange woman. And as we went, I became aware of a noise. I tried to place it, but it was everywhere. A continuous deep rumble pervaded the world. It seemed to come from the bowels of the earth, to reach down from the spaces of the heavens. What was it? Where did it come from? Why?

'Hear the noise?' I said to the woman.

'What noise?' She was not interested.

I felt homesick suddenly and looked back. I looked for it but could not identify our house. Each house looked like the next, all strange. And the people about me were all strangers. I panicked. I tried to pull free of the woman's grip.

'Where are we going?' I asked.

'To the station.' Her voice was more kindly.

'Why?'

'We are going to Elsburg.'

I began to whimper.

'I want to go home. I want my mother.'

The woman spoke soothingly and quieted me down. About me was the big world. There was so much of it. Motors flashed by. Trams rumbled along. Large horses dragging huge carts pranced up and down the wide Delarey Street. Shop windows were filled with new and interesting things. My head jerked from left to right. I forgot my home and my mother. All this was new, excitingly new.

At Fordsburg station our train was on the point of departure. We scrambled on. The train moved off. The engine puffed and screamed a shrill warning. We found a place near the window. The woman sat on the hard wooden seat. I stood with my nose pressed against the dirty window-pane, watching the world go by.

The engine puffed and snorted. Every now and then, when the train curved round a bend, it screamed its shrill warning. And the wheels, under me, whispered:

'On a-w-a-y. O-n a-w-a-y. O-n a-w-a-y.' Then they said: 'On away. On away. On away.' Then they said: 'On away, on away, on away.' And after that, for nearly all the time, they said:

'Onawayonawayonawayonawayonawayonawayonaway.'

Soon the houses and buildings were far behind. The land came rushing up, only to rush away again: vast stretches of green land, and brown land; land rising and falling. Sometimes hills and mountains flashed by. Sometimes we went through a mountain and were in darkness. And the engine would scream its warning and we would come out of the mountain. Tall telegraph poles come up to meet us, then rush away with clock-like regularity. And all the time the wheels said, 'Onawayonawayonawayonawayonawayonaway-onawayonawayonaway,' till I was drunk with it all.

I was hazy and sleepy and very tired when we stepped off the train at the little gravel siding at Elsburg. The sun had gone down. There was a softness over the land. It made everything more beautiful than it really was.

The woman took my hand and we set off on our four-mile walk through the beautiful land. When we got to her house at the location, I was asleep on my feet. Vrededorp was far away and I was happy and tired, so I tumbled into a strange bed and slept deeply.

[iii]

I woke in a strange place. Fear took hold of me. I longed for the familiar, for my mother and for the home I knew.

For days, till I grew used to the people with whom I lived and familiar with the place, I was miserable and painfully homesick.

In time the woman became Aunt Liza to me, a person with a name. And there was comfort in her having a name. Her husband, whom I had hardly noticed the night before, was Uncle Sam.

When I got up Uncle Sam had already gone to his work. In common with all the men, as well as some women, of Elsburg location, he worked on one of the nearby white farms.

The routine of my days at Elsburg began that morning. I made my bed. Then I went outside to the sunny side of the house with a small bowl of cold water and a piece of home-made soap. There I washed. Then I went in to breakfast. This was a plate of *mielie pap*. Maize is crushed to a powder slightly coarser than flour. A saucepan of salted water is brought to the boil, then the required amount of maize is added and stirred continuously. It is cooked in about fifteen minutes. The result is *mielie pap*. For breakfast, it is thinned down to a runny liquid. A plate full of that and a mug of black coffee was my breakfast. I had the choice of having two teaspoons of sugar either in my coffee or over my *pap*. I elected to have one over the *pap* and one in the coffee. The coffee remained bitter and I could hardly taste the sugar over the *pap*.

After breakfast I had five minutes to myself. I sat in the warmest and most protected spot I could find. I took stock of the place that was now my home.

The houses were built in two lines, as they would be on either side of a wide road, each line facing the road. Only, there was no road. What could have been the road was a strip of land, dotted with mounds and potted with holes. Here and there footpaths had worn the grass away; here and there, children had, by constant playing on the same spot, created patches of dusty sand. The location stood on a rising between a valley on the one side and a river on the other. To the east and west, the land sloped away gently.

On windy days the sand patches were stirred to life and everything, all in all the houses, was coated with the fine, gritty sand that hung like a thick mist over the place. In the rainy season, the pot-holes in what might have been the wide street, were filled and became stagnant pools. When the rainy season passed the children fished for tadpoles in those pools. If the wet spell had been long, we often found frogs in the mud after the water had seeped away.

The houses were usually two-roomed. Here and there a person had added a smaller room to the back. But where that had been done there was not the bit of land left on which to grow a few green vegetables, for each house stood in a small piece of fenced-off land. And the land belonged to the farmers for whom the people of the location worked. And behind the fenced-off little plots, spreading in all directions, were vast stretches of rolling land.

The houses were made by those who lived in them. And because they had no security of tenure few took pride in what they put up. The walls were of unbaked mud bricks held together by straw. The roofs were sheets of corrugated-iron nailed or screwed together over rafters. And the holes and open spaces were stopped up with sacking and pieces of canvas. Neither cold nor wet was ever effectively kept out.

The place, itself, seemed to fit into the bleak austerity of the land about it. There was not a tree in the valley below. To the east and west there was just the harshness of the sloping land under the curving sky. Even the sky seemed cold and remote and very far away.

Only the river promised a touch of softness in this hard place. A line of willows marked the course it took. They were the only trees in all the land about. I would go there, I promised myself. I would go down to the river and look at the trees.

Aunt Liza came out of the house. My five minutes were up. She gave me two pails.

'The well is up the street.'

I took the pails and marched out of the gate. Women and children were already there. I was the stranger and everyone turned to look at me. I looked steadily at the ground. A little boy, no bigger than myself, arrived after me.

At last, all the others had their water and went and only the boy and I were left. It was my turn but I did not know how to work the well. I looked at the boy.

'You go first,' I said.

He started towards the handle then changed his mind.

'No. It is your turn.'

I had hoped to watch and learn from him.

The bucket stood on the edge of the well. It was weighted with an iron bar. I took hold of the handle and began to unwind the rope.

'The bucket,' the boy said.

It was still on the mouth of the well. A long strand of the rope dangled down into the darkness of the well. I let go of the handle, leaned forward, and pushed the bucket in. As I straightened up, the rope jerked taut, the handle swung in a downward arc. It struck me flush on the mouth, then on the upper part of the chest. I fell flat on my back. My jaw was paralysed. I swallowed blood. Above me the handle whirled dangerously. As suddenly as it started, the handle stopped. I got up slowly. My chest and jaw were beginning to hurt.

The boy was holding his sides, laughing. Then he saw the blood dripping from my mouth. He looked frightened suddenly. His eyes opened wide.

'Are you going to die?' he whispered.

Aunt Liza stalked up to the well, raging at the top of her voice.

'The first damn thing you'll learn here is that time's not to be wasted! I'll take the skin off your damn back if you play around when I send you for something! When'll I finish all that damn washing! You'll have to learn or I'll damn kill you!'

Neighbours pushed their heads out of doors to see what the storm was about. When Aunt Liza saw my face, concern replaced her rage.

'What happened?'

I tried to speak but could not. I was too hurt to cry. In her anxiety she shook me.

'What happened?'

The frightened boy whispered: 'Is he going to die, Auntie?'

Aunt Liza turned to him. And he told her what had happened. He ended with his big question.

'Is he going to die, Auntie?'

'Of course not, Andries!' Aunt Liza snapped.

'But I saw a dog bleeding and he died,' Andries said anxiously.

'Of course you didn't know,' Aunt Liza said to me. 'Why didn't I think of that?' Her brow creased in a worried frown.

Andries' mother, our next-door neighbour, came cursing to the well, promising hell and damnation to Andries for being so long about the water. She, too, was silenced by my bleeding mouth.

Aunt Liza put her arm about my shoulders and hurried me down to the house. From across the way someone called: 'Wash his mouth with salt! That'll do it!'

When you have a cut, it is bathed with salt water. They say the sting of it is good. They say it kills the pain. When your nose bleeds, you inhale salt water up the nostrils. They say it will stop the bleeding. When you have earache you bathe your ear with warm salt water. When you have a sore throat, you gargle with salt water. If your eye is inflamed and sore, salt water eases it. When you have toothache you fill your mouth with hot salt water and get it to soak into the aching tooth. If you have stomach-ache, a large mug of warm salt water is the best cure. It either drives the sickness down or brings it up. . . . Salt was the greatest cure-all of my childhood days. And, it nearly always worked!

I washed my mouth repeatedly with salt water till the bleeding stopped. The intense pain soon passed. The inside of my mouth was sore, one of my teeth was loose, my lips were badly swollen, but no real damage had been done. And I was soon fit to go back to the well.

With the help of Andries who became my friend once he was sure I was not going to die, I learned how to handle the well. Together, we carried a relay of pails, first for Aunt Liza, then for his mother.

It was washing day for Aunt Liza. I was to discover that every day was washing day for Aunt Liza. And nearly all afternoons and nights were given up to ironing. Uncle Sam brought home a huge bundle of dirty laundry each night, and took away a neat bundle each morning. For a long time this was a mystery to me. Then I discovered it was the laundry of the white people for whom Uncle Sam worked.

Aunt Liza had two tubs out in the yard. A string of drying lines criss-crossed so that every inch of space was used when the lines were full. One of the tubs stood on stones over an open fire built in a scooped-out hollow of the ground. Near it was a huge pile of pieces of dried cow dung. She fed the fire with these.

When we had brought enough water for her washing needs, we filled the rusty rain-water tank. Then two pails filled the drinking-bowl inside the house. The water I poured into the drinking-bowl was yellow, almost opaque. I watched the sediment settle. When it was clear, I saw a black water-spider moving slowly over the sediment. Other signs of tiny life wriggled about as well. I told Aunt Liza. She laughed.

'You'll get used to it. They haven't killed me. Just don't drink the water at the bottom. They stay there. Now go with Andries and find some manure, and be quick because I'm short. You'll find the sacks in the corner. There's a piece of bread in the bin.'

I found the sacks, and a hard crust in the bin. I hurried out to Andries.

'Come!' he chanted.

He dashed away. I followed. We streaked across the virgin fields, veering slightly to the east so that we would, if we kept that course, reach the river a long, long way further on. He was getting further away from me so I called:

'Hey, Andries!'

He eased up a little. With a burst of speed I caught up with him.

'Don't run so fast.'

'We must.'

'Why?'

'Others will get all the dung.'

'Where are they?'

'Must be nearly there.'

'Where?'

'Where we get the dung, silly!'

'Where is that?'

'Shut up and come on. You'll see.'

'I'm tired.'

'Come on!'

'Let's walk a little.'

'Want Auntie Liza to lick you?'

'Why?'

'If you walk now there'll be nothing when you get there. You'll go home with empty sacks. And man, will she lick you! Seen how thick her arms are? My mother's thin but she licks like hell. Auntie Liza with her thick arms will kill. Come on!'

'But I'm tired.'

He shot away again. I had not noticed Aunt Liza's arms, but thinking of them, they became huge clubs swinging at me. I shot across the veld after Andries, forgetful of my tiredness. The space between us narrowed gradually. By the time we topped the rising of the land we were running side by side.

'There!' Andries cried.

Far ahead, a cluster of children walked across the veld, playing as they went. We eased the pace a little and trotted steadily across the wide green valley. Some way ahead, beyond the children, a herd of cows grazed under the gentle sun.

We caught up with the others. Andries was soon drawn into the play and banter. I was left on the outside. I was the new boy, the stranger. I had still to earn the right to be one of them.

Where we walked the grass was lush and taut. I could feel its sharpness on my feet where my canvas shoes had split. A little below us, to the left, in the direction of the river, were willow trees. They were stunted and their leaves were pale and transparent. They grew in two lines that were more or

23

less straight. For them to be there suggested that where we walked had been the bed of a wide, shallow river in times long gone.

The morning sun was getting warmer. The land seemed vast, unending and very quiet. And we, the children and the cattle, were the only living creatures on the earth, owned it and the sky, belonged to earth and sky. The light breeze that was about us carried the voices of the children to the cows. The cows turned their heads ponderously. One or two opened their mouths and hailed us with a placid 'Mooooo. . . .'

A cross-eyed boy who seemed to command universal respect raised his hand. We all stopped. Andries ran to me and said:

'When he says go you go looking for dung. Quickly.'

I thought of Aunt Liza's arms. I did not want the weight of those arms on my body. But I was worried about the cows. Did they bite?

'Do they bite?'

'Who?'

'Those things.' I pointed.

Andries doubled up with laughter. He turned to the others.

'Hey! He wants to know if cows bite!'

They joined in the laughter.

'He's just a dumb towny,' someone called out.

'Shut your trap!' the cross-eyed boy called. 'Go!'

They forgot my ignorance. We streaked off in all directions searching for the precious dung. Dung makes the fire that cooks the food. Dung is the fire that fights off the cold. Dung boils the washing that brings the money that pays for our bread.

We darted here and there, grabbing the dried flat cakes and shoving them into our sacks. We were not children at play. This was serious. Life depended on this. To the left of me, two boys argued over a piece of dung both had spotted at the same time. They soon came to blows. The rest were too concerned with finding dung to stop and look. I lost my

24

nervousness of the cows and darted among them, grabbing pieces of dung. I saw a huge piece and dashed for it. Another boy had seen it at the same time. We glared at each other. Two savage dogs over a bone. I remembered I was the stranger. I had to instal myself before I could expect to fight on terms of equality. I veered away and left the precious piece to him.

I filled one sack and started on the next. But now the dung became more rare. Competition became fierce. There were more dog-fights. I passed a boy on his knees, blood dripping from his nose. Two little girls were pulling each other's hair. I bumped into a boy. He pushed me over. I jumped up. He waited, his fists bunched, ready for the fight. I looked into his eyes and it seemed he was as frightened as I was. Somehow, seeing fear in his eyes, made me feel less of an outsider. I turned my back on him. I heaved the full sack on to my back and trotted away scanning the grass. I was beginning to recognize the cakes at quite a distance. The boy cursed me, a frustrated desperation in his voice.

All about me, each with sacks on his or her back, children ran; they darted first this way, then that: they stooped, grabbed, shoved dung into their sacks and were off again. The area of search widened till we ceased to be a group, till we lost contact with each other.

When I had filled both my sacks the sun was high and I was alone in a hollow strip of land. I flopped down on the ground and leaned against the sacks. I was utterly wearied. It was not just tiredness. There had been a tight desperation in the search, a nervous tension. Now that it was over I felt listless.

After a while I got up. I now had to find my way home. There was not a person in sight. If I faced about the river would be on my right. If I kept walking with the river on my right, and if I veered slightly to the left, I would be going in the general direction of home.

I heaved the sacks on to my back and climbed out of the

hollow strip. I walked steadily, anxiously, yet wearily, till I topped a slight rising. The cows grazed in the valley below. I was right. That was the way home. And down there, among the cows, were some of the children. To the left, some way behind me, were others. Yet others were far ahead, on their way home. I trudged down into the valley. I met up with some of the children and we walked in silence, each bent under the weight of dung.

Ahead of us, children walked in two's and three's. Others came behind us. Hardly a word was spoken on the journey back. The listlessness that was on me seemed on everyone else as well.

We soon left the valley of the cows and walked where everything was sombre and hard, where even the grass was stunted. We crossed deep *dongas* of eroded and eroding soil. We passed barren patches where no blade of grass grew and the earth had turned to a fine, dusty sand. The way seemed infinitely longer, returning, than it had been going. And the sacks on my back grew heavier with each step I took.

I reached home near sunset. Aunt Liza was still at her wash-tub. She straightened her back painfully. I dumped the sacks near the fire. Though the day was not hot, sweat dripped from her face. Her eyes were bloodshot. The top of her dress clung damply to her body and was wet under her arms. I noticed the thickness of her arms, and her big hands that were pitted with being in water the whole day, white as a sheet and swollen to twice their size. A tired smile softened her face.

'Tired?'

I nodded.

'First time's always the worst,' she said.

She put an arm about my shoulders and pressed me against her body. I felt strangely comforted and rewarded. The dull ache seemed to go from my back.

'Let's have some coffee,' she said.

She warmed up the remains of the breakfast coffee.

'When do we eat, Aunt Liza?'

'When Uncle Sam comes home.'

We drank our coffee. Aunt Liza went back to her tub. I found the warmest corner of the house and squatted. The coffee rumbled in my stomach. I felt warm inside and out. I leaned back against the wall and closed my eyes. . . .

Journeying from a great distance, I became aware of Aunt Liza. She shook my shoulder.

'Wake up!'

I opened my eyes.

'Come on,' Aunt Liza said.

She moved slowly, heavily; only the strength of her will seemed to hold her big body together.

The huge bundle of washing was done. The little yard was filled with clothes drying on the lines. The whites gleamed cleanly. And in the tub was a huge pile waiting to go on the lines.

I shivered and got up. I followed her out of the gate, up the wide strip of field that might have been a road, past the well, across the veld. We walked till the location was out of sight. We made for a cluster of hillocks on the other side of a valley. She stooped and picked some broad leaves that grew among the grass. She gave them to me.

'It is called *Moeroga*. Look at them carefully. You'll come by yourself to-morrow. They grow among nettles.'

I studied the leaves of wild spinach. Aunt Liza made a carrier of her apron. Deftly, quickly, she plucked the leaves. The nettles did not bother her. I worked more slowly, more clumsily. I tried to avoid the nettles but my hands were soon purple and stung as though on fire.

At last, the hollow of her apron filled. We turned back. Night was nearly on us. A fine mist hung over the veld. It grew cold. Night had fallen when we reached home.

'Build up the fire,' Aunt Liza said.

I squatted close to the fire and piled it high with dung. As the dung caught light, bluish smoke with a fragrant sweetness about it spiralled up to the misty sky. Aunt Liza came and squatted beside me. Catching some of the warmth of the fire, she prepared the *Moeroga*. I watched her work, and became aware of my gnawing hunger.

'Aunt Liza. . . .'

'Heh?'

'When does Uncle Sam come home?'

'Very hungry?'

'Yes.'

'Soon now.'

My front was warming; my back was freezing. I thought about Uncle Sam. I had not really seen him the night before. I had been too tired and worked up. What was he like? Aunt Liza had become a person to me. When I thought of her my mind said: Two huge arms that terrified Andries; a gruff but gentle voice; two bloodshot eyes in a coarse reddish brown face; a broken left front upper tooth when she smiled; great tiredness; the comfort of her rough embrace. A person. And Uncle Sam? I tried to build an image from what I had seen last night. Nothing came. Just a name: Uncle Sam.

Well, he would soon be home now. I would eat. And I would see him.

Aunt Liza crammed the *Moeroga* into a huge pot and put a stone on the lid to keep it down. I moved back from the fire. The heat was burning my face. My behind was numbing with cold. The fire gave off less smoke now. The dung glowed more brightly. And about me, in the darkness, was the noise of the cricket, the croak of the frog, and a thousand other noises I could not name. When had these begun? One moment the world had been silent, the next I was aware of all these noises. I looked into the darkness and saw the flickering lights of glow-worms go on and off continuously.

When the fire glowed at its brightest and gave off no smoke, we carried it into the kitchen and shut out the cold, the night, and the noises of the veld. I made myself comfortable on a sack in a corner on the floor and watched Aunt Liza prepare the evening meal.

She cooked a thick, lumpy *mielie pap*. When it was nearly done, she added a blob of fat. She put two iron bars across the fire, moved the *pap* to the very edge, and put on the *moeroga*.

Uncle Sam arrived. He flung open the kitchen door and brought in a gust of cold night air. He was very tall, his head was up among the rafters near the roof. But this was an illusion. I was seeing him from ground-level and he only seemed tall. In reality he was no taller than Aunt Liza. He was very thin. His face showed up the rise and fall of every bone of his skull: like skin drawn tight over a skeleton head. His eyes, small, were set deep in their sockets. They were stern, forbidding eyes. And the curve of his mouth made him the most forbidding man I had ever seen. He carried a sack slung over his shoulder.

'Hello Sam,' Aunt Liza said.

'Liz . . .' His voice was harsh.

He put the sack on the table, shut the door, hung his hat on the nail behind it, and looked at me. I lowered my eyes quickly.

'How's he?'

'Near killed himself at the well,' Aunt Liza said. 'But he picks up fast.'

'Done anything?'

'A good bit. Get the things?'

'Yes. Our debt's up to a pound.' His voice was bitter.

'Brought the washing?'

'It's outside.' To me, he said: 'Bring it in.'

'Let it be,' Aunt Liza said. 'I'm fed up with their dirt.'

I settled back in my corner. Uncle Sam sat on the bench near the fire and stared moodily into it. Aunt Liza took the *moeroga* off. From the cupboard she got three pieces of crackling. When a pig is killed, it is skinned. The thick skin is fried to a crisp brown. This is cut into square pieces and sold as crackling. There was a pig farm near Elsburg siding where the people of the location bought their crackling. Aunt Liza warmed up the three pieces. The meal was ready. She dished it into three tin plates. A dollop of *pap*, a spoonful of *moeroga*, and a piece of crackling. She sat on the bench beside Uncle Sam. He said grace:

'Thank you for the food we are now going to eat, God. Amen.'

We ate.

While we ate, four irons warmed on the fire. I marvelled at how the *moeroga* had shrunk: so much had gone into the pot, so little came out. And it was the most tasteful part of the meal. When I finished, Aunt Liza said:

'You can scrape the pot.'

With a knife I scraped the brown crust from the bottom of the *pap* pot. I discovered a delicacy, crisp and crunchy, and the tastiest part of the *pap*.

My last chore of the day was washing up. While I did it, Aunt Liza prepared my bed in the corner on the floor. Uncle Sam sat staring into the fire, picking his teeth with a used match-stick. On the fire, beside the irons, the coffee-pot brewed Uncle Sam's good-night cup. I put the dry crocks away and went back to my corner.

I took off my canvas shoes. They would last another day at most then I would have to get used to going about barefooted. Next, I took off my khaki shorts. Draughts suddenly stung my bare bottom and thighs. I hurried under the protection of the blankets. The flame from the thick home-made tallow candle fluttered. Aunt Liza poured Uncle Sam's good-night coffee. Then she cleared the table and began to iron.

I glanced furtively at Uncle Sam. The last sound he had made was to say grace. He sat, the mug of coffee in his hands, his face expressionless, his eyes fixed on one spot of the fading fire. I closed my eyes. I still had no picture of Uncle Sam. He was still not a person. He was just a name, a being, and silence, I felt afraid of him because I did not understand anything about him.

I dozed off, then woke. Aunt Liza was still ironing. Uncle Sam still sat staring fixedly at the fading fire. I dozed and woke again. Uncle Sam had gone. Aunt Liza was still ironing. The candle was nearly burnt out. The saucer on which it stood was gutted with molten tallow.

'In a minute, Sam,' Aunt Liza called.

I fell asleep.

The pattern of my days was set. Each day I would perform the tasks I had performed this day; eat the meals I had eaten this day. With skill and speed, I would perform my chores more quickly and earn time, later, for a daily visit to the river. On Sundays there would be a small piece of meat to vary the diet. Often, there was a piece of bread at midday to take the edge off my hunger. Each day Aunt Liza washed; each night I fell asleep while she ironed. In time I lost my fear of Uncle Sam's silence. There was, of course, variety. But the basic pattern of my days was as this first day had been.

[iv]

Wednesday was crackling day. On that day the children of the location made the long trek to Elsberg siding for the squares of pig's rind that passed for our daily meat. We collected a double lot of cow dung the day before; a double lot of *moeroga*.

I finished my breakfast and washed up. Aunt Liza was at her wash-tub in the yard. A misty, sickly sun was just showing. And on the open veld the frost lay thick and white on the grass.

'Ready?' Aunt Liza called.

I went out to her. She shook the soapsuds off her swollen hands and wiped them on her apron. She lifted the apron and put her hand through the slits of the many thin cotton dresses

31

she wore. The dress nearest the skin was the one with the pocket. From this she pulled a sixpenny piece. She tied it in a knot in the corner of a bit of coloured cloth.

'Take care of that. . . . Take the smaller piece of bread in the bin but don't eat it till you start back. You can have a small piece of crackling with it. Only a small piece, understand?'

'Yes, Aunt Liza.'

'All right.'

I got the bread and tucked it into the little canvas bag in which I would carry the crackling.

' 'Bye Aunt Liza.' I trotted off, one hand in my pocket, feeling the cloth where the money was. I paused at Andries's home.

'Andries!' I danced up and down while I waited. The cold was not so terrible on bare feet if one did not keep still.

Andries came trotting out of their yard. His mother's voice followed; desperate and plaintive:

'I'll skin you if you lose the money!'

'Women!' Andries said bitterly.

I glimpsed the dark, skinny woman at her wash-tub as we trotted across the veld. Behind, and in front of us, other children trotted in two's and three's.

There was a sharp bite to the morning air I sucked in; it stung my nose so that tears came to my eyes; it went down my throat like an icy draught; my nose ran. I tried breathing through my mouth but this was worse. The cold went through my shirt and shorts; my skin went pimply and chilled; my fingers went numb and began to ache; my feet felt like frozen lumps that did not belong to me, yet jarred and hurt each time I put them down. I began to feel sick and desperate.

'Jesus God in heaven!' Andries cried suddenly.

I looked at him. His eyes were rimmed in red. Tears ran down his cheeks. His face was drawn and purple, a sick look on it.

'Faster,' I said.

'Think it'll help?'

I nodded. We went faster. We passed two children, sobbing and moaning as they ran. We were all in the same desperate situation. We were creatures haunted and hounded by the cold. It was a cruel enemy who gave no quarter. And our means of fighting it were pitifully inadequate. In all the mornings and evenings of the winter months, young and old, big and small, were helpless victims of the bitter cold. Only towards noon and the early afternoon, when the sun sat high in the sky, was there a brief respite. For us, the children, the cold, especially the morning cold, assumed an awful and malevolent personality. We talked of 'It'. 'It' was a half-human monster with evil thoughts, evil intentions, bent on destroying us. 'It' was happiest when we were most miserable. Andries had told me how 'It' had, last winter, caught and killed a boy.

Hunger was an enemy too, but one with whom we could come to terms, who had many virtues and values. Hunger gave our *pap*, *moeroga*, and crackling, a feast-like quality. We could, when it was not with us, think and talk kindly about it. Its memory could even give moments of laughter. But the cold of winter was with us all the time. 'It' never really eased up. There were only more bearable degrees of 'It' at high noon and on mild days. 'It' was the real enemy. And on this Wednesday morning, as we ran across the veld, winter was more bitterly, bitingly, freezingly, real than ever.

The sun climbed. The frozen earth thawed, leaving the short grass looking wet and weary. Painfully, our feet and legs came alive. The aching numbness slowly left our fingers. We ran more slowly in the more bearable cold.

In climbing, the sun lost some of its damp look and seemed a real, if cold, sun. When it was right overhead, we struck the sandy road which meant we were nearing the siding. None of the others were in sight. Andries and I were alone

33

on the sandy road on the open veld. We slowed down to a brisk walk. We were sufficiently thawed to want to talk.

'How far?' I said.

'A few minutes,' he said.

'I've got a piece of bread,' I said.

'Me too,' he said. 'Let's eat it now.'

'On the way back,' I said. 'With a bit of crackling.'

'Good idea. . . . Race to the fork.'

'All right.'

'Go!' he said.

We shot off together, legs working like pistons. He soon pulled away from me. He reached the fork in the road some fifty yards ahead.

'I win!' he shouted gleefully, though his teeth still chattered.

We pitched stones down the road, each trying to pitch further than the other. I won and wanted to go on doing it. But Andries soon grew weary with pitching. We raced again. Again he won. He wanted another race but I refused. I wanted pitching, but he refused. So, sulking with each other, we reached the pig farm.

We followed a fenced-off pathway round sprawling white buildings. Everywhere about us was the grunt of pigs. As we passed an open doorway, a huge dog came bounding out, snarling and barking at us. In our terror, we forgot it was fenced in and streaked away. Surprised, I found myself a good distance ahead of Andries. We looked back and saw a young white woman call the dog to heel.

'Damn Boer dog,' Andries said.

'Matter with it?' I asked.

'They teach them to go for us. Never get caught by one. My old man's got a hole in his bottom where a Boer dog got him.'

I remembered I had outstripped him.

'I won!' I said.

'Only because you were frightened,' he said.

34

'I still won.'

'Scare arse,' he jeered.

'Scare arse, youself!'

'I'll knock you!'

'I'll knock you back!'

A couple of white men came down the path and ended our possible fight. We hurried past them to the distant shed where a queue had already formed. There were grown-ups and children. All the grown-ups, and some of the children, were from places other than our location.

The line moved slowly. The young white man who served us did it in leisurely fashion, with long pauses for a smoke. Occasionally he turned his back.

At last, after what seemed hours, my turn came. Andries was behind me. I took the sixpenny piece from the square of cloth and offered it to the man.

'Well?' he said.

'Sixpence crackling, please.'

Andries nudged me in the back. The man's stare suddenly became cold and hard. Andries whispered into my ear.

'Well?' the man repeated coldly.

'Please *baas*,' I said.

'What d'you want?'

'Sixpence crackling, please.'

'What?'

Andries dug me in the ribs.

'Sixpence crackling, please *baas*.'

'What?'

'Sixpence crackling, please *baas*.'

'You new here?'

'Yes, *baas*.' I looked at his feet while he stared at me.

At last he took the sixpenny piece from me. I held my bag open while he filled it with crackling from a huge pile on a large canvas sheet on the ground. Turning away, I stole a fleeting glance at his face. His eyes met mine, and there was amused, challenging mockery in them. I waited for Andries

35

at the back of the queue, out of the reach of the white man's mocking eyes.

The cold day was at its mildest as we walked home along the sandy road. I took out my piece of bread and, with a small piece of greasy crackling, still warm, on it, I munched as we went along. We had not yet made our peace so Andries munched his bread and crackling on the other side of the road.

'Dumb fool!' he mocked at me for not knowing how to address the white man.

'Scare arse!' I shouted back.

Thus, hurling curses at each other, we reached the fork. Andries saw them first and moved over to my side of the road.

'White boys,' he said.

There were three of them. Two of about our own size and one slightly bigger. They had school bags and were coming toward us up the road from the siding.

'Better run for it,' Andries said.

'Why?'

'No, that'll draw them. Let's just walk along, but quickly.'

'Why?' I repeated.

'Shut up,' he said.

Some of his anxiety touched me. Our own scrap was forgotten. We marched side by side as fast as we could. The white boys saw us and hurried up the road. We passed the fork. Perhaps they would take the turning away from us. We dared not look back.

'Hear them?' Andries asked.

'No.'

I looked over my shoulder.

'They're coming,' I said.

'Walk faster,' Andries said. 'If they come closer, run.'

'Hey, *klipkop*!'

'Don't look back,' Andries said.

'Hottentot!'

36

We walked as fast as we could.

'Bloody kaffir!'

Ahead was a bend in the road. Behind the bend were bushes. Once there, we could run without them knowing it till it was too late.

'Faster,' Andries said.

They began pelting us with stones.

'Run when we get to the bushes,' Andries said.

The bend and the bushes were near. We would soon be there.

A clear young voice carried to us:

'Your fathers are dirty black bastards of baboons!'

'Run!' Andries called.

A violent, unreasoning anger suddenly possessed me. I stopped and turned.

'You're a liar!' I screamed it.

The foremost boy pointed at me:

'An ugly black baboon!'

In a fog of rage I went towards him.

'Liar!' I shouted. 'My father was better than your father!'

I neared them. The bigger boy stepped between me and the one I was after.

'My father was better than your father! Liar!'

The big boy struck me a mighty clout on the side of the face. I staggered, righted myself, and leapt at the boy who had insulted my father. I struck him on the face, hard. A heavy blow on the back of my head nearly stunned me. I grabbed at the boy in front of me. We went down together.

'Liar!' I said through clenched teeth, hitting him with all my might.

Blows rained on me, on my head, my neck, the side of my face, my mouth, but my enemy was under me and I pounded him fiercely, all the time repeating:

'Liar! Liar! Liar!'

Suddenly, stars exploded in my head. Then there was darkness.

I emerged from the darkness to find Andries kneeling beside me.

'God man! I thought they'd killed you.'

I sat up. The white boys were nowhere to be seen. Like Andries, they'd probably thought me dead and run off in panic. The inside of my mouth felt sore and swollen. My nose was tender to the touch. The back of my head ached. A trickle of blood dripped from my nose. I stemmed it with the square of coloured cloth. The greatest damage was to my shirt. It was ripped in many places. I remembered the crackling. I looked anxiously about. It was safe, a little off the road on the grass. I relaxed. I got up and brushed my clothes. I picked up the crackling.

'God, you're dumb!' Andries said. 'You're going to get it! Dumb arse!'

I was too depressed to retort. Besides, I knew he was right. I was dumb. I should have run when he told me to.

'Come on,' I said.

One of many small groups of children, each child carrying his little bag of crackling, we trod the long road home in the cold winter afternoon.

There was tension in the house that night. When I got back Aunt Liza had listened to the story in silence. The beating or scolding I expected did not come. But Aunt Liza changed while she listened, became remote and withdrawn. When Uncle Sam came home she told him what had happened. He, too, just looked at me and became more remote and withdrawn than usual. They were waiting for something; their tension reached out to me, and I waited with them, anxious, apprehensive.

The thing we waited for came while we were having our supper. We heard a trap pull up outside.

'Here it is,' Uncle Sam said and got up.

Aunt Liza leaned back from the table and put her hands in her lap, fingers intertwined, a cold, unseeing look in her eyes.

38

Before Uncle Sam reached it, the door burst open. A tall, broad, white man strode in. Behind him came the three boys. The one I had attacked had swollen lips and a puffy left eye.

'Evening *baas*,' Uncle Sam murmured.

'That's him,' the bigger boy said, pointing at me.

The white man stared till I lowered my eyes.

'Well?' he said.

'He's sorry, *baas*,' Uncle Sam said quickly. 'I've given him a hiding he won't forget soon. You know how it is, *baas*. He's new here, the child of a relative in Johannesburg and they don't all know how to behave there. You know how it is in the big towns, *baas*.' The plea in Uncle Sam's voice had grown more pronounced as he went on. He turned to me. 'Tell the *baas* and young *basies* how sorry you are, Lee.'

I looked at Aunt Liza and something in her lifelessness made me stubborn in spite of my fear.

'He insulted my father,' I said.

The white man smiled.

'See Sam, your hiding couldn't have been good.'

There was a flicker of life in Aunt Liza's eyes. For a brief moment she saw me, looked at me, warmly, lovingly, then her eyes went dead again.

'He's only a child, *baas*,' Uncle Sam murmured.

'You stubborn too, Sam?'

'No, *baas*.'

'Good. . . . Then teach him, Sam. If you and he are to live here, you must teach him. Well . . .?'

'Yes, *baas*.'

Uncle Sam went into the other room and returned with a thick leather thong. He wound it once round his hand and advanced on me. The man and boys leaned against the door, watching. I looked at Aunt Liza's face. Though there was no sign of life or feeling on it, I knew suddenly, instinctively, that she wanted me not to cry.

Bitterly, Uncle Sam said:

39

'You must never lift your hand to a white person. No matter what happens, you must never lift your hand to a white person. . . .'

He lifted the strap and brought it down on my back. I clenched my teeth and stared at Aunt Liza. I did not cry with the first three strokes. Then, suddenly, Aunt Liza went limp. Tears showed in her eyes. The thong came down on my back, again and again. I screamed and begged for mercy. I grovelled at Uncle Sam's feet, begging him to stop, promising never to lift my hand to any white person. . . .

At last, the white man's voice said:

'All right, Sam.'

Uncle Sam stopped. I lay whimpering on the floor. Aunt Liza sat like one in a trance.

'Is he still stubborn, Sam?'

'Tell the *baas* and *basies* you are sorry.'

'I'm sorry,' I said.

'Bet his father is one of those who believe in equality.'

'His father is dead,' Aunt Liza said.

'Good night, Sam.'

'Good night, *baas*. Sorry about this.'

'All right, Sam.' He opened the door. The boys went out first, then he followed. 'Good night, Liza.'

Aunt Liza did not answer. The door shut behind the white folk, and, soon, we heard their trap moving away. Uncle Sam flung the thong viciously against the door, slumped down on the bench, folded his arms on the table, and buried his head on his arms. Aunt Liza moved away from him, came on the floor beside me and lifted me into her large lap. She sat rocking my body. Uncle Sam began to sob softly. After some time, he raised his head and looked at us.

'Explain to the child, Liza,' he said.

'You explain,' Aunt Liza said bitterly. 'You are the man. You did the beating. You are the head of the family. This is a man's world. You do the explaining.'

'Please, Liza. . . .'

'You should be happy. The whites are satisfied. We can go on now.'

With me in her arms, Aunt Liza got up. She carried me into the other room. The food on the table remained half-eaten. She laid me on the bed on my stomach, smeared fat on my back, then covered me with the blankets. She undressed and got into bed beside me. She cuddled me close, warmed me with her own body. With her big hand on my cheek, she rocked me, first to silence, then to sleep.

For the only time of my stay there, I slept on a bed in Elsberg.

When I woke next morning Uncle Sam had gone. Aunt Liza only once referred to the beating he had given me. It was in the late afternoon, when I returned with the day's cow dung.

'It hurt him,' she said. 'You'll understand one day.'

That night, Uncle Sam brought me an orange, a bag of boiled sweets, and a dirty old picture book. He smiled as he gave them to me, rather anxiously. When I smiled back at him, he seemed to relax. He put his hand on my head, started to say something, then changed his mind and took his seat by the fire.

Aunt Liza looked up from the floor where she dished out the food.

'It's all right, old man,' she murmured.

'One day . . .' Uncle Sam said.

'It's all right,' Aunt Liza repeated insistently.

The long winter passed. Slowly, day by day, the world of Elsberg became a warmer place. The cracks in my feet began to heal. The spells of bearable, noonday cold gave way to warmth. The noise of the veld at night became a din. The freezing nights changed, became bearable; changed again, became warm. Warm nights and hot days!

Summer had come, and with its coming, the world became a softer, kindlier, more beautiful place. Sunflowers began blooming in people's yards. And people themselves began to relax and laugh. When, one evening, as I came in with some washing from the line, I heard Uncle Sam's voice raised in laughter, and saw him and Aunt Liza playing, I knew the summer had really come. Later that same evening, he went into the other room and returned with a guitar. Aunt Liza beamed.

'Open the door?'

Uncle Sam nodded. He played. Soon, people from the other houses came, in one's and two's, till our little room was crowded. Someone sang with his arms on his wife's shoulders, a love song:

> *I'll be your sweetheart,*
> *If you will be mine. . . .*

Summer had come indeed.

In the long summer afternoons, after my day's work, I went down to the river. Sometimes Andries and some of the other children went with me. Often I went alone.

Often, with others, or alone, I climbed the short willows with their long drooping branches. The touch of willow leaf on the cheek gives a feeling of cool wonder. Often, I jumped from stone to stone on the broad bed of the shallow, clear, fast-flowing river. Sometimes I found little pools of idle water, walled off by stones from the flow. I tickled long-tailed tadpoles in these. The sun on the water touched their bodies with myriad colours. Sometimes I watched the *springhaas*— the wild rabbit of the veld—go leaping across the land, almost faster than my eye could follow. And sometimes I lay on my back, on the green grass; on the bank of the river, and looked up at the distant sky, watching thin fleecy white clouds form and re-form and trying to associate the shapes with people and things I knew. I loved being alone by the river. It became my special world.

Each day I explored a little more of the river, going further up or down stream, extending the frontiers of my world. One day, going further downstream than I had been before, I came upon a boy. He was on the bank on the other side from me. We saw each other at the same time and stared. He was completely naked. He carried two finely carved sticks of equal size and shape, both about his own height. He was not light brown, like the other children of our location, but dark brown, almost black. I moved almost to the edge of the river. He called out in a strange language.

'Hello!' I shouted.

He called out again, and again I could not understand. I searched for a place with stones, then bounded across. I approached him slowly. As I drew near, he gripped his sticks more firmly. I stopped.

He spoke harshly, flung one stick on the ground at my feet, and held the other ready as though to fight.

'Don't want to fight,' I said.

I reached down to pick up the stick and return it to him. He took a step forward and raised the one in his hand. I moved back quickly. He stepped back and pointed at the stick on the ground. I shook my head.

'Don't want to fight.'

I pushed the stick towards him with my foot, ready to run at the first sign of attack. I showed my new, stubby teeth in a tentative smile. He said something that sounded less aggressive. I nodded, smiling more broadly. He relaxed, picked up the stick, and transferred both to his left hand. He smacked his chest.

'Joseph! Zulu!'

I smacked my own chest.

'Lee . . .' But I didn't know what I was apart from that.

He held out his hand. We shook. His face lit up in a sunny smile. He said something and pointed downstream. Then he took my arm and led me down.

Far downstream, where the river skirted a hillside, hidden by a cluster of willows, we came on a large clear pool. Joseph flung his sticks on the ground and dived in. He shot through the water like a tadpole. He went down and came up. He shouted and beckoned me to come in. I undressed and went in more tentatively. Laughing, he pulled me under. I came up gasping and spluttering, my belly filled with water. He smacked me on the back and the water shot out of my mouth in a rush. When he realized I could not swim he became more careful. We spent the afternoon with Joseph teaching me to swim. At home, that evening, I stood beside Aunt Liza's wash-tub.

'Aunt Liza. . . .'

'Yes?'

'What am I?'

'What are you talking about?'

'I met a boy at the river. He said he was Zulu.'

She laughed.

'You are Coloured. There are three kinds of people: white people, Coloured people, and black people. The white people come first, then the Coloured people, then the black people.'

'Why?'

'Because it is so.'

Next day, when I met Joseph, I smacked my chest and said:

'Lee! Coloured!'

He clapped his hands and laughed.

Joseph and I spent most of the long summer afternoons together. He learnt some Afrikaans from me; I learnt some Zulu from him. Our days were full.

There was the river to explore.

There were my swimming lessons, and others.

I learnt to fight with sticks; to weave a green hat of young willow wands and leaves; to catch frogs and tadpoles with my hands; to set a trap for the *springhaas*; to make the sounds of the river birds.

There was the hot sun to comfort us. . . .

There was the green grass to dry our bodies. . . .

There was the soft clay with which to build. . . .

There was the fine sand with which to fight. . . .

There were our giant grasshoppers to race. . . .

There were the locust swarms when the skies turned black and we caught them by the hundreds. . . .

There was the rare taste of crisp, brown baked, salted locusts. . . .

There was the voice of the wind in the willows. . . .

There was the voice of the heaven in thunderstorms. . . .

There were the voices of two children in laughter, ours. . . .

There were Joseph's tales of black kings who lived in days before the white man. . . .

At home, I said:

'Aunt Liza . . .'

'Yes?'

'Did we have Coloured kings before the white man?'

'No.'

'Then where did we come from? Joseph and his mother come from the black kings who were before the white man.'

And laughing, and ruffling my head, she said:

'You talk too much . . . Go'n wash up.'

And to Joseph, next day, I said:

'We didn't have Coloured kings before the white man.'

And he comforted me and said:

'It is of no moment. You are my brother. Now my kings will be your kings. Come: I have promised the mother to bring you home. She awaits you. I will race you to the hill.'

From the top of the hill I looked into a long valley where cattle grazed. To the right, on the sloping land, nestled a cluster of mud huts. Round each hut was a wall built of mud.

'That is my home.' Joseph pointed.

We veered right and went down to it. From a distance, we saw a woman at the gate of one of the huts.

'There is the mother!' He walked faster.

She was barefooted. She wore a slight skirt that came above

45

her knees. A child was strapped to her back. The upper part of her body was naked except for the cloth across her chest that supported the child. Round her neck, arms, and legs, were strings of white beads. As we drew near, I saw that she was young. And her broad, round face was beautiful. Her black eyes were liquid soft. She called out a greeting and smiled. Joseph pushed me forward.

'This is my brother Lee of the Coloureds, little mother.'

'Greetings, Mother,' I said.

'I greet you, my son,' she said softly, a twinkle in her eyes. 'As the man of my house has told you, food awaits. Come.'

'See!' Joseph puffed out his chest. To his mother he said, 'He would not believe when I told him I was the man in our house.'

'He is indeed,' she said.

Circling the hut was a raised platform. We sat on this while she brought us the food; salted fried locusts and corn on the cob. She sat nearby and watched us eating.

'Show the mother,' Joseph said and took another bite at the *mielies*. 'Show the mother you are not circumcised yet.'

I showed her.

'This is strange,' she said. 'Have you no initiation schools?'

'No!' Joseph said.

'Then when do you enter manhood?'

'He does not know.'

'Is it true?' She looked at me.

I nodded.

'He's still a child!' Joseph cried. 'So big and a child!'

Christmas came and it was a feast of eating and laughter. I spent half my time at home with Aunt Liza and Uncle Sam and the other half with Joseph and the little mother.

My sixth birthday came. Joseph and the little mother and I celebrated it by the river.

Then, early one morning, just as the first cold touches crept into the morning air, Joseph came to our location.

46

I was washing up when I heard young voices shouting:
'Look at the naked kaffir! Lee's kaffir!'

I rushed out. Joseph came gravely to me.

'I come to take leave, my brother. My father has died in the mines so we go back to our land.'

He stood straight and stern, not heeding the shouts of the children about. He was a man. This was the burden of his manhood. I had learned much from him, so I said equally coldly:

'I must take leave of the little mother.'

'She is a woman. She weeps.'

We ran all the way there. . . .

When the little cart had taken them away, I climbed the hill and went down to the river. I carried Joseph's two sticks with me. These were his parting gift to his brother.

'Defend yourself,' he had said. 'I will make others.'

I walked along the river that had been our kingdom. Now, it was a desolate place. Joseph had been here with me: now Joseph had gone. Before I realized it, my tears flowed fast. There had been much between us.

So the summer passed. The autumn came. The leaves went brown on the willows by the river. They fluttered to the ground and turned to mould. The long days shortened suddenly. The cold came. Winter had come to torture us again. . . .

In the spring, I was suddenly uprooted from the familiar world of Elsberg and taken to Vrededorp where I was born.

[v]

It was late afternoon. The days were warm again. The thick buds on the old trees had turned into small leaves of a light, transparent green. Soft, downy, new grass grew on the banks of the river. And the river itself was swollen high. I lay on its bank, lost in the green dream-world of childhood. Joseph did not seem far away. I expected, at any moment, to

47

hear his strong voice hail me and dare me to a swim in our secret bathing-place. The water there would be icy cold now.

I heard footsteps.

A voice said:

'There he is!'

I turned and saw a young man and woman. I jumped up. They were well-dressed, Coloured like me, but strangers. They drew near. The young woman was attractive. Her deep brown olive face was round and smooth. She smiled and dimples showed on both cheeks and chin. She had jet black wavy hair that fell to her shoulders. She was short and plump. The young man was a head taller, a shade lighter in colour. His hair, too, was wavy, but short and with a tinge of reddish brown about it. His face was pitted with pock-marks; and there was a touch of devilment about it.

A few yards from me, she put a hand on his arm and stopped him. He said something to her in English. She replied in the same language. Then she took a step toward me.

'Hello, Lee.'

I watched them silently. How did they know my name? Who were they?

'Don't you remember us?' This time it was the young man.

The young woman held out her arms to me.

'I'm Margaret,' she said. 'Your sister.'

'I'm your brother, Harry,' he said.

Some far-away corner of my brain stirred and responded.

'Your sister,' she repeated, and though she smiled tears showed in her eyes.

'You from my mother?'

'Yes!' she said. 'We're from your mother! Your mother is our mother too! We're your brother and sister!'

'What's your name?'

'Margaret.'

I looked at my brother.

'Harry.'

I said their names carefully to myself.

'Margaret . . . Harry . . .' I remembered something Aunt Liza had told me. 'Is my mother still where sick people go?'

'No,' Harry said.

'We've come to take you to her,' Margaret said.

I thought of the train and grew excited. Such a long time since I last rode in a train. I could hardly remember it.

'When?'

'To-night,' Harry said.

Aunt Liza waited for us with coffee and fat cakes. She seemed worried and upset.

'He's happy here . . . Aren't you, Lee?'

Before I could answer, Maggie said:

'I'm sorry Aunt Liza but Mother wants him. He is her baby, you know.'

'But he's so happy here, aren't you, Lee?'

'He can't decide, Aunt Liza.'

'We could leave him for a week . . .' Harry began.

'No,' Maggie said firmly. 'Mother wants him to come back with us, you know that Harry.'

'I thought . . .' Harry said.

'You heard Mother yourself,' Maggie said.

'Then why did she let him go in the first place?' Aunt Liza said fiercely.

'That's not fair,' Harry said.

'You offered to take him till things were straight,' Maggie said. 'Mother couldn't help Natalie dying and getting burnt and going to hospital.'

No more was said. In silence, we waited for Uncle Sam. After an age of silence the door opened and Uncle Sam entered.

'Oh Sam!' Aunt Liza cried. 'They've come to take him. . . .'

'I warned you, Liz.' Uncle Sam took in the scene then shook his head. He went into the next room without greeting my brother and sister.

'Better be going or we'll miss the train,' Harry said.

'Get your things, Lee,' Maggie said.

'He hasn't anything,' Aunt Liza said.

Uncle Sam spoke from the other room:

'We've just paid off our debt at the store. I was taking him in on Saturday morning to get some clothes.'

'Come on,' Harry said.

'Say good-bye to Uncle,' Aunt Liza said.

I went into the other room. Uncle Sam sat on the bed staring at the floor. I stood in front of him, waiting for him to look up. At last I gave it up.

'Good-bye, Uncle Sam.'

'Good-bye, son.'

I was reluctant to go. Maggie called. I went to Aunt Liza. She stared at me so intently that I lowered my eyes.

'Good-bye, Aunt Liza.'

'You were happy here, weren't you, Lee?'

'Let him go!' Uncle Sam called fiercely from the other room.

'Come on!' Harry said impatiently.

II

[i]

I woke to the grinding of brakes as the train came to a stop.

'We're home,' Maggie said, raising me.

We got off the train and went out into the deserted streets. Long, empty, silent streets. From the silent street, and from everywhere about me, a low, deep, rumbling hum came to me. I remembered this incessant noise from other times: I had heard it before. In the silent, yet noisy night, I walked up one empty street and down another with my brother holding my one hand and my sister the other. Once, a white man in uniform stepped from a shadowy corner and shone a torch on us.

'Evening, *baas*,' Harry said.

'Where're you going so late?'

'Home,' Harry said. 'We've been to fetch my little brother from the country.'

'Prove it?'

'I'm Coloured; I don't carry a pass.'

For a long time he shone the torch on Harry's face.

'Trying to be smart, heh.'

'No, *baas*. Just stating a fact.'

He swung the torch down to my face. I blinked and closed my eyes.

'*He* looks like a kaffir.'

'Don't you call my brother a kaffir!' Maggie snapped.

He swung the beam up to her face, then turned it out. 'All right. . . .'

He faded into the shadows from which he had come. We set off again, walking more briskly than before.

We turned up a long, narrow street and walked nearly its whole length. Then we turned into a dark passage and climbed stairs. Harry knocked on the only door at the top of the dark stairs. There was no answer. He pushed and the door opened. We entered. The candle on the saucer in the centre of the small round table danced crazily in the draught we had brought.

'Shut the door,' Harry said.

An iron bedstead stood against the wall facing the door. Near it was the round table. In a corner, at the foot of the bed, stood a life-size tailor's dummy. An old, unpainted wooden chair was near the table. Two tin trunks and a small cupboard in a corner made up the rest of the furniture. There was no ordinary window to the room, but in the sloping ceiling, in the corner directly over the bed, was a small fanlight.

The blankets on the bed were thrown back as though someone had been to bed then got up again.

'Wonder where she is,' Harry said.

'May be in the lavatory.' Maggie went to the stairs and called: 'Mother! Mother! Lee's home!'

'Not there,' Harry said after a while.

Maggie shut the door.

'What now?' Harry said.

I sat on one of the trunks. My eyes kept straying to the tailor's dummy in the corner.

'You go: I'll stay here,' Maggie said.

He touched my head and went out. Maggie came and sat beside me. She put her arm about me and rocked gently. I closed my eyes and forgot the tailor's dummy.

Time passed. The candle flickered violently, on the point of going out. Maggie found another and lit it. Again she put her arms, about me. We rocked from side to side in an easy gentle, rhythmic motion.

After a long, long time, a sudden dull thud somewhere below us shattered the silent peace of the night. Maggie went to the door.

'That you, Mother?'

'Yes,' a gentle voice called up. 'Come and give me a hand. Bring the candle.'

Maggie took the candle and went out. I waited in the dark, my face turned to where the dummy was.

The darkness dispersed slowly as an area of light mounted the stairs. Then they came into the room, and the darkness was gone. I turned my eyes from the dummy.

Maggie and my mother let go of the big, fat, fair, woman they supported. She sank to the floor in a drunken stupor.

I looked at my mother with the clear, sharp eyes of a nearly seven-year-old. A small dark woman with a long narrow face and an air of great frailty about her: thin arms, thinner than mine; hands smaller than mine; kinky hair with a touch of brown, like mine, not wavy like that of my brother and sister; big, sombre dark eyes.

She said:

'Lee . . . My baby!'

She put her arms about me and held me tight.

'Careful, Mother!' Maggie said.

Her tears wetted my face. . . .

Maggie got a Primus stove from the cupboard, lit it, and made tea. My mother and I sat side by side on the bed. The drunk woman lay on the floor.

'I suppose you've opened your side again,' Maggie said.

'I couldn't leave Betty lying in the gutter.'

'Oh, Mother!' Maggie said helplessly. She looked at the woman on the floor. 'What about her?'

'Leave her there. I'll put a blanket over her.'

'And Lee?'

'He can come in with me.'

53

'No . . . Your side, remember.'

'I'll make his bed on the floor then.'

'I'll make it. Blankets?'

Maggie got out the blankets and made up a place for me in a corner away from the dummy. My mother poured tea for us. Maggie flung one blanket over the drunk woman.

'I must go now, Ma.'

'Be careful.'

Maggie kissed mother on the cheek.

' 'Night, Ma.'

'Good night, child.'

She hugged me.

'See you to-morrow.'

She went out. I heard her footsteps moving hesitantly, down the dark stairs. My mother put a hand lightly on my shoulder. I looked up.

'Bit strange, isn't it?'

I nodded. I wanted to tell her I did not like the dummy. But she might do something about it, and her side might bleed.

'To-morrow will be better. . . . Hungry?'

'No, Mother.'

'Want to go to sleep?'

'Yes, Mother.' I didn't really.

I took off my trousers. She knelt beside me on the floor and tucked me up under the blankets.

'All right?'

'Yes.'

She bent down and kissed me, first on the forehead, then on the lips: a kiss light as the touch of a feather.

'Good night, my baby. . . . Sleep well.'

She blew out the candle. After a while of silence, I heard the creak of the bed as she got in. I closed my eyes and drifted away to the river at Elsberg. . . .

. . . And Joseph was there with me. And he was chasing me. And I was laughing. And above my laughter was the

54

sound of his voice. *I will catch you, I will catch you.* And he drew near. And then it was not Joseph. It was the dummy, come alive: armless and headless. It drew near. *I will catch you, I will catch you.* I ran fast. It drew nearer. And now I felt it on me, toweringly, ready to crush me. And I cried out. . . .

I woke screaming. My mother stood over me with the lighted candle.

'Everything's all right. You've been dreaming. Everything's all right. There now.'

I stole a quick, furtive look across the room. It was still there.

'That it?' she said.

I looked at her face and knew, suddenly, that I could trust her in all things. I said:

'I was at Elsberg with Joseph and then Joseph was gone and it chased me.'

She got an old coat from under the bed and flung it over the dummy.

'Go to sleep now, and to-morrow you must tell me about Joseph.'

She blew out the candle and got back into bed.

'Tell you what, I'll tell you a story, one that your father used to tell. Would you like that?'

'Please. . . .'

'Then listen: Once upon a time, in a far-away land where the trees were blue, there lived a young prince. . . .'

Softly, easily, her gentle voice droned on. It took me to strange adventures inside the biggest snake that ever lived. And then, easily, it carried me off to the land of peaceful sleep.

A deep hissing drew me from the land of sleep. I opened my eyes. I remembered this was not Elsberg, the order of my days here would be different. The hissing was made by the Primus stove. The big woman who had been drunk the night before was cooking over it. I looked across the room.

The dummy was not there. I sat up. My mother's bed was made. The woman turned and smiled.

'Good morning.' Her voice was rusty and gay.

'Where's my mother?'

She brought me a mug of coffee: white, creamy, and very sweet.

'It's polite to answer a greeting.' Her eyes laughed at me.

'Good morning,' I said. 'Where's my mother?'

'There you go again! Give us a kiss, big eyes.'

It was hard to think of this woman with the rusty voice and gay, laughing eyes as the person who had lain in a drunken stupor all night. She brought her face down. I pulled mine away. Then, impulsively, I pushed it forward and kissed her.

'Now, was that so bad, darlin'?' She laughed and ruffled my hair. 'Tell you something. You stick with Aunt Betty and everything will be *all right*, heh? You be my man and I'll see you right. I'll be yours. Many a man would give his right arm to have me his, but I'll be yours, darlin'. And if you look after me when I need it, I'll be yours for ever. Now gi' us another one quickly.'

She flung her arms about me and kissed me with wet lips.

'My man?'

I nodded.

She poured me another mug of coffee. Footsteps moved up the stairs.

'Here's your mother.'

My mother came in with a big parcel.

'Hello, Ma.'

'Morning, Lee. Slept well?'

My mother undid her parcel and got out some plates. Aunt Betty dished two sausages on to each plate. My mother sliced a loaf of bread. I sat beside her on the bed. Aunt Betty sat on the chair. We ate.

'Must do something about clothes,' my mother said.

'Hasn't he enough?'

'Only what he's in.'

'Must do something then. But don't get any till to-morrow.'

'I must find the money first.'

I finished eating.

'Where do I wash, Ma?'

'Downstairs.'

I got the soap and towel and went down the stairs. The stairs were steep, narrow and short. In places a stair was broken and had been covered with a thin plank that sagged as my weight came down on it. Once I nearly slipped. I grabbed the bannister. It moved outward, dangerously. At the bottom of the stairs I turned left into a little dark passage. I fumbled in the dark till I found the door. I jerked it open: daylight rushed in.

The yard was tiny: no more than six yards wide, and just as long. And in it, taking up half the space, was a high pile of junk: twisted bicycle wheels, old tyres, a bicycle frame, broken chairs, part of an iron bed, brown with rust; pots and pans and pieces of broken crockery; rags and bones; and much other rubbish beyond recognition. Three short steps led down into the yard, and the tap was near the door. The lavatory was beside the tap. I leaped across the three steps and landed near the tap. I tucked the towel into my shirt collar and washed.

Going back, I bumped into an old Indian in the dark passage. He spoke to me in English. I couldn't understand and fled up the stairs.

[ii]

The heart of Johannesburg nestles in the heart of the valley of the Ridge of the White Waters. From there it spreads away, up the sloping land, out of the valley, in all directions. Journeying westward from the tram terminus near the city hall, one goes down to the huge market with its big square. Then, immediately past the market, and the beginning of Fordsburg, the land levels off for a short distance and begins

57

to slope upwards, very gently. To the western end of Fordsburg is a sudden dip. Trams and traffic go through a long,
deep subway. Two sets of railway lines lie across it, going
south in a smooth westward curve in one direction, and
north with an eastward curve in the other. The tramlines
climb steeply out of the subway. To the left of them is Vrededorp, to the right is Braamfontein.

Vrededorp is made up of twenty-four streets, running
parallel to each other. They are known by their numbers.
First Street is way up near the north-western hills, and
Twenty-fourth Street is down in the south-western valley,
backing on the curving railway lines.

And from the streets and houses of Vrededorp, from the
back-yards and muddy alleys, a loud babel of shouting,
laughing, cursing, voices rise, are swallowed by the limitless
sky, and rise again in unending tumult. And through, and
above, and under, all this is the deep throbbing hum of the
city. It is everywhere at once. Without beginning, without
end.

I did not stray far from the protection of home that first
morning. Twenty-second Street, the street where we lived,
was strange and alien. The noise was frightening after the
quiet of Elsberg. After a while I grew interested in the dark
stream of life about me and ventured down to the bottom of
the street.

There were small, well-built Basuto women. They balanced their shopping, baskets, paraffin-tins, bundles tied in
spotless white sheets, delicately on their heads. They went by
with effortless grace: their bodies straight, their dark faces
serene. There were the tall, swaying Zulu women, big-boned
and strong-muscled, moving with the ease and grace of
dancers, essentially feminine for all their bigness. And the
women of the Bechuana and the Barolong, their skins a
yellowish brown, were very like the Coloured women. They,
and the Coloured women, did not have the easy grace and

58

dignity of the Basuto and Zulu women. But they had a free, swinging gaiety of movement that suggested unending high spirits. They spoke loudest, laughed longest. They were more colourfully dressed than either the Zulu or Basuto women. They wore reds, blues, greens, and purples in bright, shiny materials. The Zulu women wore severe dark colours for the most. The Basuto women went in for a little more colour, but in quieter tones than the Bechuana and Barolong women.

The women paused at the stalls that lined the sidewalk, bought, and moved on. The traders were Indians. They stood by tables piled high with hard-boiled eggs, steaming sweet potatoes, Indian sweetmeats, fruit, vegetables, and all manner of edibles. They called out their wares in high, tinny voices; reedy, and sounding strange against the deep-throated African voices. Darting in and out among the women and stalls were ragged boys of all shapes, and of colours ranging from black to a pale, almost white, yellowish fairness.

Common to all the women, African and Coloured, was the *doek*. This was a kerchief they wore over their heads. It was an institution from Sixteenth Street downward. It was usually white, and always spotlessly clean. It was tied so that it covered all the hair, with two slight risings over the horns. The two ends were tucked in, one under each ear. Another, though less important, emblem among the women of lower Vrededorp was the apron. No woman ever went out without putting on a clean apron, except when going to a burial or to church. At all other times a woman was not properly dressed without an apron.

And among them moved the men, their shirt fronts open, their sleeves rolled up as far as they would go, their caps pulled low over their sullen, downcast eyes. A few men were not like that, but they were a minority. The rest moved close to the walls, not looking at people, like panthers, ever poised for the leap to savage battle.

Boys fell over each other battling for orange-peels swimming on the black water of the gutters. Near me, a fat black boy grabbed a hot sweet potato from a stall and ran. An old Indian lumbered after him, cursing. People looked on disinterestedly. The Indian gave up and returned muttering to his stall. By then two other boys had grabbed some eggs and run in the opposite direction. The old man waved his fists and screamed helplessly at them.

And all about surged the dark stream: people laughed and cursed; young women went by swaying their hips; men with caps pulled down called to them in gruff voices; carts pulled by great horses moved slowly by; children swung behind the carts till the drivers lashed out with their long whips; trams rattled out of and into the subway; trains went screaming by across it; motor horns hooted; children played in the streets till the motors were nearly on them then jumped clear; screams, laughter, shouts, cries, everything but silence. A fight started between two men. A black van came up through the subway. People dispersed, began to run. I turned and ran for home.

My mother met me at our door. We went up to a lunch of fish and chips.

'Tell me about Elsberg.'

I told her, mainly about Joseph and the little mother and the good times we had shared. I ended:

'Why do they call them kaffirs, Ma? Uncle Sam did and Harry too. And the little mother didn't like it.'

'You told her?'

'After Uncle Sam said it.'

'You shouldn't have. Your father always said it wasn't good to tell people things that make them unhappy.'

'Did he call them that too?'

'Never.'

'The little mother said I would call black people that when I get big.'

'Not if you remember the good Lord made us all.'

'Mother. . . .'

'Yes?'

'Why didn't the Coloureds have kings in the days before the white man? The Zulus had.'

She laughed and her face looked very young suddenly, younger than my sister's.

'Joseph asked you about Coloured kings?'

'Yes.'

'Well, the Coloureds never had kings, but you had. You still have.'

'Now? To-day?'

'Yes.'

'And are they black?'

She thought for a little then nodded slowly.

'Must be. Your father didn't have any white blood in him so he must have been black. Yes, your kings were black.'

'And the ones of to-day?'

'They are black too.'

Oh, if only Joseph were here now! I would go up to him and push out my chest and say: 'I am Lee of the . . .' No, not the Coloureds. Of the what, then?

'Ma . . .'

'Yes?'

'If my kings were black, why am I Coloured?'

'Oh Lee,' she protested.

'But I want to know.'

She thought for a while.

'You're only Coloured on your mother's side, that's my side. On your father's side you're Abyssinian.'

'And that is black?'

'Yes.'

I would say to Joseph: 'I am Lee of the Abyshinins! My kings were before the days of the white man and my kings are still kings to-day!' How he would envy me! If only he were here. . . . I would lend my kings to him.

She smiled.

61

'Now don't be ashamed of your Coloured mother just because you are black.'

I felt generous and loving.

'I will lend you my kings.' I thought of something. 'Where do my kings live?'

'In Abyssinia. . . . And that is the last question I'm answering. I must get back to work.'

'Black kings of Abyshina!' I cried.

My mother went down to work. I wandered up the street and crossed the road that ran past the cemetery. I lay on the soft grass. The sun shone from a clear sky that was far away. The noise of Vrededorp drifted up as an echo. I plucked a tall blade of sweet grass and chewed it. And I was far, far away, in a merry land called Abyshina. There, black kings strode the earth in all their majesty. And I was a great warrior of Abyshina, serving my kings. I was the strongest, the bravest, the most daring, of all the warriors in that glorious land called Abyshina. . . .

Lo, I am black, but comely, O ye daughters of Jerusalem, as the tents of Kedar, as the curtains of Solomon. . . .

Hunger, and some big boys starting a game of rugby dangerously near, drove me home at sunset. Half my body and all my mind were still in the merry land of Abyshina when I entered the room. My sister was there with my mother. Neither looked up as I entered. Maggie was bent over my mother who sat on one of the tin trunks. I went closer. I watched, and, watching, grew tense, felt every twitch of pain on my mother's face as Maggie worked.

In front of Maggie was a bowl of hot water. A pad of cotton-wool and rolls of bandages were on the table. Used bandages lay on the floor. Except for the lint that stuck to her raw flesh, my mother was naked from the waist up. With the aid of hot water, Maggie eased the lint from my mother's flesh. It was slow, drawn-out work. Yet, for all

Maggie's care, my mother kept gasping with pain. In places, the wound bled a little. Once, my mother moaned aloud.

'Don't hurt her!'

'Quiet, black Lee,' my mother said weakly.

'Better go out for a while,' Maggie said without looking up.

I was rooted to the spot, hurt, yet unwilling to go out and be free of the hurt.

'I want to stay.'

'Then be quiet.'

Slowly, painfully, Maggie parted the lint from the raw flesh. At last, after an age of pain, the lint came away, blood-stained and with small pieces of my mother's flesh sticking to it. With them, I sighed and relaxed. My participation had been complete enough to exhaust me.

The wound had originally covered the whole of my mother's left side, back and front, taking in the left breast and going round her back to within an inch of the spinal column; it stretched from her shoulder down to her waist. The breast and the area about it had healed and new skin was growing. The part of the back near the spine had also healed. The wound, now, was raw only in the area directly under the arm. And the upper part of the arm itself was still raw.

Maggie unwound a roll of fresh lint and cut a piece big enough to cover the wound.

'Hold the corners.'

I held the lint while she smeared a thick paste over it.

'Ready, Ma?'

'Yes.'

My mother held up her arm. Maggie put the lint over the wound. My mother drew in air through her clenched teeth. Maggie broke the seal of one of the broad rolls of bandage and wound it about my mother's body. Then she took another and another. When that was done, she did the arm. The wound here was less raw.

At last it was all over. My mother moved to the bed. I

realized then what people meant when they said a person was sick. It meant having pain that hurt very much. I thought: Mother is sick, and sickness means hurt.

'You going to the hospital to-morrow?' Maggie said.

'Yes,' my mother replied.

'When I think of those white people, I shake all over with rage,' Maggie said.

'It's nearly a year ago now, child. Forget it.'

'What white people?' I asked.

'Ma worked for them,' Maggie said. 'She was washing and the tin of boiling water fell on her. They made her come home by herself. . . .'

'Why get all worked up, child? It's all past.'

'You worked for nearly a month and then nearly died and what did that woman say? "I can't help it if she's careless enough to get hurt. She can't ask for a penny from me." '

'What's the matter, my child?' My mother's voice was very soft.

'And the whites are supposed to be civilized!'

'Tell your mother.'

Suddenly, Maggie's eyes brimmed with tears.

'Aunt Mattie says I must leave school.'

'My poor child,' my mother said.

'I did want to become a teacher and make a home for you, Ma.'

'You must see Mattie's side, my child. She's looked after you and Harry as well as her own Catherine, and it isn't easy for a woman without a husband to do that.'

Maggie wiped her eyes. Her voice was tinged with bitterness:

'Now I must go and work for the whites; clean their dirt and look after their children just like you and all the others.'

We had just finished our evening meal of bread and pork sausages when Aunt Betty arrived. With her was a bumpy, pale yellow little woman. She was no taller than I was, and

64

her behind stuck out like a huge alien bump, separate from her body though attached to it. Her cheek-bones were two bumps that stood out largest in her face. She had hardly any nose, just two holes on an almost flat surface. She was called *Hotnot* Annie and claimed to be pure Hottentot. Whenever she got excited she spoke the clicking Hottentot language. Her hair, when she took off her kerchief, was a series of tightly curled little balls, each separated from the other by a slight spacing of yellow flesh. She boasted that any comb other than an iron comb would break before going through a dozen of her little balls of hair. In a world where texture of hair was vital socially, *Hotnot* Annie was proud of her pepper-corn hair.

Aunt Betty gave me a big brown-paper parcel.

'This is my man, Annie. I am his and he is mine. We are sworn to each other since last night.'

Hotnot Annie pushed her face close to mine, made a series of clicking noises, and burst out laughing.

'Don't be vulgar!' Aunt Betty said.

'Stop it, you two,' my mother laughed.

They answered with a series of clicking noises, then roared with laughter. *Hotnot* Annie bounced her behind up and down as she laughed.

I undid the parcel. There were three pairs of shorts, two of grey flannel and one of khaki; a grey flannel jacket; four shirts and a pair of white tennis shoes.

'All for my man!'

'Say thank you to Aunt Betty, Lee.'

'Thank you, Aunt Betty,' I said.

'Your white people are kind,' my mother said.

Aunt Betty snorted.

'You didn't . . .' my mother began.

'And why not? I slave for them for next to nothing. And besides, Lina, they'll never miss it. Those brats have more than they need. I took them.'

'That's stealing, Betty.'

'If that's stealing then they are stealing my sweat every day. Call it what you will. The child will have something on his back. Winter is coming. What would you have done if I didn't bring these?'

'The Lord takes care of his own.'

'Well, He has, so be quiet.'

'Ag, the Lord will provide an overcoat for winter, and a pair of shoes and some socks,' *Hotnot* Annie said.

'Now don't you start,' mother said rather helplessly. 'You're just asking to go to jail: and how do you think I'd feel?'

'Ag,' Annie laughed. 'They're only waiting there for the Lord to come and provide. It will be a sin not to allow the Lord to provide.'

'Don't mock in front of the child.'

'You are mocking,' Aunt Betty said. 'Wanting to refuse what the Lord provides. . . . I'll see about a fire, heh?'

While they talked over coffee round the fire, I sat fondling my new clothes.

Hotnot Annie began a story.

'Once upon a time . . . a long, long time ago. . . .'

Her voice was light and caressing, pure now, freed of all its earlier vulgarity. It was the voice of the eternal story-teller, the trader in dreams who nursed the dreams of all the ages and clothed them with words. The words dripped on my consciousness, sank into my being, and carried me away to the magic long ago of once-upon-a-time.

When Annie ended, my mother told a story. Then, after my mother, Aunt Betty.

They took me on strange adventures among strange people. And there were no words between me and the story, only the story, which was the reality. And when I came out of the reality to take a piece of bread, the sharp, clear, infinitely simple words were there to guide me back to reality.

That night I entered a world in which the dividing line between reality and dream was so fine as not to exist. And I lived many quiet moments of many years in that strange region that is neither of this world nor out of it.

At last I could take no more. I fought off sleep till I could fight no more. I sank into Aunt Betty's ample lap. The words receded till I could hear no more, till silence came, till I could feel no more. . . .

[iii]

The days passed, and with the passing days I became familiar with Vrededorp. I ranged far and wide, exploring the world in which I lived. I became part of the flowing dark stream. I found that only the poorest Coloured people lived below Nineteenth Street. Above Nineteenth Street lived the more respectable; children who had fathers at work and who wore fine clothes all the time. Those with straight hair and fair skins lived higher up. I longed to steal, as other boys did, from the stalls of the Indian traders. But I always panicked at the last moment. In all other respects I became one of the citizens of Vrededorp, unafraid of going out at night, even on Saturdays. Like all the other citizens, I ran whenever I saw the pick-up van. With other boys, I stood on street corners watching dice 'schools'. Sometimes I kept watch for the players. If I saw a policeman or a pick-up van I shouted a warning and ran. Young boys who were caught while watching for gamblers were sent to a reformatory. My dread, therefore, of the police was as great as that of the gamblers. For reward, the winner usually gave the watcher a few coppers. Whenever I earned a few pence in this way I rushed off to a grocery shop run by a Chinaman. My favourite buy was a pennyworth of coconut icing and a pennyworth of bread. I usually got a handful of roasted peanuts as *bonsella*. Without the *bonsella*, the 'come again' token, no little boy would shop at the same place twice. At times, if I had earned only a penny, it would go on chips, or on a huge paper-bag of 'broken biscuits'.

Sometimes I ran into Aunt Betty on the streets. She always had a kiss and a coin for me.

My mother discovered lice in my hair and clothes. She began a vain battle. Like most of the other children, I sprouted sores at the corners of my mouth. Whenever Maggie saw me, she scrubbed me from head to foot. I avoided her as much as I could. Sometimes I went to the veld above the school and dreamed long dreams on the soft grass.

In the streets, people recognized me and I them. I had been born in Vrededorp. It reclaimed me completely. The Elsberg interlude could easily have been a figment of that half-world of my imagination. I never thought of Joseph and the little mother. And there were other, more immediate, things to take the place of the black kings of Abyshina.

[iv]

The long summer days hung over Vrededorp. And to ease the length of each day, I searched for new forms of adventure. One day, some boys down Twenty-second Street asked me to go coal-hunting with them. There were four of us. We each had a little sack.

We climbed over the high, pronged fencing that cut off the railway lines from the streets of Vrededorp.

'Watch out for police,' a boy called.

We ran between the lines, picking up pieces of coal. Goods trains trundled along; expresses flashed by. We shouted and waved at them. When they had gone we carried on with our search. The boldest of our numbers, a pot-bellied, bare-chested black boy saw a large pile of coal near a stationary wagon.

'Here!'

We followed him. We were shoving coal into our sacks when one boy suddenly shouted:

'Trap! Run!'

I turned. Two men, one black, one white, were nearly on

68

us. I dodged an outstretched arm and shot away, leaving my sack. Heavy feet thundered after me. From somewhere behind I heard a boy scream in pain. The thundering feet were very close. If they caught me I would go to a reformatory and get lashes. I ran as hard as I could. Oh, God! The fence is so far away. Run, Lee, run. They'll lash the skin off your back at the reformatory. I'll never steal coal again, *baas*. Never again. Those boys made me do it. I streaked over the lines, heart pounding. I sensed a hand reaching out for me. I dodged. The man behind me over-balanced and went down heavily. I was safe. The fence was near. I would have time to climb it and fling myself to the ground on the safe side. I reached it and shot up to the top. Then the seat of my pants got caught on one of the prongs. I worked furiously to get it loose. I looked back and saw the man drawing near. It was the black one. He raised his stick and flung it. It caught me on the side of the face. The weight of my body, falling, ripped my pants off the prong. Dazed, I fell on the Vrededorp side of the fence.

When I became aware of the world, I was surrounded by a crowd of angry, shouting women. One of them had the stick which had felled me. She brandished it at the man on the other side of the fence.

'He's my prisoner,' the man said. 'And that is my stick. I'm coming over for them.'

'Come!' the woman shouted. 'Come, you dog of the white man! We will show you where your manhood was lost!'

'A child,' another said bitterly. 'See the blood on his face. A child!'

'They were stealing,' the man said.

'So you, a grown man, must use a stick of battle on an unarmed child. Come over and we will kill you! I will kill you with my own hands!'

'It is my work,' the man said. 'A man must work to live.'

'So you, a black man, must go on even after the white man has given up!'

69

'A black man!'

'But it is my work,' the man protested.

'Our work is to protect our children. Stone the dog! He has sold his manhood to the whites!'

The man turned and ran. A rain of stones followed him. They flung stones long after he had gone.

The woman who had picked up the stick examined my face. There was a cut on the side of my right eye.

'There is much blood but it is not bad. The cut is small. More to the left and the eye would have been gone. . . . Is your home near, my child?'

'Yes, Auntie.'

'Then run home so that your mother can clean your face.'

I trotted home with blood running down the side of my face. It was early afternoon so she would still be working. I tiptoed past the door where she worked and climbed the creaking stairs as quietly as I could. I opened our door then stopped dead.

My mother was lying on the bed, her eyes closed, her face strangely twisted.

'That you, Lee? Come here . . . Mother's very sick so you must do something for her.'

I walked slowly to the side of the bed. She opened her eyes.

'Lee! Oh God!'

She half-raised herself, then flopped back and went limp. Death became real, suddenly. The fear of it was on me. I whimpered:

'Ma! Don't die, Ma. Please. . . .' I shook her.

I hardly noticed Aunt Betty's entrance. She pushed me away and turned to my mother. I went to my favourite trunk and sat sobbing, my bloody face buried in my hands.

From a long way off, my mother's voice came to me.

'The child, Betty.'

'I'll see to him, Lina.'

'His eye. . . . Blood. . . .'

'Be quiet. I'll see to it.'

She came over, examined my face, and said:

'It's a small cut. The blood frightened you.'

She bathed my face and put vaseline on the cut. Then she led me to the bed.

'See.'

My mother looked at my face.

'It frightened me. . . .'

'It was enough to frighten anybody. . . . I came as soon as I got your message. I met Oupa Ruiter on the way. He gave me his keys so we can move into his room to-night. I'll have to go with you, Lina. I've been sacked.'

'Why?'

'The bitch didn't want me to come to you. Said I needn't return if I came.'

'You should've stayed, Bet.'

'And leave you alone with a frightened child? Don't be silly. You rest. I'll see to the moving. . . . Get some water, Lee.'

On the stairs, I met the old Indian coming up.

'You can't go in. My mother is sick.'

'Tell her,' he said in halting Afrikaans, 'tell her I spoke to the landlord but he will not let us stay. We must go to-night. I am sorry it comes when she is sick, but I must go too, and there is nowhere for me.'

I got the water and returned. I gave them the old Indian's message.

'I'd better start packing,' Aunt Betty said.

'I'll help,' I offered.

'When I've sorted things. Go'n play now, but don't go far. I'll call you.'

I looked at my mother. Her eyes were closed but her face was composed. I went downstairs. I sat on the pavement edge and watched the passing life. I had nothing better to do so I tried to widdle through my left trouser-hole. I was just getting to be good at it when I saw Maggie coming up the

71

street. I flung sand on the little puddle I had made, got up, and walked to her.

'Hello, Mag.' I fell into step beside her.

'You look dirty, Lee. . . . What happened to your eye?'

'Accident. . . . Mother's sick. She fainted. Aunt Betty's there. We're moving. To-night.'

'Moving. . . . Where to?'

'Don't know. Why is mother always sick?'

'She's not always sick.'

'Why is she?'

'She's not strong and she tries to do too much.'

'Like when she burned?'

'Yes.'

'Why can't we all live together, Mag?'

'We will one day.'

She went upstairs. I went back to the pavement edge. Sitting there, piddling, it seemed to me there was no sense in life. Things happened and no one seemed to know why.

III

[i]

Oupa—grandpa—Ruiter was a drover. He was a sheep specialist. He knew and loved sheep: they were his friends as no men could be. He had spent the best part of his life—as near a hundred years as not to matter—with them.

When a farmer in the Transvaal sold five hundred or a thousand sheep to a farmer in either the Orange Free State or the Cape, Oupa Ruiter would lead the flock on the long journey from the one place to the other. He would return with another flock, either for a farmer or for the great Johannesburg cattle market. Then, after a few days of drinking and resting and seeing old friends, he would set out again.

He had done this since his boyhood days that began in the distant years after the Great Trek. All the years of his life had been spent walking through the land; from east to west, then back; from north to south, then back. He knew every corner of the land, the name of every mountain and river, the piece of history behind every hill. He knew the mood of the weather too.

Hotnot Annie called him the last of the great Hottentots. She spoke of him with awe and was humble in his presence. She said he was the last member of her race who, as a boy, had looked on the face of the great Adam Kok, whom she claimed to have been the last king of the Hottentots.

Oupa Ruiter was small and wiry, built on the same pattern of bumps as *Hotnot* Annie. His skin was a rusty golden yellow,

73

dry as old parchment. His head was covered with white pepper-corn hair. His small eyes were almost completely hidden by the many folds of his eyelids.

All Vrededorp knew him. Always, on his return from a long journey, people welcomed him in a very special way. He never had to pay for food or drink. And if he wanted to talk they hung on every word he said. And if he wanted to be silent, they were content to sit with him. He was more than just an old man. He was a symbol of something important to all the citizens of Vrededorp.

Aunt Betty had found a dray-cart and our belongings had gone on that earlier in the evening. Now, with my mother between her and my sister, we walked up Fifteenth Street.

Oupa Ruiter waited for us on his veranda.

'Angelina, my child,' he said in a loud cackle.

'Sorry to bother you, Oupa,' my mother said. 'It's only for a few days, then I go to Krugersdorp.'

'Bother!' he snapped. 'You've too much pride. Just like your mother! You know you can stay here as long as you want to. I don't forget what your father did for me. Only time I fell sick. . . . Over thirty years ago. . . . Come, come in. . . .'

The room was twice the size of the one we had left. Brown paper was stuck over the window. The flame of the solitary candle was too weak to dispel the darkness. Shadowy things were strung across the ceiling on lines that criss-crossed.

'This calls for the lamp,' Oupa Ruiter said.

He lit the oil lamp that hung from the centre of the ceiling. It bathed the room in light. The shadowy things were sheep's entrails.

The old man saw me staring.

'Fodder, boy, fodder! And don't pull up your nose at the smell. You'll be glad to take one of those down when your own guts are empty and screaming. Nothing like 'em. The best fodder in the world. And all from my little friends.'

74

The smell of sheep waste was everywhere in the room. Our things were piled in a corner near my mother's bed, which the old man had set up and made. Maggie went to the window, tore off the paper, and opened it. Aunt Betty began to unsort the pile of our things.

'You staying with Ma, Aunt Betty?' Maggie sounded depressed.

Aunt Betty nodded.

'Then I'll go. . . . Thank you Oupa Ruiter.'

'Pretty wench you've grown into,' the old man touched Maggie's back. 'You'll soon make a slave of some fool man.'

' 'Bye, Ma,' Maggie called miserably from the door and went out.

'What's the matter with her?' Oupa Ruiter said.

'She's young,' Aunt Betty said.

'Yes,' the old man said, suddenly serious. 'Yes. The young.'

'Better lie down, Lina,' Aunt Betty said.

My mother stretched herself on the bed. Oupa Ruiter went and sat on the edge of the bed. He took my mother's hand in his own gnarled and sinewy old hand.

'Well, my child. . . .'

'It's hard, Oupa.'

'I remember you and your sister with your mother. You were always the quiet one, proud and quiet. . . . A long time ago. Only the children of friends are left now. And they are grown up and have children. Some are old. . . . Yes, it's hard, child. Make this your home as long as you like. I'm never here. And even if it is hard, don't admit it. . . . Want to eat?'

'No, Oupa.'

'Where will you sleep Oupa Ruiter?' Aunt Betty asked.

'Are you blind? My bed's on the veranda. I let down my canvas and it's a room. . . . Do *you* want to eat?'

'No thank you, Oupa,' Aunt Betty said.

'Come, boy.'

I followed him out. He had a narrow canvas bed on the

75

veranda. He had built shelves against the wall and on these his few personal possessions were stacked. In one corner was a paraffin-tin with holes knocked in its sides. Near it was a pile of coal and a small bundle of wood. He pulled a huge piece of tobacco from his khaki drill jacket and took a bite.

'Now we'll cook. Can you make a fire?'

'Yes, Oupa.'

'Then go to it.'

I laid the fire and carried it out into the street. Oupa Ruiter pushed the dried sheep's waste out of the intestine with his thumb, turning the meat inside out as he went along. His room had no yard so I had to get water from the yard next door. He washed and salted the meat and put it into the pan. It would go on as soon as the fire was ready. He fished out a sixpenny piece and gave it to me.

'Two pounds of yellow rice.'

I walked the short distance to the Chinaman's grocery shop. A thin boy moved to my side.

'Hello.'

'Hello.'

'I saw your things going into Oupa Ruiter's. My name is Benjamin but I'm Dinny. Shake.'

I took his hand.

'I'm Lee.'

'Play to-night?'

'Yes.'

My turn came. I said:

'Two pounds of yellow rice and monkey-nuts *bonsella*.'

I smiled at the tall, lean-faced Chinaman in the hope of a big *bonsella*. It worked. I needed both hands to take his fistful of monkey-nuts. Dinny's eyes popped. I stuffed the nuts into both pockets.

'You never give me so much!' Dinny accused.

'You never buy so much,' the Chinaman retorted. 'And you call me names.'

'That's a lie!'

The Chinaman grinned and said:

'Ching-go-ma, tie-boss-ee, one-cigarette-and-two-toffee. . . . Who shouted that at me this morning?'

A broad grin cracked Dinny's face. He tried to wipe it off but failed.

'I didn't mean it.'

'You said it.'

'Tuppence mealie meal.'

After he had got and paid for the mealie meal, Dinny held out both hands for his *bonsella*. Grinning, the Chinaman only put a few monkey-nuts into his hands. Dinny looked at the nuts, then at the man. He picked up his meal and walked slowly to the door. There he turned. His voice was charged with venom:

> *'Ching-go-ma,*
> *tie-boss-ee,*
> *One-cigarette-and-two-toffee!'*

He streaked away. The Chinaman chuckled softly and said:

'Here, boy.'

I collected another lot of nuts.

The fire had stopped smoking when I got back. Oupa Ruiter carried it on to the veranda. He put two iron bars across the fire and put the saucepans on. He added onions and potatoes to the meat. I sat on the floor near the fire. He sat on the edge of his bed, stirring the food, chewing his tobacco. The food began to give off hunger-making smells. My stomach rumbled loudly. The old man laughed.

At last it was cooked. He dished up into four plates.

'Better take these to the women.'

I went in with two plates. Aunt Betty sat sewing on the edge of the bed. It was clean and tidy. The hanging intestines had been moved to one corner. Almost, it was a completely different room, bigger, lighter, cheerful—a room that had been turned into a home. My mother turned her head.

'He knew,' she said.

'Can't fool that old man,' Aunt Betty said.

From up the street, Dinny's piercing voice rang:
'Lee!'
I had finished eating. I went to my mother.
'Can I go'n play with Dinny?'
'Who's Dinny?'
'A boy.'
'He's all right,' Oupa Ruiter called. 'I know him.'
'Don't go far and don't come back too late and be careful.'

We met under a street lamp. For a while we stood facing
each other, each touched with uncertainty. He had mocked
at the Chinaman. He might mock at me. I felt withdrawn
and reserved. Perhaps he liked fighting. I didn't. Perhaps he
would want to fight with me when he got to know me better.
He pulled his hand out of his pocket. It was filled with
many-coloured marbles. He chose three, one blue, one red,
and one green. He offered them to me. I shook my head.
'No.'
'O go on, take them.'
'No.'
'Why not?'
'You'll want them back. . . . And you'll call me names.'
'I won't.'
'You called the Chinaman names.'
'He's stingy.'
'You'll call me kaffir.'
'No.'
'My friend Joseph's black. All black. He's a Zulu and his
mother too. You'll call them kaffir.'
'Ag, I won't man!' he screamed. Then, suddenly, his voice
became wheedling. 'I won't man. 'Strue's God, I won't. I
won't even call a damn kaffir a kaffir any more. Take them,
please. I'll only win them back.'
I took them. I remembered my pockets were stuffed with

78

monkey-nuts. I took out two handfuls and offered them to Dinny.

'You're a pal, man, Lee man,' he purred. 'You're a damn pal.'

We set off down the street, munching nuts. About us, people moved. On one of the verandas a man sat in the shadows playing a guitar. We stopped and listened for a while. Almost, he made the instrument speak. Its language was sad. The story it told was an unhappy, unfulfilled lament of frustration.

'Come on before I cry,' Dinny said. 'Damn him.'

A woman came out of the house and shouted at the man:

'If you worked as well as you play we'd have something to give the children!'

The man shouted back at her. We carried on down the street. Their cursing voices followed us.

Farther down the street a man and woman were fighting in a room. The door was open and a group of grown-ups and children stood in the street, watching. We joined the crowd, pushed our way through till we had a good view. The man's face was smeared with blood and blood dripped from his mouth. The woman held him by the front of his shirt and kept butting him in the face with her head. His white shirt was in shreds and stained red. He fought till he broke loose. The woman grabbed at him. He stepped back. She grabbed again. He kicked her in the stomach. She screamed and doubled up. He hit her on the side of the face. She went down like a dead weight. The man swung about and rushed at us, cursing. The crowd scattered in all directions. Dinny and I streaked down the street.

'Jeez what a fight!' Dinny said gleefully. 'Just like the fillums. Our fights are never like that. My mother is not strong enough so my brother has to beat up my father when he beats my mother.'

We slackened our pace.

'Want a woman like that when I'm big,' Dinny said.

'Strong. Anybody bothers me, I'll just say to her *moer* him. Boy, that'll be nice.'

We passed a group of young men and women courting on a veranda. Some held hands, others leaned against each other. The young men sang softly.

I'll be your sweetheart,
If you will be mine.

'Love!' Dinny said disgustedly.

We passed on without looking at the lovers.

'Got a sister?' Dinny asked.

'Yes.'

'Lucky stiff. I wish I had one.'

'Why?'

'Tips!'

'What's that?'

'Jeez, you're dumb! Tips! Don't you know what that is?'

'No.'

'Jesus Maria Monk! Where are you from man, Lee man? . . . When a fellow runs after your sister like those silly fellows there, you make him give you money. That's tips.'

At the corner of Seventeenth Street a small boy called to Dinny. He reached to below my shoulders. He was dressed in an orange sack. Three holes in the sack allowed for his head and arms to come through. About his waist was a piece of rope that gathered the sack in and made it hang like some monkish garb. He was barefooted, very fair, and very dirty.

'Hello, Pip,' Dinny said. 'Seen the gang?'

'They've gone begging.'

'Why didn't they damn well wait?'

'Lippy said you weren't coming.'

'Wait till I get that long lipped dog. . . . Where'd they go?'

'They didn't say. . . . Give us a rise, Dinny. I haven't eaten since yesterday.'

'Jeez man, Pip, I'm flat broke man,' Dinny said.

The boy in the sack garb moved away, in the direction of the subway.

'Poor bugger that bloody Pip,' Dinny said.

'Why does he wear that sack?'

'Why don't you give him clothes, Mister Rich?' Dinny was possessed by one of his sudden rages. 'He's alone in the bloody world. Both his people died last year.'

I remembered the remaining monkey nuts in my pocket.

'I have more nuts. We can give them to him.'

Dinny hesitated. I knew that he really wanted the nuts for himself. He looked at me and I knew he knew I knew. A sheepish grin, half-shy, half-apologetic, cracked his face.

'Come on!' he said.

We streaked off, Dinny in the lead. We dodged in and out among people. Every now and then Dinny's voice rent the air in a shrill call for Pip. We caught up with him at the bottom of Eighteenth Street.

'Lee's got some monkey-nuts,' Dinny said.

I turned out my pockets, picked out the three marbles, and passed the nuts to Pip.

'Thanks fellows,' Pip said and turned once more for the subway.

'Let's play Debs, Lee. Come!'

He shot across the wide street, heedless of the traffic, dodging speeding cars and motor-cycles by inches. In his wake, I danced in and out of the flowing stream of vehicles. Horns hooted. Drivers cursed.

'To hell!' Dinny shouted as a car just missed him.

'To hell!' I echoed gaily.

He rushed to a huge glass window filled with men's suits on dummies. He licked his right thumb and pressed it against the window.

'Debs! That's mine!'

He pointed out the suits that were his. I did not like any of the remainder, so I ran to the next window, full of women's clothes.

'Debs! All these are mine for my mother and sister and Aunt Betty.'

'Give you some suits for some dresses?'

'All right!'

'Two suits for half your dresses and things.'

'*Jou moer!*'

'All right. Four!'

'One for one.'

'That's not fair! Suits are thicker.'

'I don't care. Take it or leave it.'

'All right . . . Mean bugger.'

We made the exchanges. I saw a window filled with boys' clothes. I dashed to it.

'Debs! Debs! Debs! Debs! All these are mine!'

Dinny shot by.

'Debs! That bed, that chair, that table; they're all mine!'

We raced to the next window, reached and touched it at the same time.

'Debs! It's mine!'

'Debs! It's mine!'

'I touched it first!'

'Liar!'

'You want to steal my cakes. Thief!'

'You're the thief!'

'It's mine or I'll knock you!'

'It's mine!'

We leapt at each other.

[ii]

Morning breaks gaily in Vrededorp. There is laughter among the people in the morning. It is as though they find themselves so surprised to be alive that they cannot help laughing. There are, of course, homes where morning is sad and miserable. But these are exceptions. For the most part, Vrededorp is a place of laughter in the morning.

'Wake up!' Oupa Ruiter shouted gaily. 'The sun's mocking you. Wake up!'

I opened my eyes. Daylight streamed in through the window. The old drover stood in the centre of the room, a mug of steaming coffee in each hand. My mother sat up in her bed, a smile on her face. Aunt Betty, who slept on the floor, pulled the blanket tighter over her head to stave off wakefulness a while long. Oupa Ruiter laughed.

'No use, Bet. Day is here.'

Aunt Betty gave up the struggle and showed her head. Oupa Ruiter gave them the coffee.

'Yours is outside, boy. And there's something special for you. Wash your face first.'

I dressed and went out. On the bench near the fire, heaped on a plate, were golden fatcakes. On another, smaller plate were the three biggest fatcakes I had ever seen and, beside it, a mug of coffee. Those were mine. I took a bite out of one of the cakes before going round to the yard to wash. . . .

From some way up the street a rich, deep voice drifted down. It rang out loud and clear as an organ pipe, sustained as organ notes.

> *I am coming, Lord,*
> *Coming back to Thee;*
> *Wash me, cleanse me in the blood*
> *That flowed on Calvary.*

The voice drew near; was silent for a while; then rang out again.

> *When the trumpet of the Lord shall sound*
> *And time shall be no more,*
> *And the morning breaks, eternal, bright and fair;*
> *When the Saviour of the earth shall gather on the other shore,*
> *And the roll is called up yonder, I'll be there.*

There was a slight pause, then the voice sang on with glorious gusto.

When the roll
Is called up yonder—
When the roll
Is called up yonder,
When the roll
Is called up yo-on-der—
When the roll is called up yonder I'll be there!

Oupa Ruiter came out of the room.

'Better hurry,' he flung over his shoulder. 'The man of God wants breakfast.' His cackling laugh rang out loud. 'Well boy, did you pinch another?'

'No, Oupa.'

'Bet you wanted to.'

'Yes.'

'More fool you for not doing so. Go on!'

I took another fatcake and went into the street. The man of God came slowly down its centre. He was tall and broad and very upright. His face was dark brown. It was crowned by a massive head of white wavy hair. He had a well-trimmed white moustache that matched his hair. He was dressed in black: tight, stove-pipe trousers gripped his ankles and climbed to his waist where they were held up by a purple sash; a shiny waistcoat hid his shirt; and he wore tails. He carried his hat in his left hand, holding it a little distance from his body, and with the hollow turned up as though to collect money. He carried his Bible, pressed against his chest, in his right hand.

He stopped near me. For a while he studied me closely, then he came to me. He slipped the Bible into a pocket and put his hand on my head.

'Good morning, child. Do you know me? Have I baptized you?'

'No.'

'Ah! Then we must look after you. Can't have you going around like a heathen. An accident may happen and if you

84

are not baptized you may burn in the devil's fire for ever. It's a hot fire. The hottest fire you can think of. And it never stops burning and you never stop hurting. You don't want that, do you?'

'No.'

'Good. Where do you live? And if your mother argues you say you want to be baptized. Where?'

'Here.' I pointed.

'Old Ruiter lives there. Don't play with me, child! You'll go to hell!'

'We do!' I cried.

'That's Lina Abrahams' child,' Oupa Ruiter called from the recess of the veranda.

The man of God straightened up.

'Hello, Brother Ruiter. I didn't see you there. Didn't know you were back.'

'Morning Reverend Rogerson.'

'Morning to you, Brother Ruiter.'

'The child told you the truth. He and his mother are with me.'

'I must see her.'

'Come, Reverend. They are just having breakfast.'

'A good sign. I haven't had mine.'

With his big hand on my head, the man of God steered me to the door.

'I'd better make some more fatcakes,' Oupa Ruiter said. 'I know God loves them.'

'So he does, my brother, so he does,' the priest said blandly.

Oupa Ruiter cackled and knocked at the door.

'God is here, Lina!'

'Come in,' my mother called.

Oupa Ruiter turned back to the fire. The man of God steered me into the room. My mother and Aunt Betty were up and dressed. The two beds on the floor had been taken up. My mother's bed was made. And the room was tidy. The man of God steered me to the centre.

'Morning, Reverend,' my mother said.
'Morning, Reverend,' Aunt Betty said.

For answer, he threw back his head and sang. His deep voice filled the room, spilled out of the window and door, moved up and down the street.

> Rock of ages
> Cleft for me
> Let me hide myself in Thee.

My mother and Aunt Betty joined in. Oupa Ruiter pushed the door wide, and his reedy voice joined in too. And then, from the street, other voices joined in the singing. The hymn ended. The priest tightened his hold on my head. He kept his eyes closed. A feeling of excitement passed from him to me. He pushed out his chest and began a new hymn, lilting and strong, swinging it like the marching song of victorious soldiers. The women in the room, the old man on the veranda, and the little group of people in the street, joined in the chorus.

> T-h-e-r-e is
> Power, power
> Wonder-working power
> In the b-l-o-o-d
> Of the l-a-m-b:
> There is power, power,
> Wonder-working power,
> In the precious blood of the lamb.

In the silence that followed the stirring hymn, the man of God raised both hands and held them as in the act of blessing. I moved away from him to get a better view of his face. He opened his eyes and stared at the ceiling. Tears rolled down his cheeks, yet there was a happy smile on his face. He sang exultantly, in measured notes.

> He taught me how
> To watch and pray.

He waited. My mother and the others sang

> *He taught me how*
> *To watch and pray.*

Then he took it up.

> *To live in joy,*
> *Sing every day:*

And they echoed him

> *To live in joy,*
> *Sing every day:*

His voice was charged with happiness.

> *Happy day*
> *Happy day—*

They caught some of it.

> *Happy day*
> *Happy day—*

He ended in triumph.

> *When Jesus washed*
> *My sins away.*
> *When Jesus washed*
> *My sins away.*

He went down on his knees. We in the room knelt with him. Oupa Ruiter knelt on the veranda. The people in the street knelt where they had stood.

He prayed. And as he prayed, God became a living being for me: a brown old man with a long beard who wore black clothes and who liked singing and laughter. The preacher told God about his backache and asked that his aches and pains in his legs and feet be less this year than they had been last. He argued with God about last year's pains, and warned him not to forget this year. Then he prayed for my mother and me. He prayed long for Aunt Betty, listing all the times he had seen her drunk, recalling all the times she had used bad language. He said it was about time she did something for God. While he prayed, Aunt Betty got up and fumbled in the folds of her dress. She brought out a half-crown and gave it to him. His prayers became kinder. He told God she was just a poor weak woman in a hard world who had had no learning.

'That's not fair,' Aunt Betty protested. 'God knows I went to school. I can read and write!'

'I'm sorry,' the preacher prayed. 'She gave me no reason to know, Almighty. Which just goes to show you never can tell with us Coloured people. And forgive me, Lord. I did not mean to be unfair to your daughter, our sister Betty, who can read and write.'

'I'm out of work,' Aunt Betty hissed.

'Ah, yes, Oh Jehovah. Your daughter needs work. Help her to get it. She will not forget you when pay day comes around. Look down Our Father, and give her her daily bread lest she walks in the ways of sin.'

'Amen,' Aunt Betty said.

'And now, Almighty God. . . .'

'Food's getting cold,' Oupa Ruiter whispered.

'Bless our food and the mocking old man who made it, and let us always remember it comes from you, the Great Giver of all things in heaven and on earth. Amen.'

Aunt Betty made a place for the preacher at the table. Oupa Ruiter brought in a pot of coffee and a pile of fatcakes. The people in the street dispersed. The preacher beamed on the food. I caught my mother's eye. I pointed to the door. She nodded.

'God and I understand each other,' Oupa Ruiter snapped.

'I am his minister,' the preacher said.

'You make people afraid of him,' Oupa Ruiter said. 'I know him. He's a friend. A good friend. He goes on my journeys with me. We understand each other and it's no good your saying I mock.'

I went out and walked slowly up the street. The people who had shared in our service had gone. The street was empty. But sounds of life came from the houses. And far down, from Delarey Street, came the echoes of the sounds of traffic. The autumn sun slanted up from the east and touched the corrugated-iron roof-tops. A young woman ran out of a house a little way up the street. She trotted down towards Delarey Street.

'Hurry or you'll get the sack,' a woman's voice called after her.

A little boy came out of a house and ran up the street with his school books tucked under his arm.

I stood outside the Chinaman's shop, waiting for Dinny. A flock of doves, making an arc in the sky, flew over from the west. The Chinaman came out of the shop with a broom in his hand.

'Want to sweep, boy?'

'Yes.'

He gave me the broom. I swept the shop. I was gathering the dirt when Dinny turned up.

'Hey! Lee!'

'Wait. I've got a job.'

'Hurry up. The gang's waiting.'

I gathered up the dirt and took it to the back. The Chinaman gave me tuppence and a paper-bag filled with monkey-nuts.

'To-morrow?' I asked.

'Yes.'

I went out to Dinny. We walked down the street munching nuts. After a while, we decided to race each other hopping on one leg. Thus, hopping, we made our way into Delarey Street, down towards the subway. We swung left on to the waste lot on the way to Fordsburg station. Here Pagel's Circus pitched its tents at Christmas-time. A wide, deep, uncovered trench cut off the Fordsburg houses from the waste lot. It was a waste-water trench, now dry. Three boys waved

89

to us from the far corner of the trench, then disappeared into it.

We ran across the lot and scrambled into the trench. The gang looked me over carefully. Dinny introduced us.

There was Lippy, tall and thin as a matchstick. He had a long, loose, lower lip, the largest thing in a small face. He had sores at the sides of his mouth. Next was Sleepy. He was bubbling and wide awake. It seemed impossible for Sleepy to keep still. A long rent in his khaki shorts showed his privates whenever he moved, and he moved all the time. Finally, there was Fatty. A moving ball of fat, covered with creases in which thick greasy dirt hid. A clean line round his fair face showed the limits of the area he washed.

'Lee's joining the gang,' Dinny said.

'Yeah!' Fatty said.

'Yeah!' Dinny said aggressively. 'I'm the leader.'

'So you say,' Fatty said. 'Prove it!'

'I don't want to fight,' Dinny said.

'Ag, let him join, man,' Sleepy said.

'Scare arse!' Fatty jeered at Dinny. He looked me over carefully. 'Want to join the gang?'

'Yes.'

'What's your name?'

'Dinny told you.'

'Your name, shit arse!' he shouted.

The others watched me. I hesitated, torn between fear and anger.

'Shit arse yourself!' I yelled.

'So you want to fight,' Fatty said oddly.

I realized he had suddenly grown frightened. I jumped at him and hit him in the stomach. He grabbed at me. We went down together.

'Kill him!' Dinny shouted. 'Kill the fat dog!'

It ended quite suddenly. I found myself sitting on Fatty's stomach, pinning his arms down with my knees. I put my hands on his neck.

'Best!' Fatty cried. 'Best, please!'

'Am I a shit arse?'

'No.'

'You know my name?'

'Yes, Lee.'

I got up and moved away backward, watching him. But all the fight had gone out of him.

Dinny moved to my side. He whispered:

'Say it's your gang.'

'I'm the leader,' I said.

'O.K. by me,' Lippy said.

'Me too,' Sleepy said, shadow-boxing in front of Fatty.

'Me too,' Dinny said.

Fatty looked at me.

'Chuck him out,' Sleepy said, smacking the fat face.

'Want to stay?'

'Please, Lee.'

'Tell him he owes you sixpence,' Dinny hissed.

I pushed out my chest and walked towards Fatty.

'You owe me sixpence,' I said gruffly

He looked into my eyes briefly, then down at my feet.

'Yes, Lee. Can I stay?'

'When do you pay?'

He pulled a podgy hand out of his pocket. He opened it. Two glittering, newly polished pennies lay in his palm.

'Sixpence!'

'All I got. Pay you off to-morrow.'

I took the two pennies.

'Can I stay now?'

'Yes.'

I savoured power and importance. It went to my head. I looked at my subjects and snapped:

'You are each fined a penny!'

'Jeez!' Dinny said.

'You refuse?'

'No. . . . I'll bloody well pay. When?'

'Now.'

'Have a heart,' Sleepy cried. 'Give us time.'

Lippy turned out his pockets.

'I'm skinned,' Dinny said.

'All right,' I said briskly. 'To-morrow.'

'Who's your deputy?' Sleepy said.

'Dinny.'

'I must go'n give ma and the baby their food,' Dinny said.

We climbed out of the trench and wandered back to Delarey Street.

We parted at Fifteenth Street.

'What about to-night?' Sleepy said. 'Begging?'

'I want to steal,' Lippy said.

'Stealing,' I said.

'Meet, at the bottom of Seventeenth Street,' Dinny said.

'So long, chief.'

'So long.'

'So long.'

Dinny and I went up the street.

Dinny's home was a big room in a muddy yard. As he opened the door, smoke streamed out of the room. It was dark with the smoke.

'Come in,' Dinny said.

'That you, Benjamin?' a woman's voice called faintly from the depths of the darkness.

'Yes, ma.'

'You're late. Baby's hungry.'

My eyes grew accustomed to the fog. A thin, dark woman with long black hair sat propped up in an old bed in the far corner of the room. The bed was covered with pieces of rags. In her arms, the woman held a tiny baby, rocking it gently. The woman's black, melancholy eyes were huge in her small, drawn face.

Dinny said:

'This is Lee, Ma.'

The smoke filtered out through the open door. Dinny went

to the smoking fire in the corner away from the bed. I heard, rather than saw, him busy with pots and pans. The child began to cry.

'Hurry up,' the woman said plaintively.

'I damn well am!'

'Your language,' she wailed.

'Sorry, Ma.'

I said:

'See you later, Dinny. 'Bye, Auntie.'

I crossed the muddy yard and went home. My mother was there, cooking.

'Hello, Lee. Food's nearly ready. Where have you been?'

'Out with the gang. I'm the leader now. Look!' I showed her my four coppers. 'I swept the Chinaman's shop and he gave me two. I got the other two by fining Fatty. I get four more from him to-morrow. Dinny and the others will pay me one each.'

'All fines?'

'Yes.'

'What for?'

'Because I'm the leader.'

'But what did they do?'

'Nothing.'

'And is it right to fine them for nothing?'

'Fatty would have done it if he'd won.'

'So you fought. . . .'

I lowered my head.

'He would have beaten me if I didn't.'

'So you beat him and fined him.'

'Yes.'

'And the others. . . . Why fine them?'

'To show them I'm the leader.'

She did not say any more. But behind her silence, I sensed disapproval and disappointment. She dished up and we ate in silence. When I had eaten, I looked up and saw her watching me closely.

'Ma. . . .'

'Yes, Lee?'

'All the other boys do it.'

I did not know what else to say, and I felt uncomfortable
with my mother in her present mood. I sought to change the
subject.

'Where's Aunt Betty?'

A slight smile touched her lips.

'All right. . . . She's looking for work. I wish I could take
you with me.'

'Where?'

'To Krugersdorp.'

I did not want to leave the gang now. But I did not say so.
It might upset her. I decided not to mention the gang to her
again.

'Can I go and play with Dinny?'

'Yes.'

I got up and went to the door.

'Lee. . . .'

I turned. She stared at me for a while, then she shook her
head, a slight, just perceptible movement.

'It's nothing. . . . Your father had such dreams. You go
and play. Be careful.'

I went up the street and crossed the muddy yard to Dinny's.
He and the baby were not there. From the room next door
came voices raised in loud quarrelling.

I went out and shut the door. The quarrel next door
turned into a fight. The crash of falling furniture followed
me across the yard and out into the street. I went through
the muddy passage that linked Fifteenth and Sixteenth
Street. It reeked of piddle.

A crowd was watching a fight a little way up Sixteenth
Street. I made my way to it. Two men, naked from the waist up,
fought in a human ring. Both bled from the mouth and nose.
The darker man with the long black hair was growing an ugly
bump just above his left eye. The ring of men egged them on.

94

'Good show, Benny!' a tall man cried and coughed. When the spasm passed, he said: 'Another five bob on Benny. Any takers?'

'I'll take it,' someone called.

'Lee!'

I saw Dinny on the other side of the throng. He held the baby precariously on his left hip. I worked my way round to his side.

'That's my brother!' His eyes glowed with excitement.

'Which one?'

'The one they call Benny. His name's Joe. . . . Sock him, Joe!'

'Why are they fighting?'

'They're not fighting. They're boxing. Sock him, Joe! Kill him!'

The child started crying. Joe held up his hand. His opponent stopped. Joe turned to Dinny.

'Get that damn child home before I break your bloody neck!'

Dinny retreated fast.

The gang met that night and went stealing.

'Where do we steal?' Lippy asked.

'Twenty-fourth Street,' I said. 'Come on!'

We went down, looking at the stalls. I saw one with an old Indian in attendance. That seemed the easiest. And it was well stocked.

'That's it,' I said.

We studied the place carefully, then walked some distance from it. I told them the plan.

'Fatty is first. Grab what you can and make him follow you. Then you go, Lippy. He'll still be after Fatty so you'll have a chance to get as many eggs as you like. Take a lot. Then you, Sleepy. Grab oranges. He may not chase Lippy so you'll have to be quick. Dinny goes after you. I go last. It's most dangerous for the last man. . . . Ready, Fatty?'

95

'Ready!'

'Go!'

Fatty waddled away, gathered momentum and bore down on the stall.

'Ready! . . . Go!'

Lippy shot away, arms and legs flailing like windmills. The old Indian dashed after Fatty.

'Go!' I said.

Sleepy shot away. Lippy was helping himself at the untended stall. The old man stopped following Fatty and turned as Sleepy reached the stall. He shouted. An Indian from the next stall came to his aid.

'Go!'

Dinny was off. He ran with his bottom stuck out and his head in the air. The two Indians chased after Lippy and Sleepy.

'Go!' I said and raced down to the stall.

The younger of the two Indians was gaining on Lippy. Fatty saw this. He ran across the Indian's path and taunted him, showing the stolen sweet potatoes. The Indian fell for the ruse and gave chase. As soon as Lippy was safe, Fatty turned on a burst of speed. For all his fat he moved like the wind.

I reached the stall. Dinny was shoving oranges into his shirt-front. I grabbed hard-boiled eggs with both hands.

'Look out, Lee!' Fatty's voice rang out.

We turned. The old Indian bore down on us. I stood, petrified for the moment. Dinny shot off to the right. The Indian lumbered across, arms outspread, cutting off his escape. Dinny veered left. The Indian cut him off there too. Dinny dashed forward desperately. He ducked under the outstretched arm. The Indian struck and caught him on the shoulder. The weight of the blow sent Dinny skidding across the street on the seat of his pants. He was too dazed to move and just sat there while the Indian bore down on him.

'Dinny!' It was Fatty again.

96

The voice brought Dinny to his senses. Suddenly, a horrible string of curses flowed from his lips. His voice quivered with rage. His frenzy gave him tongue and he cursed in a language I could not understand. But the old Indian understood. And what he heard shook him into momentary immobility. Dinny jumped up and shot away. I ran off in another direction. The operation was successful!

We met at the bottom of Eighteenth Street. Our shirts bulged with food.

'What language was that?' I asked Dinny.

He grinned sheepishly: 'Indian.'

'What did you say?'

'Don't know. My old man's Indian. He says that when he's drunk and wants to beat Ma. . . . Didn't know I was half-Indian, heh?'

'What shall we do with the grub?' Sleepy asked.

'Let's have a party,' Fatty said. 'Heh, Lee?'

We bought ginger beer at a Chinaman's at the top of Nineteenth Street, then, after baiting the Chinaman for a while, we crossed over on to the field.

The moon was big, yellow and near the earth. The sky was clear. The stars stood out. Almost, one could leap up and touch their twinkling bodies. The night air was warm, tender. Far away, on the horizon, the mine dumps, white mountains, were ghostly shadows. Underfoot, the grass was tender. We stopped in a grassy hollow. Vrededorp was out of sight, beyond the rise of the land.

'Look!' Sleepy hissed.

Two lovers were on the ground nearby.

'Yah-hoo!' Dinny cried piercingly.

We all laughed loudly. The lovers scrambled up and slunk away. We flung ourselves on the grass in a circle. We heaped our food and drink in the centre of the circle.

'See!' Fatty cried.

We looked up. A shooting star curved across the heavens to the west. It exploded in a burst of light, then was gone.

'Make a wish,' Dinny said.

We turned our attention to the food. We feasted under the moon, in the Ottoman's Valley.

[iii]

One morning Maggie, Aunt Betty and I saw my mother off to Krugersdorp. Then we went back to Oupa Ruiter's. The gang was waiting there. They helped me carry my things down to Twenty-first Street where my mother's sister, Aunt Mattie, lived.

She was waiting in the yard. She looked at the gang.

'Who are these children?'

'My gang,' I said.

'No street gangs here.'

The gang dumped my things and fled. Aunt Mattie looked me over.

'What a dirty child!' she snapped. 'Take your things in, then wash yourself. See that you do it properly or I'll do it for you.'

Maggie put a comforting arm about my shoulders.

My new home was two rooms that opened into the corner of a yard. The back room was small and dark. It had one small window that opened on to the wall of the adjacent building no more than two feet away. Hardly any light came in through it. The front room was larger and lighter. It served as sitting-room, dining-room, and, at night, as bedroom. My aunt, her daughter Catherine, and my sister Maggie had slept in the small back room since the death of my father. My brother Harry and the young man who worked for Aunt Mattie slept in the front room. In her corner of the yard, my aunt had built two sheds.

My aunt was as loud and assertive as my mother was quiet and retiring. She was short and stocky and fair and had once been a very handsome woman. She chain-smoked.

Till the death of her husband she had lived on a level far

above that of the Coloureds of Vrededorp. Her husband had been caught at either diamond- or gold-smuggling. All their money had gone on the defence. Then he had died, leaving her penniless and with a small child. She had worked in the homes of white folk, had dealt in the illicit liquor trade, had sold fruit and vegetables on a push-cart. Now, as the winter drew near, she had a small horse-drawn cart and was selling firewood. At week-ends she still dealt in illicit liquor.

She looked harshly, coldly, on a harsh, cold world. She was as harsh with herself as with anyone else. The only two people who ever seemed to pierce her coldness were my brother Harry and her daughter Catherine.

Maggie gave me a towel and piece of soap.

'Better wash well or she'll scrub you.'

I went out to the tap. I washed as I had not washed before. When I had done, Aunt Mattie inspected me. She was not satisfied.

'Bring me the bath, Maggie.'

'I'll wash him, Aunt Mattie.'

'I told him to do it properly. I'll show him.'

'He's small,' Maggie protested.

Aunt Mattie glared at her till she fetched the round, iron bath. She filled it with cold water. I stripped and got in. Aunt Mattie scrubbed me till all my skin was red and sore. And, whenever I moved, she smacked me resoundingly with the back of the brush. At last, I stepped out of the water, hurt and miserable.

'Look at it!' she snapped.

The water was dark and scummy. I dried myself and dressed.

'If you don't want this to happen again, wash properly.'

'Yes, Aunt Mattie.'

'All right. . . . Help with the wood.'

I followed her to the sheds. One shed was filled with split wood tied in neat bundles and stacked up. In the other shed were unsplit logs of even length. Maggie and my cousin Catherine were tying split pieces into bundles.

Catherine was fair as a white person; blue-eyed and with long, straight, light brown hair of a golden texture.

'Hello,' she smiled at me.

I felt too miserable to respond.

I sat beside Maggie, stacking up bundles of wood. Splinters entered my fingers. As fast as I pulled them out, others went in. After a time I grew used to the splinters and the routine. By lunch-time I was working cheerfully.

My brother and Danny, the young man who worked for Aunt Mattie, came home for lunch. They had been out selling wood all morning. Danny gave Aunt Mattie a tobacco-bag filled with the morning's earnings. I studied my big brother.

He had changed much since the day he and Maggie had brought me from Elsberg. Then, he had been dapper and neat in dress; a kind of buoyant radiance had gone out from him. It had said: Life is good, brother; life is mine: what fun! Now it was gone: there was no neatness, no gaiety, no sense of strong elasticity. His clothes hung drably on him. His shoulders slouched. An oily cap sat far back on his head, showing the dust in his hair. His eyes were sullen.

I watched him, anxious for warm recognition. His eyes flitted over my face.

'Hello, Lee. Ma gone?'

'Yes.'

Only Maggie saw my disappointment. She touched my hand and beamed reassuringly.

Aunt Mattie emptied the tobacco-bag into her lap and counted the money. Maggie doled out the food. These were lean days at Aunt Mattie's, and lunch consisted of *magou* and bread. *Magou* is another version of the inevitable *mielie pap*. The meal is thinned to a thick runny liquid. It is cooked then left to cool, ferment, and turn sour. It is served cold and drunk from mugs. In the long summer months, *magou* is the main food of the very poor of Vrededorp. Maggie gave us each a mugful and a slice of bread.

Aunt Mattie finished her counting.

'You're two shillings short.'

Harry and Danny looked at each other.

'We were hungry,' Harry said.

'Well, Danny?'

'It's as Harry says . . .' Danny began quietly.

'To hell with what Harry says! You're supposed to look after my money. I pay you, feed you, and keep a roof over your head so that you should do what I want.'

'Yes, Aunt Mattie,' Danny murmured. His thin, yellow face looked drawn.

'I took you off the streets!'

Danny looked at the ground and stopped eating.

'Ma!' Catherine cried.

'Shut, Miss! How do you think I keep you at school. We go without when we are hungry, but not the great Mister Harry Abrahams. I work my fingers to the bone for you. And this is what I get!'

Harry dumped his mug on the ground and got up.

'I'm getting out of here,' he said bitterly.

He stalked to the gate.

'Mister!'

'I'm fed up with all your nagging!'

'Come back here!'

'Nag, nag, nag. That's all you do. Morning, noon, and night, you yap away at us, no matter what we do.'

'I said come back here!'

'Better come back, Harry,' Maggie said.

He turned slowly, reluctantly.

'I'm going to blow one day and you'll never see me again. You'll be sorry then.'

Aunt Mattie laughed harshly.

'It'll be good riddance of bad rubbish. . . . Till that happy day you'll do as I tell you. Better get ready to go and sell.'

'More? To-day?'

'Yes, more, to-day.'

'But it's Saturday!' Harry's voice was strained.

'You don't stop eating on Saturdays.'

'Have a heart, Mattie,' he appealed. 'Everybody else stops work on Saturday afternoon.'

'We can't afford it.'

Harry watched her for a while. Then, with a sudden decisiveness, he flung back his shoulders and shook his head. He pushed his hands deep into his pockets. A smile, half-challenging, touched his lips.

'I'm not going,' he snapped.

They stared at each other. Aunt Mattie lit a cigarette and blew out a cloud of smoke.

'All right,' she said calmly. 'You're a man. You know your mind. You're not going. Get ready, Danny, and take the boy with you. Let him learn to earn his bread.'

Danny got up and went into the shed. We heard him piling bundles of wood on his arm. Harry's firmness deserted him. His body relaxed and drooped again. Catherine sat biting her finger-nails. I turned miserably to Maggie. Aunt Mattie kept her eyes on Harry's face. Maggie looked from the one to the other, a strange, unhappy expression on her face.

'Why don't you go?' Aunt Mattie taunted.

'I will!'

He swung about and stalked out.

'Harry!' Maggie called.

'Let him be,' Aunt Mattie said.

Maggie closed her eyes and clenched her hands.

'Why don't you say it?' Aunt Mattie mocked. 'Or are you still trying to be a lady?'

Maggie jumped up and followed Harry out of the yard. I saw a sudden, convulsive move on Catherine's face. As I looked, her face moved in uncontrollable jerks. The convulsions spread to all her body.

She suffered from St. Vitus's Dance, and this family storm

had brought on an attack. Tears rushed from her eyes. She bit her lower lip, trying to stop the jerks. She jumped up and rushed, jerking, into the house.

Aunt Mattie sat staring into space. Danny came out of the shed, his arm piled high with bundles of wood. I got up and went in the shed. I came out with bundles of wood and carried them out to the cart. I looked about but there was no sign of Harry or Maggie. Between us, Danny and I filled the cart. Then he went in to where Aunt Mattie still sat staring into space.

'We're going, Aunt Mattie.'

She looked up.

'How much?'

'Two hundred bundles.'

She gave him the little tobacco-bag.

'There's five shillings in change.'

I followed him out and walked beside him as he led the horse down the street. We walked away from Vrededorp, away from the narrow, mean streets, away from the throb of the pushing crowds. We walked steadily till we got to the broad, tree-lined streets of upper Fordsburg. We stopped the cart on a quiet corner. The world seemed hushed and empty here. Peace hung over it. The broad pavements were clean. No black water ran down the gutters of these streets. No half-naked, potbellied children fought and played in these gutters. The houses were of bricks. They had curtained windows. And each house had a back and front garden. There was room between one house and the next. And each had large windows to let in the light of day. A stranger walking here, in the shade of the broad pavements, seeing the trim, fenced-off houses, and the riot of flowering colour within each front garden, would find it hard to believe a place called Vrededorp was less than half an hour's walk away. To me the contrast was so great, I might as well have stepped into another world, on another planet.

Danny instructed me.

'Two bundles for a *tickey*. And remember a tickey is three pennies, not two or two and a half. Aunt Mattie'll be mad if we are short. Always go to the back door. Be careful of dogs. And remember to say *baas* or *missus*. All right.'

With four bundles on my arm, I went off to canvass my first house. Behind me, Danny's voice rang out, making a melodious sound of the one word:

'Firewood!'

I opened the gate and went to the back of the house. My heart thumped violently. Was there a dog? Would the white people chase me away? I reached the backyard. I saw no dog. I moved tentatively towards the kitchen door.

'Yes?'

I jumped and spun round. A white man, half-in, half-out of a little shed, stood looking down at me.

'Firewood, *baas*,' I whispered. My throat was constricted.

The kitchen door opened. I looked quickly at the white woman who came out, then I turned back to the man.

'What is it?' The woman spoke to the man.

'This *skepsel's* selling firewood. You don't want any, do you?'

The woman moved round till she stood beside the man. I looked at the ground while I waited.

'I think the wood's only an excuse,' the man said. 'He looks guilty as hell. If he'd found the place empty. . . .'

'Stop it!' The woman laughed. 'He's only a child.'

'There are no children among them. They thieve before they can walk or talk properly.'

'Don't be silly!'

'Look at his face. He can't even look at you.'

'He's a child, frightened like any child would be with strangers.'

'Guilty conscience, if you ask me.'

'Nonsense. . . . How much is the wood, boy?'

'Two for tickey, missus.'

'That your last four?'

'No, missus.'

'All right, leave the four here and get eight more.'

I hurried out to the cart.

'You've been long,' Danny said.

'Eight more,' I said excitedly.

'Good fellow. Hold that sack.'

I hurried back. The woman came out of the kitchen. The man stood by, amusement in his eyes.

'In that corner, boy.'

She counted while I stacked up the wood. She offered me half a crown.

'Have you change?'

'I can get it, missus.' I took the money.

'Better keep it till he brings the change,' the man said.

'Nonsense.'

'He won't be back.' His eyes challenged me. 'Your chance, boy.'

I collected a shilling from Danny and brought it back. The woman was waiting for me with a large slice of home-made bread, a thick coat of butter on it.

'Thank you, missus.'

'Thank you, boy.'

I looked at the man then turned away quickly. Without knowing how, I realized I had angered him. I hurried out, confused.

I shared the bread with Danny. We rested while we ate. Then we went off again. He took one side of the street, I took the other. We went up one street and down another. Our cries rang over the quiet streets.

'Firewood!'

'Firewood!'

Sometimes, people chased me away. Sometimes, they set dogs on me. Twice, they cheated me. The first time a woman took six bundles and went into her kitchen. I waited a long time. Then a man came out.

'What are you waiting for, boy?'

'My money, *baas*.'

'What money?'

'For the wood, *baas*. Six bundles.'

'She paid you.'

'The missus didn't pay me, *baas*.'

'I saw her pay you, you dirty little black liar. Get out before I lose my temper! Lying about white people. Get out!'

I ran.

Danny took it calmly.

'Aunt Mattie won't be mad about *that*.'

At the second place, they took ten bundles and paid for four. They swore that was all they had taken.

More often, they just bought their wood and paid for it. Sometimes, they were friendly and gave us something to eat.

We sold a third, then half, then a little more than half our cartload.

Shadows invaded the broad streets. The sun turned orange and sank rapidly. Bright lights went on in the houses about us. I turned to Danny.

'Those the same as the street lights?'

'Yes.'

'Why don't we have them in our houses?'

'Because we are not white.'

'Are they only for white people?'

'Yes. . . . We'd better be going home.'

We turned for home.

'Danny. . . .'

'Yes?'

'Why are those lights only for white people?'

'I don't know, man. . . . Because they are on top.'

'And their houses are nice.'

'*Ja*.'

'I'd like to live in a nice house.'

'We all would.'

'Would you, honestly?'

'Sure, kid.'

'Did you? Once?'

He looked at me and smiled.

'No.'

'Not even when you were with your mother and father?'

He put his hand on my head and tugged playfully at my mop.

'I never had a home, kid.'

'Do you like it at Aunt Mattie's? I don't.'

'She's all right once you understand her.'

We reached home just as the Vrededorp street lights were lit. I carried the wood in while Danny and Aunt Mattie went over the money. I finished carting the wood in and went into the big room. Aunt Mattie and Danny sat facing each other across the table. The money was stacked up in little piles on the table. She looked briefly at me as I went to a bench against the wall.

'How was he?'

'Good.'

'That's something. . . . I'm selling to-night, Danny. I have two tins of *skokiaan*. I have someone to help with the selling but I need someone to watch. They say the police will be about.'

'I'll do it,' Danny said.

Aunt Mattie looked at me.

'We don't want him here. What'll feed him?'

'A tickey's fish and chips and a penny's bread,' Danny said.

'And the bioscope?'

'Four pence.'

She counted eight pennies from the pile of coppers and pushed them to me.

'Keep out of mischief.'

'Been to the bioscope before?' Danny said.

'No.'

'You'll like it.'

I pocketed the coppers and went out. About me the Satur-

107

day night crowds were thick and loud. Mine boys, money in their pockets, thronged together. They talked at the top of their voices. They laughed often and loudly. They told each other where the most potent *skokiaan*, a foul-smelling rot-gut home-brewed liquor, could be had. Amid laughter, they discussed the current prices for women's bodies.

Rubbing shoulders with the often-blanketed giants, were the small, smooth house-boys and kitchen-boys. They came from the homes and hotels of the white people of Johannesburg and its suburbs. On Saturday nights they were dressed in bright suits and ties that looped out in front of them. Their jackets were short and very tight, the bottoms of their trousers were very wide. Sometimes house-boys wore suits made of two different coloured materials. The left half of a jacket would be a bright green, the right a bright orange. The right trouser leg would be of the same colour as the left half of the jacket; the left the same as the right of the jacket. They wore very pointed patent leather shoes, polished till they gave off mirror-like reflections. Fights often flare up between mine· boys and house-boys on Saturday nights. The townsmen and the countrymen did not get on well together.

And there were the housemaids, dressed in their brightest and best. They pranced awkwardly up and down the streets on their high-heeled shoes. Their dark mouths and cheeks were brightly painted. They wore hats, white gloves, and hid their beautiful legs in cheap, shiny stockings. They laughed and chattered loudly. Later, as the night wore on and they found partners, they would take off the silly hat, the uncomfortable shoes, the gloves and stockings. They would relax and dance till daybreak at some *maraba*, egged on by the thumping noise of a broken-down piano. Till daybreak . . . That is, if the police do not come.

I pushed and fought my way through the dark crowds that were everywhere. The crowds thinned a little as I reached Fifteenth Street. I hurried up to Dinny's, half-fearing he might not be there. But he was. He sat feeding the baby in the smoke-filled room. An Indian lay drunk across the foot of his mother's bed. His mother lay on her back, staring dejectedly at the soot-stained ceiling. At the little table near Dinny, a well-dressed and well-groomed young man sat. His long black hair was combed back in beautiful waves. It shone with grease.

'Lee man!' Dinny said happily.

I waited for him. The young man stared sullenly at the table. The drunk man snored. The woman kicked at him under the blankets. Dinny finished feeding the child and took it to his mother.

'I'm going out with Lee, Ma.'

'Where?'

'Bioscope. All right?'

'Yes. But come straight back.'

We went out and took the route round the top, by the side of the cemetery, to Twentieth Street. That way we would avoid some of the crowds.

'God man, it's nice to see you. The others said you won't come to-night. Only Fatty and me said you'd come.'

'Where are they?'

'Waiting at the bioscope.'

'Perhaps they've gone in.'

'We were all going to wait for you till the last show. I was going to tell my ma to tell you. D'you see the end of *Sunken Silver* last week?'

'No.'

'Oh boy! Walter Miller was in the water, out. The little crook had knocked him out with a hammer. He was floating. Two crocodiles with helluva big mouths were rushing at him. The crooks had the girl and his pal. Oh boy! How'll he escape?'

'You like the bioscope?'

Dinny looked at me as though I had asked the silliest question.

'Don't you?'

109

'I've never been.'

'What! . . . You lie!'

'Honest.'

'Oh boy! God man, Lee! You're going to see something!'

'That your old man?'

'That drunk on the bed? Yes. He only comes home once in a while. The other fellow's my brother.'

'He wears nice clothes,' I said.

'He's a cissy. He puts stinking oil in his hair and runs after girls. He's a waiter in a club.'

I told him about my selling of firewood.

'So you got a job, you lucky dog!'

'I don't like it.'

'I had a real job once. Good money too. But I had to leave it when ma got sick and the baby came. It brought in three bob a week. Good money.'

'Where?'

'The tinsmith. I worked for Boeta Dick. . . . Say, Lee, do you want a job there?'

'What'll I do?'

'Smear tins for Boeta Dick to solder.'

We neared the bioscope. The gang saw us, waved, called. Under a street lamp nearby a dice 'school' was in progress. Lippy grabbed my arm as we stopped at the bioscope door.

'Look, chief! Look!'

His left eye was black and puffy. His long lip quivered with pride.

'What happened?' Dinny asked.

'Cockeye and his gang beat me up. I told them our gang would fix them to-night.'

'Who's Cockeye?' I asked.

'A cross-eyed dog from Seventeenth Street,' Dinny said.

'Only three in the gang,' Sleepy said. 'Let's go.'

'We're going in the bioscope,' Dinny said.

'We'll fight them to-morrow,' I said.

'But they're waiting for us,' Lippy protested.

'To-morrow!' I shouted.

'O.K., O.K., chief.' Lippy stepped back.

'How much?' I asked Dinny.

'Fourpence, if you pay at the window; two if you slip it to Sheriff.'

The fellow at the door was a stocky black man. He was dressed in the colourful garb of a cinema cowboy: check shirt, ten-gallon hat, a bright kerchief round his neck, leather cuffs, chaps, and high-heeled boots with spurs. Two guns were strapped to his waist. A sheriff's star shone over his heart.

'You slip it to him,' I said to Dinny.

'Shell up,' Dinny said.

We gave him our money.

Dinny made a sign to Sheriff. Sheriff winked. A while later, he came to the door. Dinny gave him the money. He slipped it into his pocket and returned to his post near the ticket window.

Two couples entered the foyer. Sheriff made a sign. One of the men winked. The two men barred the ticket window while they paid. We sneaked in past the legs of the grown-ups. In the darkness, one of Sheriff's henchmen guided us to the front seat where a score or more other little boys sat, who had entered as we had.

Suddenly, a train came rushing straight at me from the silver screen. I shut my eyes and screamed. I was not alone.

The bioscope in Twentieth Street was Vrededorp's most powerful and direct link with the outside world. Through it we kept touch with the scientific advances of our time. From it, we drew our picture of the world of white folk. Our morals were fashioned there. The young men of Vrededorp slapped their girls as they had seen men slap girls on the screen. The girls modelled themselves on the ladies of the screen. Once, a Vrededorp murder was modelled on a murder we saw on the screen. People wept bitterly at screen tragedies; more bitterly than at their own, real-life tragedies. Often, the illusions of the screen became the reality of some frustrated boy's or girl's life; and drab Vrededorp became the illusion. There was a boy who became Douglas Fairbanks. He jumped off roofs, leapt on fast-moving cars and leapt off before the shocked drivers realized what was happening. He drowned in one of the mine dams. He was trying to get into the pipe that pumped the water up from the bowels of the earth.

Illusion and reality often merged at the bioscope. . . .

When I got home Harry and the girls were still absent. The big room and the yard were full of drinking people, black and Coloured. Strapping men and drunken women leaned against each other and talked with wild animation. The sweet-sour smell of *skokiaan* hung over the place. Aunt Mattie and another woman went among the drinkers, serving. Aunt Mattie had a money-pouch tied round her waist. A woman began to sing.

'Shut up!' Aunt Mattie snapped.

The woman's man protested.

'Will you pay my fine if I'm caught?'

'Only a little music, sister.'

'I won't have it. The police are about. Be quiet or go.'

'All right, sister. All right.'

I went back to the street. Danny stood at the corner, keeping a look-out for the police. I went and kept watch with him.

'Hello, kid.'

'Danny.'

The street lamp showed the smiling curve of his lips

'Longing for your ma?'

I said nothing.

He punched me playfully.

'Cheer up, kid. To-morrow is another day.'

We watched till we were the only two people in the street,

till even Delarey Street became deserted. No trams ran; no trains rumbled across the subway bridge; odd cars went through at long intervals. Even the dogs that scavenged in the gutters had gone.

'Look,' Danny said.

Far up Delarey Street, coming to us, two women walked.

'That's Maggie and Catherine,' Danny said.

At the same time, people came out of our yard in a bunch. We heard Aunt Mattie's voice:

'I tell you there's no more.'

'I will sleep here,' a man's drunken voice said.

'You must go. I have no room.'

'You take all my money, now you chase me.'

'You must go. Get out!'

The people passed us. The drunk followed, protesting bitterly. Aunt Mattie came out and stood with us on the corner.

'That the girls?'

'Yes,' Danny said.

'Go and meet them. I'll clear up.'

When the four of us got back the place was clean: the beer-tins were out of sight, the floor was swept, the table tidy. All that remained was the heavy smell of *skokiaan*. Aunt Mattie and the woman who had helped her were having a private drink. There was a drink waiting for Danny. The two girls pulled faces at the smell.

'Had a good time?' Aunt Mattie asked.

The girls said nothing. Danny sat near the table sipping his drink and pulling faces at the taste.

'To hell with you all!' Aunt Mattie said in sudden anger.

'I must go,' the woman who had helped said.

Aunt Mattie paid her. With her going, an uneasy, strained silence hung over us while we prepared for bed. Catherine and Maggie made a bed on the floor of the big room. We then all went into the small room and knelt in front of Aunt Mattie's bed. With the stench of *skokiaan* about us, we prayed.

113

Aunt Mattie stood over us with a short rod. Danny led the prayer.

> *Our father.*

We followed:

> *Our father,*
> *We charge in heaven.*

Maggie and Catherine started giggling. Aunt Mattie lashed out with the rod, striking at their arms and shoulders. I peeped through my fingers. Danny's face had gone red, his lips trembled. The girls stopped giggling. Aunt Mattie stopped beating them.

'Again, Danny.'

> *We charge in heaven.*

The girls chortled and got another beating. Their laughter infected me and I, too, took a beating. Just as we quieted down, Danny burst out giggling. We joined in and were all beaten. Pain soon sobered us.

'Again,' Aunt Mattie said.

'Oh no!' Catherine cried, and collapsed with laughter.

Plump Maggie held her sides. Tears ran down her cheeks. Danny leaned his head against the bed and shook. I screeched with uncontrollable laughter.

Aunt Mattie beat us till we laughed and cried at once.

'I'll get the damn devil out of you!'

She got a bucket of water and threw it over us. We sobered.

'Again!'

Danny said:

> *We charge in heaven.*

The girls said:

> *Which art in heaven.*

Danny said:

> *Hello, be thy name.*

114

Maggie sank to the floor, writhing in the agony of a new gust of laughter.

'Please God, I'm bruised . . .' she moaned.

Once, in the early hours of the morning, Catherine's voice woke me.

'Come to bed, Ma. It's nearly morning.'

Aunt Mattie sat huddled near the door, a shawl over her shoulders. The long candle had burned down to nearly nothing. Beside me, on the floor Danny snored evenly. I heard Catherine move on the bed in the other room. I closed my eyes. Sleep claimed me once more.

Groaning woke me. Harry was in the room, near the door. He was on his knees, being violently sick. Aunt Mattie knelt beside him, holding his head. The two girls, in their night-clothes, stood in the doorway between the rooms. Danny sat hugging the blankets about his naked waist. A fresh candle had burned itself half-away. Harry groaned. A rush of muck spurted from his mouth. Aunt Mattie compressed her lips. Tears shone in her eyes. She wiped the muck from his lips. Her voice had a strange newness to me:

'Oh God! How have we sinned?'

I sank back into sleep.

IV

I began work at the smithy on the Monday morning. My wages were half a crown a week. My hours were from six in the morning till six at night, with an hour's break for lunch. My boss, Boeta Dick, was a tall, bent, reedy consumptive. He had a parched yellow skin, drawn tight over his jutting bones. His cheeks were so sunken it was as though he were permanently sucking them in. His eyes were far back in his head. He coughed violently. And, beside his seat was a bucket of sand into which he spat. Changing the sand daily was the only part of my job I hated.

The smithy was divided into two parts. At one end were the machines that cut, shaped, and put the tins together. The men who worked on the machines were on a regular weekly wage. At the other, smaller, end, was a row of small furnaces, each with its own small bellows and pile of fuel. Here, at each furnace, a man sat soldering the seams of the tins as they came from the machines. The solderers were on piece-work. To average two or three pounds a week they had to do a mountainous amount of soldering. Each solderer had a boy to cart the tins from the machines to him, then to smear the seams of each tin with sulphur powder so that the lead took easily. And, after checking, to cart the tins out to the yard where the lorries collected them.

Dinny had, on the previous day, instructed me in the mysteries of counting tins. I had a sheet of paper and a pencil. I made twelve marks on the same line. Each mark stood for a dozen tins. As each dozen tins were smeared and soldered, I cancelled off one mark on the paper. When the twelve marks were cancelled, the result was a gross. But neither Dinny nor I knew what a gross was.

On that first day I drew six rows of strokes and cancelled them; I made tea for Boeta Dick; I went near the strange, roaring machines whenever I had a chance.

There were four other boys. Three were about my own age and size. The fourth was bigger. Everyone called the big boy Mad Nondi. He fetched and carried for two of the solderers.

Toward late afternoon, as I stood in line with the other boys, waiting for tins to come off the machines, Nondi nudged me from behind. I turned. He opened his eyes wide, poked out his tongue, and snorted at me.

'Saucer eyes!'

I looked away. He pushed me in the back.

'What's your name, thin stick?'

I dared not ignore him so I said:

'Lee.'

'Saucer-eyed Lee!' he cried and burst out laughing.

I willed myself not to look at him. He kicked me in the seat. I staggered against the boy in front. The boy in front staggered against the one in front of him. The boy in the lead nearly fell against the machine. Nondi's laughter pealed above the rattle and drone of the machines.

When the working day ended Nondi met me outside the smithy gate. I prepared myself for an ordeal. Instead, he linked his arm through mine and marched off in the direction of Vrededorp with me, babbling words I only half-understood.

An old black man with a push-cart stood outside Braamfontein Station. Nondi brought me to a halt.

'Fatcake, big eyes?'

'I've no money.'

'I have.'

'I don't want anything,' I said.

'Why not?'

'You'll fine me if I take it.'

'Go to bloody hell! . . . Two fatcakes, father! Two fat fat-cakes! And let them taste like the foods of the heavens so that this big-eyed, small-headed fool can taste the heart of corn and learn to understand. . . .' His words flowed on faster than I could follow.

The old black man laughed and spoke in one of the Bantu languages. Nondi answered in the same language, eyes shining, arms waving. The old man threw back his head. His deep-throated laughter rang out. Nondi pointed at me, flung back his head, flung out one arm, and spoke at the top of his voice. The old man laughed till tears ran down his face.

The old man gave us a big, golden fatcake each. He filled two white enamel mugs with steaming coffee. A crowd came out of the station. Some came to the stall. We moved away, giving them room. We ate in silence. Nondi offered the old man money but he would not take it. We set off again. Nondi was silent for the rest of the way. His last outburst seemed to have sapped him. We parted in Delarey Street.

There was peace at Aunt Mattie's that night: an uneasy peace, but peace for all that.

Catherine was doing her homework. Harry and Danny were chopping and tying wood for the next day. Harry was subdued and looked green and sick. I washed, then went and helped with the wood.

It grew dark. We lit candles.

'Come on!' Aunt Mattie called us to supper. The week-end liquor trade had been good so we had stew and rice. Maggie arrived in the middle of supper. She brought cold meat which was shared out among us.

Aunt Mattie went off to *Stokveld* after supper. *Stokveld* is the trade union of the women who deal in illicit liquor. Each pays a weekly contribution. The total amount thus collected is given to a different member each week. The union also helped arrested members. Often, a well-known '*Skokiaan* Queen' was sent to prison without the option of a fine. In such cases the *Stokveld* helped with the home and children till the member came out of jail. They met every Monday evening. Danny built a small fire after Aunt Mattie had gone. It was not cold. We were in the middle of summer. Christmas was drawing near. But a fire is a thing of friendship as well as of warmth. A young man called Jacob Loff turned up. He was Catherine's boy: a stocky, muscular, good-looking Coloured man. Beside him, Catherine looked very frail, very white, and, suddenly, not a girl but a woman. His coming brought a new radiance to her bearing.

Next, a girl called Emily arrived. She was tall, thin, and very dark, almost black. Her kinky hair was made into two tight, neat plaits. She had large, limpid eyes, and a shy wayward smile. This was Harry's girl. She had a habit of looking quickly at Harry's face then away at the ground. Her teeth, when she smiled, shone white and perfect from the setting of her dark face.

Maggie embraced her. As well as being my brother's girl, she was my sister's favourite friend and soon became my favourite young woman.

The circle was complete.

Danny carried the fire in. We made ourselves comfortable. Maggie began a song. The others joined in.

> *A room*
> *Dim-lit by candle-light,*
> *Soft voice*
> *Singing on the night,*
> *A glowing fire*
> *Red with love's desires:*
> *Fire*
> *Voices*
> *Room*
> *Conspire;*
> *And drabness*
> *To his deep dark hole retires.*

Danny looked longingly at Maggie. Harry started 'I'll be your Sweetheart'. Emily sang with a private little smile tugging at her lips. Catherine and Jacob held hands. I leaned against Maggie's comfortable body.

They turned from singing to story-telling. The fire glowed warmly. A free, hopeful, happiness hung over the room. They took turns at telling stories. I closed my eyes. Maggie put an arm about me. I drifted off to the soft music of Emily's voice. . . .

[ii]

The long summer days passed. The big sun shone fiercely on the world of Vrededorp. The coon shows began to assemble and practise for the great New Year festival of song and dance. A lazy slowness came over the inhabitants of Vrededorp. They moved slowly about the streets while the hot, dry sun beat down.

At nights they gathered in little groups in the streets. Sometimes they stood talking, sometimes they sang and danced.

The summer sun set late. The summer moon rose early. So, when it was not day, the world was bathed in a soft half-light. The summer sky seemed to move further away from the earth: the summer stars drew nearer, hung just above the highest roof-top.

Young men and women walked under the moon on the Ottoman's Valley. And sometimes, a male voice, serenading its love, drifted down to the crowded streets. Then, old women exchanged looks and smiled. Often, in the summer, there was 'trouble in the family' because the moon and the Ottoman's Valley and the soft night air, and oh, so many other things, had made a girl give in to her lover and get 'into a family way'.

And there were the groups of little boys walking the streets with yard-long sticks of sugar-cane. And the way the cane-juice ran out of the side of your mouth as you chewed.

And there were the girls playing skipping or high-jump or one of a large number of ball games.

And there were the dice-schools of the bigger boys and the young men.

And on Saturday afternoons there were the rugby matches on the Ottoman's Valley. There Hakkies, 'the greatest full back in the world' had his days of glory, and the colourful play of a little Malay fly-half made him the most sought-after young bachelor in Vrededorp. There too, one Saturday afternoon, I basked in my brother's reflected glory when he caught the ball inside his own half, sold four opponents the dummy, and outpaced the rest to put the ball between the posts, and then convert the try. His Emily and I shouted ourselves hoarse as they chaired him.

There were the days at work. I grew used to my job and the machines; used to changing the basin of sand into which Boeta Dick spat, I grew unafraid of Mad Nondi. In an oddly curious way we became friends. From him I learned that a gross was one hundred and forty-four; from him I learned to count up to a thousand. He taught me a smattering of English. Sometimes his mad words fell into order in my mind. When that happened he revealed vivid depths of feeling. And always, when he had money, he wanted me to share in spending it. Often, Nondi laughed and cried for no apparent reason.

And there was the gang. We still went out thieving at nights. At times we fought rival gangs. Often we went up to the Ottoman's Valley in the long summer nights. We were the scourge of loving couples with our rude remarks and raucous laughter.

At home, time did nothing to alter the uneasy tension between us, the children, and Aunt Mattie. Her private fight with Harry often made the house a place of misery that we deserted whenever we could. But on Monday nights it was peaceful. Harry's girl and Catherine's boy came. There was the friendly circle of song and story. And Danny nursed his secret love for Maggie.

People talked about a depression. Money grew even scarcer than it had been. More men hung about street corners. More women sold their bodies to the mine boys. There was less food. But the sun was shining, and while it shone nothing seemed quite as bad as it was.

The Reverend Rogerson walked the streets of Vrededorp each day. The people fed him. And in return, he sang and prayed to his God. On Sunday mornings, white men and women, dressed in the uniforms of the Salvation Army, marched through the streets of Vrededorp. Hundreds of little boys and girls danced behind the stirring music of the brass band.

Two days before Christmas Maggie said:

'Would you like to spend Christmas with Ma, Lee?'

'Yes.'

'All right, we'll go to-morrow.'

'You coming too?'

'For to-morrow but not for Christmas. I must be at work on Boxing Day.'

[iii]

The man said:

'That is the Petersen house. The last one, right at the top of the hill. Well, I must leave you here.'

He turned left for the upper end of Krugersdorp location. We went straight on. The little house stood on the crest of the curving hill that overlooked the location. Where we walked the track was sandy. Fine particles jumped from the living earth and stung our eyes. And everywhere, beyond the little house, green rolling land, undulating gently, swept away to the greenish blue horizon far, far away in the mists of distance.

We were half-way between the house and the location when a woman came out of the house.

'It's mother,' Maggie said doubtfully.

The woman raised an arm and waved, hesitantly.

'It *is* mother!' Maggie cried.

'Mother!' I yelled.

We started to run, oblivious of the harsh heat of the sun and the cloud of choking dust we raised. As we neared my mother, Maggie began to laugh. Tears streamed down her face. My mother hurried down to meet us.

'You look well, Mrs. A. . . . Better than I've seen you in a long time.'

'I am,' my mother said.

'And the wound?'

'Almost completely healed. You don't have to tear the bandage from the flesh any more.'

'I'm so glad.'

'How's Harry?'

'The same. I don't know what to do about him, Ma. He's drinking. I think Emily's giving him up. She's very unhappy about it.'

'Mattie loves him,' my mother said sadly. 'But he should've had a man to guide him.'

'If only he had a job,' Maggie said helplessly. 'He could have married Emily.'

My mother sighed and turned to me.

'And how's my Lee?'

'I'm working, Ma!'

As we walked to the house, I poured out the whole story. We entered the house. There were two bedrooms and a large kitchen.

'Granny and your Uncle Petersen's little girl are away on church business. They won't be back till sunset.'

'Then we'll have you all to ourselves, Mrs. A.,' Maggie said.

Later we went down into the valley behind the house. We walked where cattle grazed in the afternoon sun. I went in front, running here and there, exploring. Far to the right, a line of stunted willows suggested a dried-up river. The grazing cattle clustered thickly there. The earth, where we walked, was covered with tiny yellow flowers, their bodies erect, their faces to the sun. And the sun glowed hotly over the peaceful land.

I passed patches of *moeroga*.

'Shall I pick *moeroga*, Ma?'

'Not to-day.'

We climbed out of the valley. This hill was steeper than the one we had come down. I saw a body of *springhaas* sunning themselves on a cluster of rocks. I picked up two stones and rushed up the sloping land. The rabbits shot away in leaping lines, gliding across the veld at incredible speed. By the time I flung my stones they were out of sight.

I reached the crest of the hill and stood waiting for my women. There was the valley out of which I had climbed, and beyond it, the hill on which Granny Petersen's house stood. Beyond that clustered the houses of the location. Then there was a space of green sweeping down to the station and Krugersdorp. A hill rose behind Krugersdorp and swung away, like a curving ledge, in the direction of Johannesburg. And behind the hill, hidden in the mists of distance, more hills and more valleys rolled away in waves: away, into an eternity of space.

I looked in the opposite direction. It was the same. The earth rolled on in undulating waves; rolled on to a point beyond the strength of my eyes. And, standing there, I knew that if I stood on the furthest point to which vision could carry me and looked ahead, the land would still stretch away as far as the strength of my eyes could see.

A strong sense of space and grandeur overwhelmed me. I longed suddenly for Nondi to be on this hill with me.

'Nondi!' I cried at the top of my voice. 'Nondi!'

Space carried my shouts away. Then, Nondi's voice seemed to come back to me from a long, long way off.

'Lee!'

I opened my arms wide. And it was as if I embraced all the

land I looked upon, and all the people who lived in the land. An irrepressible shout swelled up in me and I let it out with all the power of my lungs.

'Y-a-h-o-o!'

My mother and Maggie drew near.

'What's the matter with you?' my mother called.

I looked at them and they seemed strangers suddenly. . . . I turned my back on them and ran to a solitary tall tree, far to the left. . . .

Granny Petersen was my mother's aunt by marriage. She was small, black as night, and toothless. Her face was so wrinkled, it was impossible to see through the folds of loose flesh and get a picture of its shape. She wore the numberless petticoats of her generation. This swelled her figure to a thickness that made her tiny face seem oddly out of place. In respose, her shrivelled-up little body looked lifeless. But she had sharp, shrewd eyes that flickered in all directions and missed very little.

Now, as she presided over the supper-table, the oil-lamp from the central ceiling rafter shone full on her white, pepper-corn curls. Her sharp eyes glowed out of her shadowy face. Her grand-daughter, the little full-faced dark brown girl of three, sat near.

Granny Petersen finished serving. We all stood with heads downcast while she prayed. It was a long prayer. It began with the food we were about to eat. Then it went on to the house, the chickens and the eggs they were to lay, the cow and her calf. It even remembered the dog. Then granny prayed for my mother, my sister, myself, and the whole of 'that branch of the family, O Lord'. The prayer swung from our branch of the family to her own. She prayed for her son who worked on that 'devil's cart', the railway. She asked God to spare the trains he went on. He had two children to feed and clothe. And this, Dear Lord, reminded her of that wicked woman who had left her son with two young girls and gone off with another man to the pleasures of the evil city. 'You know what to do with such as her, O Lord, don't you. You will punish her and show her that sin does not pay. . . .'

By the time Granny Petersen had finished praying, the food was cold. My mother looked at her food, then at granny.

'I'm sure the Lord would like us to have our food hot, Auntie.'

'Thank you, Angelina, but I think I've lived with the Lord much longer than you have.'

I caught the shadow of a smile on my mother's face as she bent over her food. Laughter-loving Maggie choked and begged to be excused.

We were half-way through our meal when there was a knock at the door. Things happened fast. Granny whisked the two pots under the bed. The little girl gathered up the spoons and took them to the washing-up bucket in the corner. Then granny took our half-eaten plates of food and pushed them far back under the bed.

'Now talk and laugh!' she snapped.

My mother said something. It was drowned by Maggie's laughter. Old granny opened her mouth and cackled away as though genuinely amused by something funny.

The knock sounded again.

'I think there's someone at the door.' Granny's voice was loud enough for those outside to hear.

My mother went to the door. The location priest and his wife came in.

'We thought we might call on you to-night, Sister Petersen,' the priest said.

'It is very thoughtful of you, Reverend.'

'But do not let us keep you from what you were doing,' the priest said, looking at the bare table and the fire with nothing on it.

'Yes,' the woman said. 'Have your supper and don't mind us.'

'We have already eaten,' granny said. 'But do come and sit down.'

The priest bit his lower lip as though in deep thought.

'Anything wrong?' granny asked.

The priest turned to his wife.

'You did take the medicine to the sick old man, my dear?'

A look of horror spread over the woman's face.

'Dear God, forgive me. I forgot.'

'I must ask you to excuse us, sister,' the priest said.

'I understand, Reverend,' granny murmured.

They hurried out.

'See if they've gone,' granny said.

My mother went.

'They've gone.'

Granny got the food from under the bed.

'Seems you were right, Angelina. The Good Lord seems to want us to eat warm food to-night. I'll put it all back into the pot to warm up.'

'Why not pray while it's warming,' my mother said.

A wicked glint showed briefly in granny's eyes. She prayed. There was no need for her to remind God how hard times were. He knew. He knew, too, that she had done her best by the preacher and his wife. Why, only to-day she had walked her poor old legs sick collecting for the preacher's rent. And she had fed them three times this week. And God knew how big their appetites were and how little she had. There were others who had more. It was up to God to stir their hearts so that they, too, took a share in supporting the priest and his good wife. And God had no right to be angry with her because she could not, like Our Lord Jesus, feed half the world on five loaves and two fishes. Anyway, God should not forget she was giving the priest and his wife Christmas dinner tomorrow. As for this little thing of to-night, well, she and God understood each other. They both knew what hard times meant even if younger people had silly thoughts. Amen.

When we had finished our meal it was time for Maggie to start back. My mother and I walked down to the station with her.

[iv]

The six days after Christmas were days of glory in Vrededorp. The grand carnival of coons was the heart-beat of these days.

There were six coon teams in Vrededorp that year. Each team tried to outdo the others in uniform, dancing and singing. A team was made up of between twenty and thirty men and boys. Their uniforms were of the brightest and shiniest silk materials. And each team wore a different combination of colours.

My brother, Harry, was a member of the Twentieth Street team. On my first evening back from Krugerdorp, I watched him dress. His shirt was bright red with shining green ruffs and breast pockets. A green handkerchief, tied pirate fashion, covered his head. Over this he wore a red straw hat with three tall green feathers. White gloves covered his hands. His knee-breeches were yellow, with black piping. A broad purple sash circled his waist. The ends hung down below his left knee. He wore red shoes with big shining buckles, and long white stockings that tucked under his breeches. His cheeks were rouged and powdered. Side whiskers and a moustache of burnt cork completed his turnout.

In marching position, each team made a triangle. There were eight guitarists in a line. In front of them walked a line of banjoists. This was slightly shorter than the line of the guitarists. Next came two lines of bone players. Each had an evenly shaped set of bones in each hand. They rattled these, producing a sound like that of castanets. Next came the tambourine players. They completed the orchestra. In front of them were the dancers, in two lines. Each dancer carried a beribboned stick which he twirled while pirouetting about the street. Finally, there was the leader, the apex of the triangle. He was the most elaborately made-up member of the team. His uniform, though of the same colour scheme, was different from that of the rest of the team. He was the brightest in a galaxy of bright peacocks. He did not dance all the time, like the others. But when he did, great artistry invaded the mean streets of Vrededorp, and all my world came out to watch it and be carried away by a *dagga*-smoking, dice-playing, Coloured boy who, for a brief moment in time, carried the gods of grace and beauty in his heart and mind and twinkling feet.

All through those six days, the lucky men, those at work, rushed home at the end of the day, changed quickly into their carnival clothes, and hurried to the meeting-places of the coon teams. There they met the unemployed who had whiled the long day away, waiting for assembly time. The teams fell in. The guitars and banjos struck up. The bones clicked. The tambourines banged and rattled. A whistle blew. The team set off, down the centre of the street. The leader twirled his stick. Those behind him danced.

Thus, they went up one street and down another. And the folk of Vrededorp marched with them. And sometimes, when two teams met, there was a battle of dancing for the right of way. The teams would stop, facing each other. And the two leaders would dance against each other. That was a sight! They whirled and leaped; made intricate patterns with their sticks; danced on their brightly coloured handkerchiefs; on their bellies; on their hands. Right of way went to the victor. The vanquished made a passage and played the victors through. And oh, how the victorious leader danced through that human passage!

Every now and then, a team stopped in front of a house. They made a circle. The guitars and banjos played till the people of the house came out. Then there was silence. The people of the house chose the song they wanted to hear and the singer. The music struck up. The singer sang the verses

129

alone. The whole team joined in the chorus. The soloist went around, collecting, after his song.

All the coon teams amalgamated on New Year's Eve. A giant coon procession sang and danced its way about Vrededorp into the new year. There was laughter and feasting, and great gaiety. On this, the last night of the old year, the stern coon rules were relaxed. Women and girls could walk in procession with their husbands and lovers. We, the young children, wore paper hats, waved rattles and let off crackers. I was with the gang and we had a wonderful time letting off squibs under people's feet and watching them jump.

Once, I caught brief sight of Harry. A pretty, long-haired, brown girl walked beside him. As I looked, he turned and kissed her. I wondered about Emily. I shouted to him. The din of music, rattles, crackers, and human noises drowned my call.

Midnight came. Whistles hooted. People shouted and flung paper hats in the air. They went about kissing strangers. Once, I caught sight of the Reverend Rogerson. He towered above a crowd that surrounded him. He sang Auld Lang Syne at the top of his voice.

My mother had returned to be with us on New Year's Day, so I left the gang and ran home. People had been saying 'Happy New Year' to each other. I would do the same to her. It would please her. And perhaps I would be the first one. I fought my way home through the crowds.

Before the sun was up, a fleet of double-decker buses carried the great majority of the citizens of Vrededorp to a wooded green place far away from the town. There, people danced and sang and laughed and loved and drank and fed till the sun went down. Then they returned wearily. The week of glory was over. Ahead lay a year of drabness and want before they could have another week of glory. This week would be something to remember in the lean days ahead. . . . The coons packed their uniforms away lovingly. . . .

V

It was a mad day at the smithy. There had been one fist fight. The boss, Mr. Wylie, had himself stalked storming through the place. After months of hardly any orders, there was a big rush order. Mr. Wylie said he had been losing money for months and was fed up. Two machinists and one solderer were sacked on the spot. The rest worked feverishly, goaded by panic. Jobs were scarce that year. Nearly all Vrededorp was at home. We were the lucky ones.

Boeta Dick worked till sweat rolled into his eyes and turned them a bright pink. He grew short of breath. He opened his mouth and panted audibly. He had a wet rag on his lap at which he sucked every now and then. When he spat into the bucket his spittle was a bright pink. His panic touched me and I ran between the machines and him, and then, when I had brought and smeared a huge stack of tins, I squatted beside him and soldered.

In all the smithy only Nondi was unaffected by the panic that possessed us. He went about casually, mumbling to himself. His boss grew angry and shouted at him.

'Shut up and hurry up, you mad dog!'

Nondi flung back his head. The 'mad' look came into his eyes. He flung out one arm and spoke at the top of his voice.

'A dog! Yes! No dog can fear as fears a man. The fears of dogs are fears of truth. I'll be a dog without your fears!'

The echoes of his laughter rang above the noise of the

131

machines. His boss had his soldering-iron in molten lead.
The man was beside himself with rage. He swung the iron.
Drops of lead spattered the side of Nondi's face and ate into
his skin. Nondi let out a piercing scream and clapped both
hands to his left eye. He went on his knees, pushed his forehead against the floor, and moaned.

The smithy foreman hurried down from the machines.
Mr. Wylie came running from his office.

'You saw nothing!' Boeta Dick snapped. 'Understand?'

'Yes.'

'What's wrong?' Mr. Wylie asked.

The foreman raised Nondi's head.

'How did this happen?' The foreman looked at Nondi's
boss.

'Better get him to hospital,' Mr. Wylie cut in. 'You can
find out later. Bring him out. I'll get the car.'

The foreman and another supported Nondi between them
and went out to the yard.

Nondi's boss came over to us.

'You'll stand by me, Dick,' he appealed.

'Go to hell!' Boeta Dick snapped.

'He was mad. You saw it.'

'He was just a kid. A good kid. Funny but good. Don't
look to me for help.'

I felt proud of my boss.

'You'd better get while the going's good,' a machinist
called.

Nondi's boss turned to the machinists. He spread his hands
appealingly.

'Have a heart fellows. I've got a wife and two kids. Stand
with a fellow. You saw he was mad.'

There were only two white men among the machinists.
They worked the two most difficult machines. I had never
heard them speak. Now one of them snapped harshly.

'Get, damn you! And that's the only mercy you'll get here.'

Nondi's boss lowered his head and walked slowly to the

door. And in my mind, I walked with him under the cold stares. And it seemed a long, long walk.

Mr. Wylie returned some time later.

'The boy will be blind in that eye. . . . Where is the man?'

'Gone, sir,' the foreman said.

'Gone? Where?'

'He ran away, sir.'

Nondi returned two weeks later, as the day was ending. He was cleaner than I had ever seen him. He looked fatter, too. He walked into the place and began to laugh.

'Hello!' he cried and made it sound a song of joy.

'How's the eye?' someone asked.

'To hell and blind!' he shouted and went into the office.

The six o'clock hooter went. I lingered in the yard till he came out.

'Ah, big eyes!'

'Hello, Nondi. Coming back to-morrow?'

'Not me!' He waved two pound notes. 'Me, I'm going, brother!'

'Where?'

He pointed at the setting sun.

'There! I'm going to see what it's like where the sun sets.'

'What for?'

'Don't be dumber than a dog, big eyes. I want to.'

'Where will you sleep? What'll you eat?'

'Where dogs sleep: what dogs eat.'

'And your people?'

'I am my people.'

'But your mother and father.'

'I am my people. . . . Don't be worried, big eyes, I'll be all right.' He hugged me then punched me affectionately. 'So long, big eyes.'

'You going now.'

'Now!'

He saluted, smiled, and walked briskly in the direction of

the setting sun. I stood watching him. Perhaps he would turn. I wanted to wave. But he did not turn.

Good-bye, Nondi! Poetry was dressed in filth and nobody recognized her.

[ii]

The long days and warm nights sped along, chased each other, and were lost in time. And time, men, and something within me, conspired against me and my innocence. The darkness of the land rushed on to meet me.

One day, someone came with the news that my brother had been arrested in a dice game.

On a bleak Monday morning, my mother, Aunt Mattie, and Danny went through the subway to the court where he was tried. He was sentenced to fourteen days but there was the option of a fine because it was a first offence. Aunt Mattie refused to try and raise the fine. Maggie was bitter about his.

On the following Saturday Maggie, I, and the girl Harry had kissed on New Year's Eve, climbed the hill above Vrededorp and went down into a valley. Harry was at Diepkloof Reformatory and we were taking him food. Deep in the heart of the valley, we saw men breaking stones. They wore striped prison uniform. And when we drew near, we saw my brother among them.

When he saw us, Harry flung down his pickaxe and waved and shouted. An armed white man struck him across the face with the back of his hand. Harry staggered back, regained his balance, then bent forward and retrieved his pick. My sister strangled a cry. The other girl cursed softly and bitterly.

We went up to the white man. Prisoners stole quick, furtive glances at us then carried on breaking rocks.

'Don't you know the law?' the white man snapped. 'You're not allowed so near the prisoners!'

'We'd like to see my brother,' Maggie said.

'They're not on holiday!' the man snapped.

Maggie looked at the man's feet, then, unwillingly, she said:

'Please, *baas*.'

'You! Prisoner Abrahams!'

Harry jumped to attention.

'*Ja, baas?*'

'Know these people?'

'*Ja, baas*. That's my sister and my little brother and,' he seemed to hesitate, 'my girl.'

I looked at my brother's face. He had the expression of an unhappy, whipped dog, hurt terribly without quite knowing why.

'You can greet them!'

Harry dropped his pickaxe and hurried forward. The man put out a big hand and shoved him back. My brother staggered and sat on the hard earth with a bump. Maggie's chin trembled. Harry's girl breathed heavily through her mouth. Slowly, Harry picked himself up.

'I didn't say make love to them! Go on, greet them!'

' 'Lo, Mag.' Harry looked at the ground.

'Hello, Harry.'

'Enna. . . .'

'Harry,' his girl murmured.

'Hello, Lee.'

'Hello, Harry.'

'All right!' the white man snapped.

'Can we give him . . .' Maggie began.

'No! Wait till they're marching back.'

'But. . . .'

'The *baas* is right, Mag,' Harry cut in. 'Go'n wait.'

'You're learning, Abrahams,' the white man said.

Harry raised his pickaxe and struck the hard rock. We walked away to a safe distance and sat on the ground, watching the prisoners.

The afternoon sun slanted westward, but only slightly. A

lone eagle circled overhead. Once, it spread its great wings and swooped down low. No doubt to see what manner of men these striped beings were. Then, with movements of great power and grace, it climbed. It made an almost straight line up. I watched it grow smaller, hazy, and then merge into the blue sky that had suddenly grown infinitely far removed from the world of men. I longed, suddenly, to be like that eagle, able to fly right out of the range of this place, so that I would not have to watch my brother breaking rock under the hot sun.

Beside me, the two young women sat brooding. At length Enna burst out:

'I nearly gave that brute a piece of my mind!'

'And Harry would have suffered later,' Maggie said tiredly.

'Nothing one can do!' Enna cried.

'One can keep out of their reach.'

'Tell *him* that,' Enna said.

'It's up to you if you're going to be his wife.'

'It's this business of not humbling himself to white people. I've talked to him about that but he won't see it.'

'Perhaps he can't.'

'Other men do.'

'They didn't have our father,' Maggie said softly.

'Your father give him his airs?' Enna was interested.

Maggie smiled.

'If you like.'

'It's foolish,' Enna said. 'How's he going to feed a wife and family with all this pride. It's silly not to see it's not the same for the whites and us.'

'Yes.' Maggie grew thoughtful. 'But you wouldn't have thought it silly if you heard my father. And I don't know if it is so silly either.'

'You've got to work for white people.'

'And crawl in front of them? . . . Tell me, Enna, are you in the family way?'

For a while the girl glared defiantly at Maggie, then she lowered her eyes and nodded.

'Then you must help him,' Maggie said quietly.

'And what of me?'

'You want him to marry you, don't you? . . . He will.'

'You don't like me. You would have been happy if it had been that black, woolly-hair Emily.'

'I didn't say so.'

'But you would! I can see it!' Enna burst out crying.

'My poor brother,' Maggie murmured.

Enna did not hear.

After this, there was a long spell of silence between us. Far away, on the other side of the land where the prisoners worked, a shining, black macadamized road cut through the veld and curved away to Johannesburg in the one direction, and the north in the other. Cars, big shiny spiders from where I sat, sped along the road in both directions. One of these turned off the road and came bumping across the veld to the white man who watched the prisoners.

Two white men and two black men got out of the car. The black men carried knobkerries. They went and stood guard at each end of the line of prisoners. The three white men talked together. The one who had been there all the time, pointed to where we sat. Then he and one of the other two got into the car. It bumped away to the curving road and picked up speed as it hit the road. It was soon out of sight. The new white man tucked his rifle under his arm and strode briskly towards us.

'Better get up,' Maggie said.

The white man walked more slowly as he drew near. He was bigger and looked more brutal than the man we had dealt with earlier.

'Hello,' he said gruffly.

'Hello, *baas*,' Maggie said.

'Want to see Abrahams?'

'Yes please, *baas*.'

He looked at Maggie then back at the line of prisoners.

'Abrahams!' His voice boomed across the silent space.

My brother straightened up and looked.

'Come here! Quick man!'

Harry flung his pickaxe down and trotted across the space that was between us. He grew uncertain as he neared us, and we grew uncertain with him.

The white man got a packet of cigarettes from his shirt pocket, pushed one between his lips, and held the packet to Harry. My brother lost his uncertainty. He took the cigarette and accepted a light from the white man. He inhaled a huge gulp of smoke, held it, then let it out with a sigh. His lips were swollen and there was a stain of dried blood at the side of his mouth.

'Your lip,' the white man said. 'What'd you do?'

'I saw them and waved,' Harry said.

'You fellows ask for trouble.' The white man shook his head gently and smiled. 'That the only thing?'

'The other *baas* knocked him down,' Enna protested.

'Quiet, Enna,' Harry said.

'It's true!' said Enna.

'Quiet!' Maggie snapped.

'You two brother and sister?'

'Yes,' Maggie said.

The man's eyes crept over Maggie's ample body.

'Must've been unpleasant for you. I'm sorry. . . . All right, *kêrel*, relax.' He left Harry with us and walked back to the line of prisoners.

'Thank you, my *basie*!' Enna called fervently after him.

'What for?' Harry said bitterly.

'Because he's kind. They'd be kinder if you appreciate.'

'You don't know him,' Harry said.

'There you go again! What's the matter with you, Harry?'

'Stop it, Enna,' Maggie said.

'I saw him peel the skin off a fellow's back this morning,' Harry said. 'You never know whether he's going to kick you or give you a cigarette. He likes it like that. The other fellow's better.'

'Forget them now,' Maggie said. 'How are you?'

They looked at each other for a while. Harry's face grew bleak.

'All right,' he said.

'Really?'

'They kick you around, but what do you expect!'

'There you go!' Enna said.

'And the food?' Maggie asked.

'You get hungry and you eat it.'

'Ma sends her love.'

'How is she?'

'All right.'

'Any message from Mattie?'

'She couldn't raise the fine, Harry.'

'Tell them I'm all right.'

He sucked hard at the almost vanished cigarette-end.

'I brought some,' Enna said.

She gave him two packets and matches. He lit a fresh one. I heard the white man's booming voice and looked across. The prisoners stopped working. Those who had cigarettes lit up.

'Kind *basie*,' Harry murmured.

'I know about Enna,' Maggie said. 'Want me to do anything?'

'Better not tell them till I come out.'

There seemed nothing more to say. They stared at each other for a while. Enna grew restless. Maggie noticed it.

'You'll want to speak to Enna,' she said. 'There's a nice piece of chicken from my work in the parcel. Take care.'

'I'll be out soon,' he said, and it was a prayer.

'You will,' Maggie said and turned away abruptly. 'Come, Lee.'

' 'Bye, Lee,' he called.

We walked up the sloping land till we came to a huge

boulder. Here we waited for Enna. The big sun was nearing the horizon and turning orange. Far up in the heavens, a line of fleecy clouds raced through the sky. Though peaceful and windless on earth, a storm raged in heaven. Was the eagle caught in that storm?

Down in the valley, Enna flung her arms about Harry's neck and clung to him. A car left the road and bumped across the veld to the prisoners. The echo of the white man's voice came up to us:

'Abrahams!'

Harry ran back with his parcel. He stood in front of the white man for a while, then, stuffing his parcel into his shirt, he joined the line. The white man blew a whistle. The prisoners shouldered their axes and formed fours. One of the two black policemen went to the head of the column. The other went to the rear. The car bumped to a standstill. The white man got in. A whistle blew. The prisoners marched away, an army in striped shirts, carrying pickaxes. And among them, one of them, marched my brother.

Enna reached us and leaned against the boulder sobbing. We watched them till they curved away with the curve of the shining road.

'A gang of prisoners will always remind me of my brother,' Maggie said.

One fine autumn day, three white boys pounced on me as I walked home from work. It was between Braamfontein Station and the Vrededorp subway. The sun had gone down and the world was bathed in the half-light that precedes night. I was walking beside the iron railings that fenced off the railway land from the street. I was running a piece of wood along the iron bars and noting the variations of each tinkle. Suddenly three boys were about me.

'I'll have this one,' a ginger-headed lad said.

'What's the matter?' I asked.

'You're going to fight me,' he said.

'We fight fair,' another said.

'I don't want to fight,' I said.

'You'll fight!' said ginger-head.

'Why?'

'I want to kill you!'

'I've done nothing,' I cried.

'You're black,' the third lad said.

'Ready!'

Ginger-head came at me with fists raised. I dodged his first blow and noticed what beautifully clear blue eyes he had. Then his left caught me smack in the left eye.

'Please. . . .' I appealed.

'Fight, black coward!'

A blow on the chest sent me reeling against the iron rails. I clutched the rails and steadied myself. I saw the three of them briefly. There was no excitement about them. They were more like grown-ups than boys. This was a calm, quiet, methodical business.

'Come on,' Ginger-head said, coming in again.

Better fight, Lee. But, somehow, I had no will to fight. I had no reason to fight, no desire. I raised my hands and warded off the blows as best I could. Ginger-head cracked me on the nose and drew blood. This, because it hurt, stirred me to rage, I rushed in with flailing fists. Ginger-head gave ground under the flurry. But I did not land a single solid blow. He dodged, slipped, and caught all my punches. Then, as my flurry ended ineffectively, his fist sank into the pit of my stomach. I gasped and doubled up. He swung at my unprotected head and caught me on the ear. I went flat on my back, dazed and hurt.

'Get up!'

I raised myself to a sitting position. The other two yanked me to my feet and propped me against the iron rails. Ginger-head hit me again, but I did not know where. Then, as in a dream, I heard running feet. Someone shook me. The fog cleared. I looked at the black man who supported me.

'Why did they beat you, son?'

'They say because I'm black,' I said tiredly.

'Come,' the man said, giving me support as we walked towards Vrededorp.

Another time, a white man on a cycle cleared his throat and spat as he flashed by. The muck struck me in the eye. . . .

My mother found a job with a little room attached. I sometimes spent part of an evening with her in her little box-room. The Boer family seemed thoughtful and considerate.

Harry came out of jail, subdued, quiet, and depressed. The scraps between him and Aunt Mattie grew more bitter. At last, he left the house and set up house with Enna in a room in Fifteenth Street.

Catherine and Jacob Loff got married suddenly one day. Then I discovered that a child was on the way.

My tenth birthday came and went.

Soon, the sharp, highveld winter was on us. It was very cold that winter and many people died in Vrededorp. Food was scarce so a hungry Reverend Rogerson walked the streets, looking pinched and blue. A number of Vrededorp men broke into grocers' and butchers' shops and stole food and money. Those arrested received stiff sentences because crime was on the increase.

Aunt Mattie's rent arrears were so big, the Indian land-lord refused to give her any more grace. She found a house in Sixteenth Street and we moved there. In the removal, Aunt Mattie lost half a crown. It was the only money in the house. She remembered last putting it on the mantelpiece of the new house.

We were all there. Maggie, Catherine, Jacob Loff, Harry, Danny, and myself. She taxed each in turn, and accepted their word when they disclaimed all knowledge of the money. Then she turned to me:

'Then it must be you!'

'I didn't take it.'

'You must have!'

'I didn't!'

'Don't shout at me, you little thief!'

'Better search him,' Maggie said quietly.

I held my hands above my head while Aunt Mattie went through my pockets.

'He must have hidden it,' Aunt Mattie snapped at last.

'He's been with us all the time,' Maggie said.

'He's a little thief!'

'I'm going,' Harry said harshly, and went.

'Haven't you hurt him enough,' Maggie said.

Aunt Mattie turned from me, still convinced I had taken the money. I went out and walked aimlessly about the bleak, cold world.

It was a Saturday night. Dinny and I walked down Delarey Street on the way to the Bioscope. The Saturday-night crowds milled about us. A heavy hand fell on my shoulder. I turned and looked into the face of a big, brawny, black boy. His glazed eyes had the *dagga*—Indian hemp—smoker's film over them. I tried to pull away. He hit me in the stomach, winding me. Dinny slipped into the crowd and disappeared.

'Don't fight, sonny!' the big boy rumbled. 'See this. . . .'

I looked at the whip fashioned of coils of thin wire.

'Your skin peels if I hit you with this. Try'n run away and I'll show you.' He clouted me on the side of the head. 'Get up!'

I obeyed. He swished the whip.

'Now run!'

I dared not.

'Come on!'

I followed him through the crowds. He moved with the easy, springy grace of a wild animal. He pushed people out of his way. They looked at his face and did not make the protests they felt.

We met two of his kind near the subway. Each had a little

boy in tow. One little boy was Coloured, the other was black. The two big fellows were smoking *dagga*.

'Wait!' my 'boss' snapped.

He went over to the other two and had a smoke with them. His drugged eyes glittered more unnaturally when he returned.

'Come!'

We went through the subway, up Market Street, past the big market, into the very heart of the town. This was my first sight of Johannesburg proper.

The streets were very broad and very clean. Tall buildings rose high in the sky. And the streets were bathed in a myriad lights. The pavements were lined with shops. The shops had huge glass windows, each brightly lit for all the world to see what was in it. And everywhere, as though flung into the sky and held by nothing, coloured lights went on and off, spelling out things I could not read. Sleek motor cars flashed by in all directions. Well-dressed white people paraded the pavements, sat in clean, spacious cafés, lounged in wonderful bars. And everywhere, here, people feasted. I passed a window where four people sat at table watching a man carve up a chicken for them. I passed another where a man and woman sat, heads close together, a huge box of chocolates and glasses of coloured drinks in front of them.

My 'boss' took me to a crowded corner. He took off his cap and pushed it into my hands. He fondled the wire whip. Then he punched me in the ribs.

'I'll cut your skin to ribbons if you don't beg. Beg!'

He crossed the road, and watched from the darkest corner he could find. I stood trembling.

A white man passed, stopped and turned back. He looked at me, then flung a sixpenny piece into the cap. A couple passed. The man flipped a penny. It fell at my feet, rolled into the gutter. I ran after it. The woman laughed. For a while after that nothing happened. People went past as though they did not see me. I shook the cap.

'Penny, please, *baas*. Penny, missus.'

An elderly lady put a shilling into the cap and murmured: 'Poor thing.'

A group of slightly drunk young men came along. They made a ring about me and made bets with each other about flicking pennies into the cap. Passers-by stopped and watched. They ran out of pennies and used threepenny- and sixpenny-bits. This went on till one of them saw three unescorted girls on the other side of the road.

After they had gone, my boss came over and emptied the cap, leaving only a few coppers in it. He had hardly got back to his quiet doorway when a black boy of his own size stopped beside me. He breathed heavily.

'Where's your boss?'

'Over there.' I pointed.

My boss came out of his shadow and hurried across.

' 'Tecs,' the stranger said. 'Got my boy and another man and his boy.'

'Van?' my boss asked.

'Yes.'

A Black Maria turned a corner far up the road. The stranger shot off.

'Run!' my boss snapped. 'Watch the cap.'

I clutched the cap to my bosom and raced after him. We ran all the way to Vrededorp.

Dinny waited for me outside our house. The night was cold and he shivered. But he had done forced begging and wanted to be sure I got back.

The black boy waylaid me three times and forced me to beg for him. He became the curse and terror of my life. In the end, in spite of his threats to kill me if I did so, I told my brother.

I took Harry and Danny to where he hung out. He was with friends. I pointed him out.

'You the fellow who took my kid brother begging?'

'Not on your life!' he cried.

'The kid says so.'

The black boy glared at me.

'Did you say that, sonny?'

I decided he would kill me in any case now if he could.

'Yes. Three times.'

'All right,' Harry said.

'Any of you others fighting for him?' Danny asked.

A big black giant smiled and shook his head.

'A man fights for himself, brother.'

'I'll take him, Harry,' Danny said. 'Kid's my friend.'

'He's my brother,' Harry said.

Harry took off his jacket and gave it to me.

'Come on, fellow.'

'I don't want to fight. Look, I won't do it again. I swear.'

Harry moved forward, my ex-boss moved back.

'Look man,' he pulled a ten-shilling note out of his pocket and flung it at Harry's feet. 'Take that. That'll pay the kid.'

'I hear you smacked him down,' Harry said.

He leaped in suddenly. There was a flurry, and then my ex-boss was on the ground with a bleeding mouth and nose. Harry raised his foot. The others looked on calmly. I turned away and braced my body.

I went on no more forced begging expeditions. . . .

A stranger called Chris Fortune came home with Maggie one night. He was small, dapper, and very fair. His coming cast a shadow over Danny. He belonged to one of the best families in Vrededorp. His manners and clothes were those of a gentleman. He was one of that small, dying band: the skilled Coloured artisan. He was a cabinet-maker.

His coming brought a bubbling gaiety into my sister's heart. And on that first night, my mother was at Aunt Mattie's. While he drank tea and talked with Aunt Mattie in the front room, Maggie hugged my mother in the kitchen.

'Mister Right, Ma!'

'Are you sure, my child?'

146

'As sure as I'll ever be, Ma!'

'All right, my child.'

I liked the look of Maggie's young man. I liked the way he looked at her. I liked him for giving me a sixpence on that first night.

Danny left us a few days later. He slipped away as quietly as he had lived among us. I never saw him again.

Enna gave birth to a boy. I visited their room a month after its birth. A stale smell hung over the place. The one window was shut. The bed was unmade. A pile of dirty crocks were stacked in a corner. Cigarette-ends lay in the dust coating of the floor. The baby lay bawling on the bed. Enna stood oiling her long tresses. Harry sat sullenly in the only chair in the room.

'Hello, Harry, I've come to see the baby.'

Harry stood beside me while I looked at the tiny creature.

'It's like you,' I said.

'Think so?'

'Yes.'

'Hope he doesn't grow up like him,' Enna said.

'Better sweep this pigsty before you start talking,' Harry said.

'I don't take orders from you!'

'Look at the place! Aren't you ashamed?'

'Aren't *you* ashamed of never working?'

Their voices grew louder.

'I've been looking! You know that!'

'But you never get anything!'

'Suppose you could!'

'Other men do!'

'You should've got another man!'

'Aren't I sorry I didn't! And all those chances!'

'Don't flatter yourself! No decent man would put up with filth!'

'You're right! You're not a decent man!'

'I must go,' I said and fled.

I did not really know my brother. We had never spent time together. We had never talked. There were too many years between us. He was my big brother but that was about all. There was the blood-relation and a series of meetings. When I first met him in Elsberg he had been gay and spruce, clear-eyed and sure of himself. Now I left him, dirty, unshaven, baffled, bitter, a father, seething with futile rage, yelling at the top of his voice in a filthy room.

I thought of the other girl who had loved him, dark Emily. Would it have been different if she had been with him? Why, loving him, did she leave him? And as I thought of this, I became conscious of the beginnings of a new awareness. Something was happening to me and the way I saw the world in which I lived.

[iii]

Often, at the smithy, I cleaned Mr. Wylie's car during the lunch hour. For this he gave me a shilling at the end of each week. Boeta Dick had raised my wage to three shillings. Thus, I went home with four shillings every Saturday afternoon. Half this sum paid for my food and keep. I took a shilling as pocket-money. The other shilling Aunt Mattie put away for me. Once or twice she had borrowed from my savings. She had always asked first. She had always returned it to my little hoard that she kept in her mattress.

One lunch-time, after I had cleaned his car, Mr. Wylie said:

'There are some sandwiches on my desk. Take them.'

He drove off. I went to the office. The short-sighted Jewish girl was in her corner, eating her lunch and reading. She looked up.

'Mr. Wylie said I can have that.' I pointed.

'All right.'

I took the little package and turned to the door.

148

'Lee.'

I stopped and turned to her.

'That is your name, isn't it?'

'Yes, missus.'

'Miss, not missus. You only say missus to a married woman.'

Her smile encouraged me.

'We say it to all white women.'

'Then you are wrong. Say miss.'

'Yes, miss.'

'That's better. . . . Tell me, how old are you?'

'Going on for eleven, miss.'

'Why don't you go to school?'

'I don't know, miss.'

'Don't you want to?'

'I don't know, miss.'

'Can you read or write?'

'No, miss.'

'Stop saying miss now.'

'Yes, miss.'

She laughed.

'Sit down. Eat your sandwiches if you like.'

I sat on the edge of the chair near the door.

'So you can't read?'

'No miss.'

'Wouldn't you like to?'

'I don't know, miss.'

'Want to find out?'

'Yes, miss.'

She turned the pages of the book in front of her. She looked at me, then began to read from *Lamb's Tales from Shakespeare*.

The story of Othello jumped at me and invaded my heart and mind as the young woman read. I was transported to the land where the brave Moor lived and loved and destroyed his love.

The young woman finished.

'Like it?'

'Oh yes!'

'Good. This book is full of stories like that. If you go to school you'll be able to read them for yourself.'

'But can I find a book like that?'

'Yes. There are many books.'

'The same one with the same story?'

'There are thousands.'

'Exactly like it?'

'Exactly.'

'Then I'm going to school!'

'When?'

'Monday.'

'I've started something!' She laughed. 'But why didn't you go before?'

'Nobody told me.'

'You must have seen other children go to school.'

'Nobody told me about the stories.'

'Oh yes, the stories.'

'When I can read and write I'll make stories like that!'

She smiled, leaned back suddenly and reached for her pen. She opened the book.

'Your surname?'

'Abrahams, miss. Peter is my real name, Peter Abrahams.'

She wrote in the book.

'Here, I've put your name in it. It's for you.'

I looked at her writing.

'That my name?'

'Yes. I've written "this is the property of Peter Abrahams".'

'But which is my name?'

'Those two words.' She pointed. 'Well, take it!'

I took the book. I held it gingerly. I moved to the door, backward. She shook her head and laughed. The laughter ended abruptly.

'Oh God,' she said and shook her head again.

'Thank you, miss. Thank you!'

Her eyes looked strangely bright behind the thick glasses.

'Go away!' she said. 'Go away . . . and good luck. . . .'

I hesitated awkwardly at the door. Was she crying? And why?

Yes, thank you, miss. Thank you!

[iv]

'You know he will have missed half the lessons, sir. It's middle of term, my class is overflowing, and he's big and old enough to be in standard four. . . . Why didn't you come at the start of term?'

'I was working, miss.'

'Now look here! Do I really have to tell you, a Coloured teacher, that education is only compulsory for whites and no one cares whether this boy goes to school or not? Do I have to read you the illiteracy figures among your own people? You're Coloured, I'm not: do I have to tell *you* about the condition of you people and your children?'

'No, sir. . . . But.'

'I know, Sarah. Your class is three times as big as it should be; you haven't slates or pencils for all of them; some are so big they're ready to have babies or grow beards; you haven't enough benches; you can't control them. I know all that. But set this against it. A boy at work hears a story and the story makes him come here. He says "Please, I want to learn". Are we to turn him away because he hasn't observed all the rules? Is your community so rich that it can afford to do that? . . . Listen! I've an idea. We'll press these big ones. We'll make them do the work of three days in one. . . . Boy! Peter!'

'Sir?'

'Afraid of hard work?'

'No, sir.'

'All right! I'll make you work. I promise you'll read and write by the end of this year. The rules will be hard. If there is any trouble or slackness I want the teacher to send you to me and I shall use the cane, hard. All right?'

'Yes, sir.'

'See, Sarah. The boy and I are in a hurry. Help us. We haven't much time. . . . Take him away!'

'Yes, sir.'

'Hello, Sarah! Another?'

'Yes. He and Visser are in a hurry. Visser's thinking up a new scheme for making the big ones do the work of three years in one.'

'Oh, my God!'

'It's killing.'

'One thing to be said for the old boy. He's interested in Coloured education, and he's the only principal about whom I can say that in all the years I've been here. And a Boer! You know he's been in an asylum.'

'Yes. Mad Boer poet. Easy enough for him to sit at his desk thinking up beautiful schemes. We have to do all the dirty work.'

'Cheer up, girl. He's not so bad. I must go'n silence my screaming brats. See you.'

'Come.'

'All right. You may sit down. This is our new boy, Peter Abrahams. Make room for him in the corner at the back, Adams.'

'Please, miss. . . .'

'Yes?'

'There is no room. We're so tight we can hardly move our arms to write.'

'Peter must have a place. Make room as best you can.'

'Yes, miss.'

'Now! Put up your hands those of you who have whole slates. Not one?'

'They're all cracked, miss.'

'It doesn't matter if they are cracked. Up now . . . One . . . two. Only three?'

'Mine is my own, miss.'

'What you mean, Margaret, is that it is one you bought and not one supplied by the school.'

'Yes, miss.'

'Then say what you mean. All right, you may put down your hand, Margaret.'

'Please, miss. . . .'

'Yes, Thomas?'

'My slate is cracked across the middle. I can let him. . . .'

'Peter.'

'Peter, miss. I can let Peter have half. And please, miss, there's a little room here and he can sit with me.'

'That is very good of you, Thomas. Thank you. But isn't that where Jones sits? He'll be back to-morrow and want his seat.'

'He's not coming back, miss. His father's gone to jail so he must go to work to help his mother.'

'Are you sure of this?'

'Yes, miss.'

'It's a shame. You liked Jones so much, didn't you, miss?'

'That's enough out of you, Adams. Thank you, Thomas.'

'Is your father alive, Peter?'

'No, miss.'

'Then things are not too easy?'

'No, miss.'

'Take this card. You'll see children standing in line during the lunch break. Join them and show this and you'll get a free lunch. That's all. You can go to your place.'

'Thank you, miss. I'm sorry to make more work for you.'

'Come back here, Peter. . . . I don't want you to think any more about making work for me or anybody. Understand?'

'Yes, miss.'

'We are here to teach and help you. I'm sorry I made you think that. You've often said something you don't mean, haven't you?'

'Yes, miss.'

'Well, it was the same. Don't think about it. And don't repeat what you heard me and the other teacher say about the principal.'

'Yes, miss.'

A B C D E F G,
H I J K L M N,
O P Q R S T U,
V W X Y Z makes the Alpha-bet.

Two times one are two,
Two times two are four—old woman scrubs the floor.
Two times three are six—the hen has many chicks.
Two times four are eight—for school I won't be late.
Two times seven are fourteen—haven't a thought in.
Two times nine are eighteen—oh golly!
Two times ten are twenty—these sums are very plenty!

C is a letter in the alphabet,
A is a letter in the alphabet,
T is a letter in the alphabet:
Put them together and you have a cat.

'Please, miss. . . .'

'Yes?'

'Are all the books in the world made from the alphabet?'

'Yes, all the books in the world are made from the alpha-bet.'

'Jee-zus!'

'What?'

'Nothing, miss; thank you.'

'Hey! Look at the new one among our hungry lot. He's in our class. Peter Abrahams. Hey! Peter Abrahams! Like lining up with the other cattle for a bit of bread and dirty cocoa? They spit in the cocoa!'

'Ha-ha-ha-ha!'

'Shssss! Old Visser's heard you!'

'Hey! No use running away, you little coward! I know you! Come here!'

'Sir. . . .'

'I heard what you said. I've a good mind to expel you!'

'Didn't mean anything, sir.'

'Of course not! That's the trouble with you and this country and all of us. We don't mean anything. We abuse, deny, outrage, insult, and don't mean anything. You're looked down upon. Have you learned nothing from it? Must you look down on someone else? Go away! If I hear any more remarks from you or anyone else. . . . Teacher!'

'Sir?'

'Is there no way we can protect these children from the vulgar remarks of others while they get their food?'

'No, sir.'

'They're being humiliated for being poorer than their fellows. Snobbery among the oppressed!'

'Let's not play with him. He's got woolly hair like a kaffir.'

'Go to hell! Yours may be straight but your skin is black!'

'. . . . And that is the story of Joseph who had a coat of many colours.'

'Is it a true story, sir?'

'Yes.'

'Please read us another one, sir.'

'You're one of the three-class students, aren't you?'

'Yes, sir.'

'Then off to your history class. . . .'

155

'Ah, Abrahams. So you're letting things slip after only six months.'

'No, sir.'

'Are you calling the teacher a liar?'

'No, sir.'

'Are you tired of working hard? Letting me down? None of the others have, you know. Do you want to do only the ordinary classes?'

'No, sir.'

'You'd better tell me all about it.'

'It's arithmetic, sir.'

'What about it?'

'I can't do it, sir.'

'Have you tried?'

'Yes, sir.'

'Hard?'

'Yes, sir.'

'This record says you show no real interest in it.'

'I've tried, sir.'

'Do you mean the record is untrue?'

'No, sir. I mean I've tried hard to be interested.'

'And failed?'

'Yes, sir.'

'You know, of course, that I don't make the laws about examinations.'

'Yes, sir.'

'Well, unless you get a certain average for arithmetic your very high average in all the other subjects won't help you. That is the law, and I didn't make it. I want to push you through as fast as I can but you must work at arithmetic. Relax a little with the other subjects if you like.'

'I like the other subjects, sir.'

'I know. But to get where you want to go you can't only do what you like. . . . Where do you want to go? What do you want to do?'

'Those stories, sir.'

'In the book the young woman gave you?'

'Yes, sir.'

'I was wondering whether you had begun to forget them.'

'I'm trying to read it now, sir.'

'Getting anything out of it?'

'A little.'

'Well, there you have it. Between you and the further knowledge that would help you get everything out of that book, stands arithmetic. It's like a lion barring your road. You either turn back because you cannot cope with it, or you kill it, and go on. There is no other way. The makers of our educational laws have not provided for poets. I want you to kill that lion and go on. Arithmetic is silly in a poet's armoury but you must master it and get that average. . . . I promised you my cane if you were ever sent to me. We must keep our promises. Let down your trousers, then go back and let the sting of the cane help you kill the lion. . . .'

'But if the earth is round, sir, why don't things fall off it? Why don't people and things and the seas fall off it?'

'Because, my dear Arendse, it has a gravitational pull which prevents all these things happening.'

'Then, sir, will you please explain this pull thing to us?'

'Yes, sir.'

'Please. . . .'

'Oh, my aunt! Do you, Arendse, and all you others, do you realize that there is a strict set scheme for each class? Certain things are taught in standard one, certain things in standard two and so on. Gravity and science are things you shouldn't know anything about till next year.'

'But, sir. . . .'

'Well?'

'That means that till next year we've just got to accept your word about everything you say about the earth. And for a year we'll go on wanting to know how things stick to the earth if it is round.'

'And you know Mr. Visser told us always to ask if things didn't seem very clear to us.'

'All right! Sit down, Flora, and you Arendse. Mr. Visser's specials! . . . But before I go on to gravity, Peter's been snapping his finger. What is it you want to know, Mr. Abrahams?'

'When you talked about how to prove the earth is round, sir, you said the curve of the land was sure proof. But the land is full of hills and valleys so how can one see this curve? And none of us have been to the sea so we don't know whether it does curve. So you see, sir, if you answer Arendse's question before proving the earth is round it will be hard to believe in this pull, because you won't need it on a flat earth.'

'You are the original flat-earthers. Now listen! . . .'

'Hello, Peter.'

'Hello, Ellen.'

'Walk with me to the end of the playground.'

'I can't.'

'Please. . . . Or don't you want to?'

'I want to but I can't.'

'Why not?'

'Why do you ask me when you know I have to line up!'

'Please don't be angry.'

'Then don't ask when you know the answer.'

'I only asked because you don't have to line up.'

'I want to eat.'

'I brought an extra lunch.'

'For me?'

'Yes.'

'Why?'

'I like you. You're the best boy in Visser's special.'

'Arendse gets better marks.'

'Only in the things you don't like.'

'His average is better.'

'I heard a teacher say your intelligence was better. And I

agree. Come. I'm shy. I don't want to give you your lunch where everybody can see.'

'I thought you were poorer than me. You are thinner.'

'We're poor in everything except food. My ma works where they waste a lot of food and she brings a lot of it home. There's chicken in your sandwiches. I can't get fat no matter how much I eat. Suppose I'd better tell you I've got a bad chest.'

'Why?'

'Here, take your sandwiches. We're far away from the others now. Let's go'n sit under that tree. . . . Nice?'

'Hmmm.'

'I'm glad. I'll bring you all the nicest things. I've some sweets for after.'

'I've nothing to give you.'

'I don't want anything. I just want you to be my boy if you like me. That's why I told you about my chest. My granny says one must always tell the truth. But even if you don't like me, I will still bring your lunch every day. What I mean is every day as long as my ma stays with us. She may go away and then there won't be any more food. . . . Do you like me?'

'Yes.'

'Really? Cross your heart?'

'Cross my heart.'

'I thought you did, but I wasn't sure. But I knew you'd never tell me if I didn't ask you. And it's not easy for a girl to tell a boy she likes him.'

'It's not easy for a boy.'

'Not if he's like you. . . . Have some of mine, please. I can't eat all of it. And a man must eat more than a woman. I told my granny all about you. She wants me to bring you home. But you must not come if you don't want to.'

'I want to! I'll carry your books this afternoon.'

'Good. Oh, I'm so glad you won't be in the line-up again. It made me want to cry when I heard them say things.'

'Wish I could give you something. Here, I've a top and some marbles.'

'Keep them. . . . Just be my boy.'

'I am your boy and I think you're the nicest girl in school.'

'I'm dark and I have kinky hair.'

'Who cares! I like you!'

'I want you to top the class for me!'

'No. You must be first. That's what I want. Will you?'

'I'll try if that's what you really want.'

'You'll be first, I'll be second and old Arendse third. I want to be proud of my girl.'

'All right! I'll do it. . . . There's the bell. Golly, we'll have to run. We'll be late.'

'Give me your hand.'

'Not too fast, please. It'll make me cough.'

'Old Visser's proud of his specials, Sarah. Nearly a dozen of them have passed the standard two exam. The first five topped even the regular standard two class. Makes one feel the awful grind was worth while.'

'Yes, he is good. . . . What is it, Peter?'

'Mr. Visser said you might like to see the prize he gave me for my essay.'

'Oh . . . Let me see. I didn't know there was a prize for an essay. . . . Poems of John Keats. . . . But you can't read this yet.'

'He told me to tell you I couldn't read *Lamb's Tales* once and that brought me here.'

'The old devil! And I just had nice thoughts about him.'

'He wants you to read the Everyman text to me.'

'Here it is: "Everyman, I will go with thee and be thy guide in thy most need to go by thy side." Does it mean anything to you?'

'No, miss. But Mr. Visser said I should say it will one day.'

'The old devil! And they thought him too mad for a white school! . . . Run along, Peter.'

BOOK TWO

I

[i]

I attended school regularly for three years. I learned to read and write. *Lamb's Tales from Shakespeare* was my favourite reading matter. I stole, by finding, Palgrave's *Golden Treasury*. These two books, and the Everyman edition of John Keats, were my proudest and dearest possessions, my greatest wealth. They fed the familiar craving hunger that awaits the sensitive young and poor when the moment of awareness comes.

> *Bards of Passion and of Mirth*
> *Ye have left your souls on earth!*
> *Have ye souls in heaven too,*
> *Double-lived in regions new?*

With Shakespeare and poetry, a new world was born. New dreams, new desires, a new self-consciousness, was born. I desired to know myself in terms of the new standards set by these books. I lived in two worlds, the world of Vrededorp and the world of these books. And, somehow, both were equally real. Each was a potent force in my life, compelling. My heart and mind were in turmoil. Only the victory of one or the other could bring me peace.

At home, meanwhile, life had run its course.

Loff had paid down a deposit on a plot of land in the new

Coloured town of Albertville. He had built the first room and he, Catherine, and the baby, had moved in. They were building the second room and kitchen. I sometimes went along to help at week-ends.

I saw my brother Harry in the streets of Vrededorp. Sometimes I saw Enna and the little boy. I rarely went to their room. My brother and his wife fought interminably and their home was a place of embarrassment to any outsider.

Both Enna and Catherine were again pregnant.

Aunt Mattie had aged suddenly. Her feet had swollen with rheumatism. She walked slowly and with great pain. A new, subdued tiredness hung over her. The loud stridency left her. I rubbed her swollen feet every night before going to bed.

Only my mother and Maggie seemed unchanged. Maggie now slept in at her work and only came to Vrededorp at week-ends. Then my mother would come down from her place of work in upper Vrededorp. We would walk together in the sunshine. I would tell them about my days at school, about the new things I had learned. And they, for their part, seemed to understand that some change was taking place in me. Often, on Saturday or Sunday evenings, their friends would come in. There would be coffee and bread fried in dripping. And they would sit talking about old times or tell stories. Quite often, Aunt Mattie would sit in a corner listening while tears ran down her cheeks.

Maggie and Chris Fortune had fixed the date for their marriage and were saving up for their furniture. The day was very near and they had found a house in City and Suburban, where only the most select Coloureds lived. But Maggie very nearly called off the marriage because Chris Fortune's very fair mother had hesitated about meeting Maggie's very dark mother. However, the mothers met, and the marriage took place.

Maggie, all in white, made a very lovely bride. Half Vrededorp came out to watch her. My mother wept with pride, Aunt Mattie with the long look of memory in her eyes.

Maggie wanted me to live with them. But City and Suburban was far from the Vrededorp school and my mother and Aunt Mattie were alone now. Beside, I was not really sure Chris Fortune would welcome me.

With Maggie gone, Aunt Mattie's only source of income was the little she got from my mother and the illicit liquor trade. I helped with the trade at week-ends when the mine boys invaded Vrededorp in search of drink and women.

The long depression that was lifting all over the world seemed permanent in Vrededorp. Desperately lean times had come to stay in our lean world.

[ii]

I still saw the gang but the fun had gone out of stealing from the stalls of Indian traders. And whenever they went begging I found some excuse for not going with them. In the end, an awkward restraint grew up between me and them. Only with Dinny did I achieve the old intimacy sometimes, but even that did not last long. I was ripe for something new, the new things my books had revealed, to take the place of the old life. But what? And how was I to achieve it? I felt lonely and longed for something without being able to give it a name. The horizons of Vrededorp were inadequate. Where was I to find the new horizons of my needs?

Impelled by something I could not explain, I went, night after night, on long lonely walks into the white areas of Johannesburg.

Night after night, I left black Vrededorp and walked along broad, clean, tree-lined streets. I walked slowly and felt the cool breeze and heard the sweet silences of these streets. I threw back my shoulders, raised my head, and filled my lungs with clean air. There was living, breathing space, and I felt better for being in it.

On either side of these broad streets were strong houses,

made of bricks. Here, had the streets been noisy, the strong walls would have kept the noise out of the houses; here, had the wind howled, had the rain lashed, these houses would have been dry and quiet and warm.

I looked into the windows of these houses. There was the magic of electricity. A boy could read *Lamb's Tales* without strain in such light. And, often, I saw whole walls of books. What a sight! Sometimes, I saw people at table, eating from finely fashioned plates on a snow-white cloth. And the chairs in these rooms were big and comfortable. And the rooms had space. From some, where a window was open, came the kind of music I never heard in Vrededorp.

Sometimes, on these nightly walks, I had the urge to piddle. But the notices on the public lavatories I passed drove me away:

RESERVED FOR EUROPEANS ONLY.

Sometimes I grew tired, but the park benches I passed said:

EUROPEANS ONLY.

Sometimes I had the price of a cup of tea as I walked past cheerful-looking little cafés. No visible sign was up. But I knew these, too, were:

RESERVED FOR EUROPEANS ONLY.

Really, these streets and trees, almost, the clean air I breathed here, were:

RESERVED FOR EUROPEANS ONLY.

I was the intruder. And like the intruder, I walked carefully lest I be discovered.

I longed for what the white folk had. I envied them their superior, European lot.

The familiar mood that awaits the sensitive young who are

poor and dispossessed is a mood of sharp and painful inferiority, of violently angry tensions, of desperate and overwhelming longings. On these nightly walks, that mood took possession of me. My three books fed it.

[iii]

One day, Aunt Mattie was caught in the act of serving drink. Suddenly, as if from nowhere, the place was full of black and white policemen. The leader of the policemen grinned as he took the one-shilling tin of *skokiaan* from my aunt's trembling hands.

'Got you this time, heh!'

'Yes, *basie*.'

He turned to the mine boys and their women.

'Get before I take you too!'

There was a general stampede. A few minutes later Aunt Mattie and I were alone with the group of policemen.

'Better tell me where the rest of the stuff is. It'll help you.'

'I'll show you, *basie*.'

Black policemen dug up two drums of *skokiaan*. They poured the foul-smelling, well-loved liquid down the drain. Then they knocked holes in the drums. I had invested my last few shillings in the contents of those drums. We would have cleared twelve pounds at least. My share of it would have been two. Now, I was broke, and Aunt Mattie was on her way to jail.

'Ready?' the white man said.

'A minute, please *basie*.'

'Hurry up! We haven't all day.'

'It's my feet, *basie*.'

'Should've thought of that before. Hurry!'

'Get my boots, Lee.'

I got them and helped Aunt Mattie force her swollen feet into them.

'Lee. . . .'

'Aunt Mattie?'

'Look after this.'

It was the tobacco-pouch in which she kept her money.

'Listen carefully. Lock up as soon as I've gone. Use that money and take the tram to Albertville. Tell Catherine and then go'n tell Maggie. Perhaps your mother can help too. Got it clear?'

'Yes, Aunt Mattie.'

'My *basie*. . . .'

'Well?'

'Think there'll be a fine?'

'This is your first time?'

'Second.'

'When was the first?'

'Years ago.'

'Then you should get off with a fine.'

'Has my *basie* any idea how much?'

'I should say a month or between six and ten pounds.'

'Tell them that, Lee.'

'Yes, Aunt Mattie.'

'Come on.'

'Yes, I'm ready, *baas* . . . .'Bye, Lee.'

' 'Bye Aunt Mattie.'

I watched my aunt hobble painfully down the street, on her way to the subway and Fordsburg prison. Then I went back to lock up before taking the news of this calamity to the rest of the family.

The family put all their savings together, and borrowed more. But it was not till all Aunt Mattie's furniture had been sold as well, that there was enough to pay the fine. This took a little time, and Aunt Mattie had to spend a few days in jail. She came out looking haggard.

She spent a few days with Catherine. Then she went out and found a job as a housemaid in Mayfair, on the other side of the railway tracks from Vrededorp.

I now had no home in Vrededorp. I agreed to go and live with Maggie. But my savings had run out. I decided to leave school. I would find a job to pay my own way. Somehow, I would find a way to carry on learning. Night school, perhaps. I was in my fifteenth year.

II

'Carry your bags, missus. . . .'

The old woman frowned at her marketing list and shook her head.

I shot away to another likely customer.

'Carry your bags, missus. . . .'

Three other boys jostled with me for the job. A market policeman approached down the line of vegetable stalls. We none of us had permits to operate as market carriers. We could not afford the fee. If the boys with permits caught us, they gave us a beating. If the police caught us, we went to jail. Two of the boys veered away and disappeared into the moving crowd. The policeman was nearly on us. The tall, red-headed woman watched us with an amused glint in her eyes. The boy beside me moved slightly to the left. He could now dodge behind the cabbage stall and be gone in a flash. There was a crowd between me and safety, and the policeman was nearly on top of us.

'Your bags, *please*, missus. . . .'

The red-head grinned at my desperation.

'So-long, mug,' the boy said and disappeared behind the cabbage stall.

I had left things too late. The policeman was on top of me. There was no way of escape. A wall of shoppers barred the way. The red-head's eyes shone with amusement. Panic gripped me.

The policeman gripped my arm.

'Come along!'

'Where to?' the red-head asked quietly.

'It's all right, lady. He knows he shouldn't be here. You know, of course, you should only use boys with permits. If everyone did that there wouldn't be so many thefts in the market and our job would be easier.'

'But I don't need a permit for a boy I bring along.'

The policeman stiffened. The hold on my arm tightened.

'I beg your pardon, madam?'

'I said he's my boy,' red-head said coolly.

I felt as bewildered as the policeman.

'But I saw. . . .'

'He's my boy.' Red-head's voice was cold now.

I sensed the policeman's mounting anger. He swung me about violently. He glared down at me. His face was red.

'That true, boy?'

'Don't answer him, Peter! Take your hands off the boy!'

For a while they stared at each other, then the policeman released my arm.

'Now you'd better go, or else take me to your inspector.'

The policeman studied my face as though he never wanted to forget it, then he raised his eyes to the woman's face.

'I beg your pardon, madam.'

He swung about and walked away, his neck as red as his face. The anger died out of the red-head's eyes. The sternness passed from her face. Her body relaxed, became less stiff and commanding. Her lips creased. Her eyes twinkled. She chuckled softly.

'All right, Peter?'

'All right, missus.'

How did she know my name? . . . She caught the thought and chuckled again.

'Look at your left hand.'

My name, in large capitals that covered the back of my hand, was there.

'Not such a mystery after all, heh?'

'No, missus.'

A half-friendly, half-amused smile touched her lips and kindled her eyes. I fell victim to all red-heads for all time. She gave me her basket and bag.

'Come on. . . .'

I followed her from one stall to another. I received her shopping. The vegetables went into the bag, the fruit into the basket. I pushed through crowded places after her, jostled against people. I passed market policemen with new self-assurance. I exchanged hurried words of gossip with others of my kind who were also protected from the police and boys with permits by the baskets and bags they carried. And the huge market was a hive of buzzing industry.

She stopped at the corner where they served tea. I could not follow her to the neat little tables. But she made the waitress send her black boy to me with a cup. The stares of passing whites embarrassed me. But I felt safe in the protection afforded by the red-head. Safe and confused because I had run up against a white person who did not react and behave in the way I understood so well. It made it so much more difficult to know where one was with whites. It complicated the business of building up defences.

My red-head finished her tea, looked at a few more stalls, then looked at her diamond-studded little wristlet.

'Time to go home, Peter.'

'Tram, missus?'

'No! No trams for us, Peter! We've a car!'

The policeman with whom we had had the run-in earlier was standing at the big door. He studied my red-head coldly, insolently. In a frankly insulting manner, his eyes moved over her body, from her trim ankles to her flaming hair. He looked briefly at me. I knew there would be trouble for me if ever I ran into that man, no matter where. I memorized his face.

The red-head paused a few yards from him.

'Give me the basket, Peter.'

'It's all right, missus.'

'Give it to me, lad!'

The policeman walked away as she took the basket from my arm. We crossed the street. I looked back. The policeman had come back to the door and stood watching us. He moved slowly down the steps.

'Following?'

'Yes, missus.'

'Thought he might,' she laughed. 'Better keep out of his way.'

'I don't need telling,' I whispered.

'Heh?'

'Nothing, missus.'

She paused and looked at me as though she saw me for the first time. Behind us, the policeman slowly crossed the street. We moved to a shining black car, sleek, big, and beautiful. It's body was close to the earth, like the big black spiders I had sometimes watched on the Ottoman's Valley.

I dumped my sack on the ground beside the rear wheel. Red-head unlocked the driver's door then gave me the keys.

'This one's for the back. Put the vegetables there.'

I piled the bag into the luggage compartment. The policeman stood, arms akimbo, watching from the edge of the parking space. I returned the keys. She put the basket of fruit on the back seat.

'Our friend's watching you, Peter. Waiting.'

'Yes, missus.'

'Don't think you're safe here.'

'I'm all right, missus.'

'Can't you find another job?'

'I tried.'

'What as?'

'Messenger boy.'

'And?'

'Hundreds of others also want to be messenger boys, missus.'

'So it's the market.'

'I sell newspapers in the evenings, missus.'

'You'd better stay away from the market for a few days.'

I stole a quick glance. The enemy had moved a little nearer. The red-head was in the car and he was poised, ready to rush on me the moment the car drove off.

'I'm not always going to carry in the market, missus.'

'But you can't be a messenger boy.' She sighed then grinned. 'I'm afraid you will, Peter. You'll be a market carrier when you're an old man.'

'I won't!' I'd almost forgotten she was white.

'I'm afraid you will, boy. . . . Anyway, get in. Can't leave you to him.'

'I'm all right, missus. I can run.'

'Get in!'

I reached for the back door.

'In front. On the other side.'

I got in beside her. She started the car. It purred gently, then moved forward with the easy strength of a powerful black spider. We passed the policeman. The woman looked at him and inclined her head slightly. A wicked grin creased her face.

The car purred and gathered speed as we climbed the slight rise that led to the heart of the city. The red-head touched a knob. In a few seconds the car was filled with the popular music of the gay thirties. I stared at the spot from where the music came. Maggie's house in City and Suburban had electricity and she had talked of getting a radio. I was used to the idea of radio. I had seen and heard sets as I passed shops. But a radio in a car!

'I'll put you off at the station. All right?'

'Yes, missus.'

She lit a cigarette. I glanced furtively at her. My eyes touched her face for a second then moved away quickly.

'Look if you must!'

But I could not after that.

All too soon, we reached the station. She pulled up. She took a crisp new ten-shilling note from her bag and pushed it into my hand.

'Thank you, missus! I'll carry your bags whenever you come to the market! I'll carry them for nothing for a year, missus! 'Stru's God!'

She grinned and pushed the door open.

'Only a foolish fairy princess appears more than once, Peter. Good-bye.'

I got out. The car shot away with the door still open.

'Good-bye, missus!' I called. But the car was already swinging round a corner. . . .

For three months, after giving up all hope of a messenger's job, I had carried baskets and bags for mean white women for coppers they gave grudgingly. In that time, I had been accused of theft, I had been called all the pet names of abuse reserved by whites for blacks; I had carried heavy loads to the tram stop and women had conveniently forgotten to pay me. I had watched and polished cars and, an hour or two later, I had had to be content with a penny flipped in my general direction. Sometimes I had been lucky and I had received the standard three pennies for the journey from the market to the tram stop. Sometimes the fee had been doubled. When that happened it meant I had hit upon what we market boys called a 'real lady'. 'Real ladies' were few and far between. A market boy was lucky if he got one once a week. And to earn anything he had to carry for at least fifty ladies a week. I had been as lucky as most. Like most, I had been caught by a boy with a permit. He had taken every penny from me and then given me a beating for poaching on his 'territory'. Unlike most, I had so far escaped being caught by the police. But as with the rest, the permit-holders and the police had been the scourge of my three months at the market. Life at the market had been hard, rough, and brutal.

At nights I had been in a scramble of another kind, that

of the newspaper boy. I had fought bitterly to be able to sell a dozen copies of the Johannesburg *Star* and earn a penny.

Now, the red-head had appeared and thrown me completely off my balance. . . . The ten-shilling note was still in my pocket so it was true. . . . I walked across Johannesburg in a daze.

I was still in my daze when I fell over a black man scrubbing the front of a third-rate hotel just above Malay Camp.

'What with you!' he snapped. 'You blind or drunk?'

I sat up beside him.

'Sorry, mister. I was thinking.'

He threw back his head, leaned back on his haunches, and laughed. I saw nothing funny in my sitting in a puddle of water, but his laughter reassured me. There was no need to jump up and run. At last he quietened down.

'You think with your eyes, boy? . . . No. I know what it is. It is not thinking. It is dreaming. It is a thing all boys do. In your mind you were not in this place. You were in another place. A fine place. And you were another person. A fine person. Maybe a rich person who could do wonderful things. Am I right?'

'Yes. . . .'

'See! Once, a long time ago, I was a boy too. So I know. But you must not call it thinking, it is dreaming. Sometimes a man thinks and does not see. But he stops before he falls. The man who dreams only wakes after he has fallen. . . . You are not hurt?'

'No.'

'Only wet, heh? It is the price of your dream.'

I got up and squeezed some of the water out of the seat of my pants. I walked away.

'Look out for cars when you dream!'

An idea hit me. I went back to him.

'I'm looking for work, mister.'

He looked me up and down carefully, then got up. I

followed him into the hotel. He went into an office and came out with a short, fat, red-faced white man. The white man looked me over.

'Jim says you want work.'

'Yes, *baas*.'

'I'm no Boer.'

'Yessir.'

'Name?'

'Peter, sir.'

'Surname?'

'Abrahams.'

'Thought you were Coloured.'

'I'll work hard, sir.'

'Don't mind having a Coloured boy. Don't have to mess around with passes then. One lot for Jim's enough. But I don't want any nonsense about your being better than him. Do as he tells you.'

'Yessir.'

'How old are you?'

'Nearly fifteen, sir.'

'It's against the law for you to be in the bar. Remember I've warned you. If a policeman finds you there you remember I've warned you and you went in there without my orders. Understand?'

'Yessir.'

'Even if I send you there.'

'Yessir.'

'All right. Now for terms. Pound a month. If you don't work out your month you get nothing. Got to be here every day. You're fed while you're here. And you're under Jim. All right?'

'Yessir.'

'All right, Jim.' He went back into his office.

'Come,' Jim said.

My working day at the hotel began at five in the morning and ended after midnight. Each morning, I got up in the dark, dressed by moonlight, and set out. I walked through dark and silent streets. Occasionally I passed shadowy black folk. Occasionally, the clatter of milk-carts, the clang of horses' hooves, rang loud through the silent streets. Sometimes, if I were a little late, the water-carts had passed and the streets were wet and shining. Usually, I walked alone through the broad, empty streets of the city while all the world slept. And at night, after the day's work, I walked through the same, empty, silent streets. The only difference was that I often encountered policemen at night. They usually accepted my word that I was on my way home from work, and let me be. In all the time I worked at the hotel, I never once walked through the streets of my city in daylight. And because of the silence of the streets during my passage to and from my work, I heard the drone of the city clearly: the deep hum without end that seemed to come from the very bowels of the earth. I called it the song of the city and spun a web of tired dreams to it. It became the companion of my dark journeys.

The day's work began in the bar. Jim was hard at work when I arrived. First, we carried the large number of empty beer bottles out to the yard. Then, while Jim washed the hundreds of glasses, I emptied the ash-trays and swept up a mountain of ash and cigarette-ends from the floor, carpets and chairs. The horrible stench of stale beer and stale tobacco pervaded the rooms of the bar. We opened doors and windows and toiled silently till a cool freshness crept into the room, battled with the foul stench, and drove it out. We polished counters and mirrors, cleaned windows. By the time we had the bar fresh, clean, and shining, daylight had been with us for many hours. Jim gave the bar a final inspection then grinned at me. The conversation of the morning began.

'It is good, heh, Beet?'

'Peter, Jim.'

'Beter. It is no matter, Beet or Beter.'

'Never mind.'

'Come, Beet. We will eat now.'

At the door, he paused and looked back.

'It is clean now till to-morrow.'

'Yes. Till to-morrow.'

That little conversation became our morning ritual.

In the yard, at the back, was a small room. It was stacked with crates of beer bottles. It had one free corner in which a small table stood. This was our rest-room and eating-place. On the table was a primus stove, two small saucepans, two chipped enamel mugs, two enamel plates, and two rusty spoons and a knife with only half its blade. I got water in one of the pans while Jim lit the stove. I put the water on and sat on an empty crate. Jim got a pile of left-over sandwiches from the bar. I made coffee which we sweetened with condensed milk. While we ate we talked.

Once, Jim had wanted to go out at night without the boss knowing. He had brought a sheet of headed paper, pen and ink, and an old pass to use as model. I had dated the paper and copied the white man's words:

PLEASE PASS NATIVE BOY JIM
WHO IS IN MY EMPLOY

I had copied the white man's signature.

Next morning, over our breakfast, we had talked about passes.

'The pass was all right, Jim?'

'I did not need it, Beet. I saw no police.'

'I will do it whenever you want.'

'Good. But it is wrong that a boy should do it for a man.'

'But why don't Coloureds have passes too?'

'It is because they are not so many, Beet. If your people were as many as the black people, they too, would have to carry passes.'

'Why?'

'It is a thing of fear, Beet. If you have many enemies and you are not sure you have conquered them, then, always, you want to know where they are, what they do, where they go. If it is possible, you want to know what they think. For that, passes are very good.'

'Do you carry many?'

'For a man one pass is many, boy. But these we carry . . .'

He listed them.

When Jim left his Pedi village in the Northern Transvaal he had to go to the nearest police station or Native Affairs Department. There he got a *Trek Pass*. This permitted him to make the journey to Johannesburg. On reaching the city he got an *Identification Pass* and a *Six-Day Special Pass*. He paid two shillings each month for the *Identification Pass*. The Six-Day Special was his protection while he looked for work. He did not find work during his first six days in the city. He did not go to the Pass Office to renew his Six-Day Special. He was picked up on the eighth day and spent two weeks in jail as a vagrant. That taught him to attend the Pass Office regularly.

He found his first job in a suburb of the city. He got a *Monthly Pass*. This was regarded as his contract of service. Like all house boys, he got part of the week-end off. Like others, he wanted to visit places like Vrededorp and Malay Camp, to drink a little, find a woman if he were lucky, and get to know the life of the city. But these places were outside the district in which he was registered. To go there without fear of being picked up, he got a *Travelling Pass*. When he got to know black people of the city and wanted to visit them on his Sunday off, he got a *Day Special Pass* from his employer, made the journey, and got a *Location Visitor's Pass* from the superintendent of the location where his friends

178

lived. Armed with these two, he could enter the location freely. He had decided, after a time, to lodge with his friends at the location. His employer had agreed. The local superintendent had contacted the Pass Office. Except for that one short spell in jail, his record was clear. The superintendent had agreed. He had got his *Lodger's Permit* and moved in.

He had met a woman, a nice young one. Good to look at. One who could laugh and who had reminded him of the one he had left in his village. It had been a good thing. They had gone out at nights. To walk without fear after nine at night he had to have a *Night Special Pass*.

But he had been happy with his laughing woman. And it did not matter about the passes while he was happy. And, as it is with a man, he wanted more of his woman. He wanted her to sleep in his bed every night. And he wanted to be home to be in that bed every night. All men are like that. And his woman wanted that too. So, they had gone to the superintendent. And after a time the superintendent had given them a little room and they had lived as man and wife.

But now there had been trouble at his work. While he had been a man alone, the hours of work had been of no moment. And working late had not mattered because he had slept in. But a man wants to go home to his wife when he has one and is happy with her. And this wish of his, this wish of a man to be with his woman, had made trouble between him and the white woman. And the trouble had grown till there had been only bitterness. In the end he had given notice and asked for his pass that would make him find other work, and for his money. The white woman had refused to give him his pass till he had worked out the notice month.

But before that month had passed the white woman had called in the police. She had lied and said he had stolen. He had gone to jail for two months.

He had returned to the location after he had served his time. But his woman had gone. Another man and another woman lived in the room. And so he had found this place where he now worked.

He had ended with a crooked smile:

'A man's life is controlled by pieces of paper.'

'Are those all the passes?' I had asked.

'Those and the Poll Tax and Hut Tax receipts.'

'Are they passes too?'

'The countryman cannot pass without those, Beet.'

He had suddenly burst out laughing then. Bubbling laughter had shaken his body and forced joyous tears down his cheeks.

'What's the matter, Jim?'

'I almost forgot the best pass of all, Beet! It is the only one that makes me laugh!'

'Yes?'

'You have been in school, Beet.'

'Yes.'

'Well, if you were a black man who dressed and spoke like white people, you would have that pass. It is for the black men who are educated and say only the things the white people want them to say. If you, Beet, were one like that you would have this pass.'

'What is it?'

'I saw a man with one. He was proud. He looked at all my passes and said he did not have any. He said he was free of them. I said: "How is it?" He said: "I am educated so I'm exempted." I said: "So you carry no pass?" He said: "No." I said: "But what if the police stop you?" He said: "I show them this!" And he showed me a pass! I said: "It is a pass." But he said: "No." And grew angry with me. . . . So there it is, the pass that is not a pass!'

On this particular morning, Jim talked about the woman who had gone while he was in jail. Though it had all happened over a year ago, the memory of her laughter was strong with him. He spoke of her as one in a cold climate speaks with longing of the sun. His strong body leaned

180

against the crates. He sipped his coffee slowly. His weary, bloodshot eyes stared into space. Almost, I felt the person of the laughing woman, so strongly did he evoke her. I wondered about her. Where was she? What was she doing? Did she ever think of him? Did she know how much he longed for her? Would they ever meet again? And what would happen if they did? . . .

We finished our breakfast. Work took the place of talk.

With buckets and mops we climbed the iron stairways that led to the forty-odd rooms to be cleaned. Jim went to one door. I went to the next. I knocked. There was no answer. I went in.

First, the slops. I cleaned the wash-basin with the remains of the drinking-water. I took up the bucket into which the white man had emptied his dirty water after washing. Keeping it as far from my body as possible, and without looking at it, I clattered down the stairs. Empty the bucket. Rinse it. Up again. Make the bed. Sweep the room. Dust it. Smelly room. Leave the door and window open. So to the next, and the next, and the next.

When all the beds were made, all the floors swept, all the slops emptied, there were the forty windows to be cleaned. After that, there were the door-knobs to polish. Then there were the landings to be swept and scrubbed. Then there was the yard and the front. The fat little manager came on an inspection tour in the late afternoon. He always found something else to be done.

Jim and I rarely had our lunch before five in the afternoon. We were usually too tired to do more than nibble at the food. But the silent rest was welcome. After 'lunch' and an hour's rest during which I invariably went to sleep, we shifted crates of bottles. We moved the empties out and the full ones in. This lasted till the bar opened and the white men returned to their rooms. We split up then. Jim went to work in the bar cellar. I went upstairs to attend the needs of the roomers.

'Boy!'

'Yes, *baas*?'

'Get me some drinking-water!'

'Boy!'

'Yes, *baas*?'

'Come and clean up this mess!'

'I say, boy. . . .'

'Yes, *baas*?'

'Come here.'

'Yes, *baas*?'

'Tell the manager—get him by himself—tell him I've a visitor. I want a tray. He knows what. Say it's for two.'

'Yes, *baas*.'

I went and returned with a tray. There was a plate of fresh sandwiches, two glasses, two big packets of cigarettes and a bottle of whisky. I knocked. The white man opened the door a slit and peeped out. He opened it wider and took the tray. I saw a woman's back.

'Here, boy!'

I took the coin. He shut the door in my face.

'Boy!'

'Yes, *baas*?'

'Boy!'

'Coming, *baas*!'

'Boy!'

At last the calls grow less, then cease. The bar is shut. Jim comes wearily up from the cellar. I go wearily down from the rooms. The day's work is done. There is food but we turn away from it.

'Good night, Jim.'

'Good night, Beet.'

Ahead is the long tramp home through the dark and silent streets.

Each day was like the one before. The work of each day was like that of the day before. We did the same things each day, the same things each night. When I got home to Maggie's place, she and her husband were asleep. When I left, each morning, they were still asleep. I became permanently tired, permanently sleepy. My eyes grew bloodshot, like Jim's. I moved with the heavy slowness of a leaden man, like Jim. I ate less and less. I just was not hungry. Only tired. Always tired. So the first week passed. Each day like the other. Days without name. I forgot the feel of the sun. I developed a dry cough that hurt my chest. I did not think about anything. I was too tired. There was only the work, and, at the end of the month, the pound.

On the Friday of my second week, I jerked awake about half-past four in the morning. It was automatic. I reached for my trousers. I had to get to work. Then I saw Maggie as she got up from the chair where she had sat. Her face was tear-stained.

'Matter, Mag?'

She took my trousers from me and pushed me back into bed.

'Go to sleep, Lee.'

'I must go to work.'

'Go to sleep little brother. You're not going back to that place. Ma's been here twice. Each time she waited till the last tram. How do you think I feel when you live here and I haven't seen you in two weeks?'

'But the work. The pound.'

'Not there. Go to sleep. Your coughing woke me.'

I wanted to resist, to argue, but I was too tired. I lay back and shut my eyes. . . .

The sun was high when I woke. Beams of sunlight fell across my bed under the window. Nearby, for my bed was in a corner of the large kitchen, a kettle sang gaily. Maggie came through from her front room.

'So you're awake.'

'Hello, Mag.'

'I thought you had sense, Lee. Killing yourself at whatever

183

this job is! How'd you think I'd face ma? Tea? How do you feel?'

'Tired.'

'Tired! You're sick!'

She gave me breakfast in bed. I went off to sleep again. I woke in the late afternoon feeling like a person again. I could think again. Yes, it was silly to have kept on with that job. It would have killed me. Maggie had saved me.

I went back to the hotel in the late afternoon. Jim was behind in his work.

'You're late, Beet. White man's gone to find another boy. If you start now maybe he'll forgive you.'

'I've not come to work, Jim.'

'What's the matter?'

'It's too hard. I'll find another job.'

'All work is hard for us, Beet.'

'Not like this.'

'Maybe not, and maybe more hard.'

'It will kill you, Jim.'

'You mean it, this thing?'

'Yes, Jim.'

'I'm sorry. I like you, Beet. It was good to work with you.'

'I'm sorry to leave you, Jim.'

'Maybe you'll be lucky. . . . Here is the white man.'

I turned. Another boy, a black boy this time, walked behind him. The white man frowned when he saw me.

'Why're you so late? And you're not working!'

'I'm not working here any more, sir.'

'Not working! Then why are you here?'

'I want the money for which I've worked, sir. My sister says it's against the law if you don't pay me for my work. Two weeks.'

The man's face went red. He took a step toward me. I moved back.

'Against the law!' He spluttered. 'You! . . . You! . Damned!' Words failed him. He rushed at me.

I dodged him and ran out.

'It'll kill you,' I said as I passed the new boy.

[iii]

I went back to the market and the market-boy's cry:

'Carry your bags, missus. . . .'

I was back in the scuffling, scrambling world. The sun shone again. I learned to laugh again, to run and shout like a boy again. My remembrance of the hotel soon became a thing of the past, unreal, like a bad dream.

Summer gave way to autumn.

'Carry your bags, missus. . . .'

'Look out! Cops!'

Sometimes I met the old Vrededorp drover, Oupa Ruiter, collecting sheep at the market. I usually tended his flock while he went on little personal errands. Sometimes I helped him herd his flock through the busy city traffic and left him on the outskirts of the town. Once, I got permission from Maggie and my mother and went on a three-day journey with him. Something of the vast majesty of the land entered my heart in those three days.

My fifteenth birthday came. My mother came from Upper Vrededorp. Chris Fortune and Maggie bought me a Meccano set. We had a sumptuous rice meal. And, to end the evening, I read them a 'Wild West' story I had written.

Winter came: a mild, promising winter.

The police got so strict at the market that winter that the boys without permits dared not enter it. The foolhardy few who did were caught. With the majority, I hung around the tram stop. Often, there were vicious fights at the tram stop. Too many dogs were after too few bones. I collected two black eyes.

On a corner on the far side of the parking square, was an eating-house for black men, 'The Burning Meat'. The market boys went there whenever they had the price of a meal.

For three pennies one got a piece of meat swilling in a thin, oily soup, and a large hunk of bread. The place itself belonged to the flies. Almost, we, the humans, were there on sufferance. Flies walked over the resin-covered floor, copulated on the long benches and tables where the humans sat, blackened the ceiling, and made the window opaque. They walked over the counter on which cooked meat was displayed. They fought and did their business on the meat. And their impudent drone filled the room and made it necessary for the humans to raise their voices when speaking. I, and all the others, often had to pick out dead and dying bodies that had fallen into our soup. Sometimes, if a person opened his mouth to put in food, a fly would shoot in. Really, 'The Burning Meat' belonged to the flies. But we had nowhere else to eat, so the flies tolerated us.

All manner of black men came to 'The Burning Meat'. I recognized those new to the city by their uncertainty, by their tentativeness, and the anxious friendliness in their eyes. The men of the city, the city born, had cold, expressionless faces, and there was a hint of arrogance in their bearing. The educated men I recognized by their shame and furtiveness. They came in quickly, quietly, looked at no one, ate hurriedly, and slipped out again. And if it happened that they saw another of their kind, they deliberately sat with their back to him, gobbled their food even more hurriedly, and slunk away even more furtively.

On the other side of the parking space, the side furthest from 'The Burning Meat', an old Zulu with a push-cart sometimes sold coffee and hot fatcakes. His pushcart and his person were spotlessly clean. Educated black men, and even some Coloureds, ate there without being ashamed. But for us, the market boys, coffee and fatcakes were a luxury we could rarely afford. One mug of coffee and one fatcake cost fourpence and was not half as filling as the threepenny meal at 'The Burning Meat'. But I had coffee and fatcake whenever I could.

One day a slim, neatly dressed, collar-and-tie young man stopped for coffee and fatcakes. While he ate he read a paper. I saw the paper's name: *The Bantu World*. I knew the names of all the big Johannesburg papers because I sold them. But I had never come across *The Bantu World*. I twisted my body to see better. Yes, the pictures on the front page were of black people! All the papers I sold had only pictures of white folk. I tried to read what it said about the black people's pictures. The young man raised his eyes and looked at me over the top of the paper. I straightened up.

'Can you read?'

I nodded.

'Really?'

'Yes.'

He looked me over. A half-smile touched his lips and creased his handsome face.

'All right. Here, read this to me.'

I took the paper and read aloud.

'By God, you can, too!'

'I told you. I went to school.'

'Then what are you doing here?'

'Working.'

'At the market?'

'Yes.'

'Why?'

'I want money to learn some more.'

'And you're one of those who stop white women and ask to carry their bags. . . .'

'Yes.'

'Couldn't you find a better job?'

'No.'

'Did you try?'

'I tried hard.'

'And that is why you carry white women's bags?'

'Yes.'

'Incredible!' He shook his head and burst out laughing. 'Like another coffee and fatcake?'

While I ate, he kept looking at me. He seemed unable to control his laughter. He was laughing at me. It hurt. I could endure the laughter and mockery of whites. But this, from a black man, hurt. I put down the mug and walked away. He came bounding after me, and grabbed my arm.

'You are wrong, my friend, you are wrong. I wasn't laughing at you. I was laughing at myself. I'm sorry. Come back and I'll explain. Honestly.'

He led me back to the stand.

'Have another coffee and cake with me. . . . I really was laughing at myself. At myself and all the others like me. You see, we despise you. Among ourselves, in our clubs and homes, we say it is you and those like you who make things difficult for us. We see you barefooted, dirty, running about the streets and markets. It makes us ashamed. We say the whites see you and think all blacks are like you. We say they never meet us, the educated, the teachers. So, to them, all blacks are the same. And we blame you for it. We do not try to find out about you, we just blame you. And how wrong we can be! It was that which made me laugh. You showed me how foolish and prejudiced our own people can be. That was all. I felt ashamed of myself and my laughter was against me and hid my shame. All right?'

'All right.'

'What do you want to learn?'

'To write stories.'

'I cannot help there. But maybe I can help with a job. Do you know the Bantu Men's Social Centre?'

'No. But I can find it.'

'Good. Go there. Ask for Mr. Peter Dabula. Describe me to him and tell him I said he might have a job for you.' He studied me again. 'Tell you what. You go home and have a good wash. Put on your best clothes and try and get a pair of shoes. Then go along. I'll phone Mr. Dabula and tell him you're coming.'

'Thank you very much, sir.'

'You haven't got the job yet, my friend.'

'Thank you all the same.'

'Here, keep this paper. Although it's by and about black people, it's controlled by whites. . . . Good luck, my friend.'

I watched him walk away in the direction of Fordsburg, then I swung about and hurried home. . . . Please God, please, please let me get that job. Amen. . . .

[iv]

Maggie was mystified by my goings-on.

I laid out my grey flannel shorts and jacket. I found the old pair of shoes her husband, Chris, had given me. I polished them till the leather glowed. I inspected my one whole white shirt carefully. The socks had 'potatoes' but I could hide those. I heated two kettles of water, poured them into the wash-tub, stripped, and got in. I soaped myself vigorously from head to foot.

Maggie gave up her pretended nonchalance.

'What's this in aid of?'

I grinned at her through a mountain of soapsuds that rolled from my woolly hair down my face and into my eyes.

'Got a job!'

'Oh. . . . Anyone would have thought you'd got a girl.'

'A good job. An educated man told me about it!'

'Where?'

'Bantu Men's Social Centre.'

'What's that?'

'Don't know.'

'Where's it?'

'Don't know.'

'You don't know what it is: you don't know where it is. Are you sure you've got the job?'

189

'No.'

She flung up her hands and laughed.

'Now I've heard everything!'

'A man told me about the job. It was at the market. I'm going to see a man called Peter Dabula. He said he'd telephone.'

'And where will you find this Peter Dabula?'

'At the Bantu Men's Social Centre.'

'And you don't know where or what that is. . . .'

'I'll find it.'

'I believe you, little brother. You're mad enough to do anything. I sometimes wonder what goes on in that funny head of yours.'

[v]

I found the Bantu Men's Social Centre on the outer rim of Johannesburg, on the way to Langlaagte and the white mountains of sand that towered beyond it. It was a huge building that stood in its own grounds. But for the huge sign on its front, I would have passed it by as just another European building.

I hesitated uncertainly on the pavement till two well-dressed black men speaking English passed me and went in. I followed them. There was a passage which widened into a rectangular hall. Doors led off to right and left. On the first door on the left was the word: 'Secretary'. The two men passed that and entered the second door on the left. I knocked on the door marked 'Secretary'. No one answered. Again. Still no answer. I heard voices and looked about me. To my right, a flight of stairs led to a first-floor landing. Two men leaned against a balustrade, talking. I called up to them :

'Excuse me, please. . . .'

'Yes, son?'

'I'm looking for Mr. Dabula, please.'

'Try the office.'

'I have. There's no answer.'

'I should wait. Mr. Rathebe won't be long.'

From the other side of the huge door that faced the passage came a deep voice, touched with the velvet quality of organ notes:

> *There's an old man called the Mississippi,*
> *That's the old man that I'd like to be.*
> *What does he care if the world's got trouble?*
> *What does he care if the land ain't free?*

The organ notes stopped. Another, lighter voice, without the magic quality of the first, sang the same words, tried to make them sound the same, but failed. Then, the magnificent voice sang a little more of the song. And again the lighter voice repeated it. If only the lighter voice would leave the other alone! Others must have shared my feeling, for a man came out of the door where the two had gone in earlier. He pushed the great door open. I saw part of a huge hall.

'Hlubi man!' the man called. 'The fellows want to hear Robeson. Turn it up!'

'All right.'

> *Old man river*
> *That old man river*
> *He must know something*
> *But don't say nothing*
> *He just keeps rolling*
> *He keeps on rolling—along.*

Black men appeared from everywhere and stood in silence.

> *He don't plant 'tatoes*
> *He don't plant cotton*
> *But them that plant 'em*
> *Am soon forgotten*
> *But old man river*
> *He just keeps rolling—along. . . .*

That was a black man, one of us! I knew it. I needed no proof. The men about me, their faces, their bearing, carried all the proof. That was a black man! The voice of a black man!

The glorious voice stopped. The men went back to what they were doing. The moment that had given us a common identity was over. Robeson the man had called him. A name to remember, that. I would find out about that man.

'Some voice, heh, son,' a man said to me.

'Yessir!'

'He's an American Negro,' the man said and moved away.

I followed him through the door where the greatest number went. It was a long room, spacious, and with big windows that let in light. At one end was a billiard table. Two men, in shirt-sleeves, played. At the other end were shelves filled with books. Comfortable settees were ranged about the room. Men sat reading or talking. Others watched the game. They all spoke English here.

I moved over to the bookshelves. I wanted to touch the books but held back. Perhaps it was not permitted. Typed slips showed what each shelf held; novels, history, sociology, travel, Africana, political science, American Negro literature. . . . I stopped there. American Negro literature. The man had said Robeson was an American Negro. . . .

A man got up and came over. He ran his finger along the American Negro literature shelf and took out a book.

'Excuse me. . . . Can I look at these?'

'Of course,' he smiled.

I reached up and took out a fat black book. *The Souls of Black Folk* by W. E. B. Du Bois. I turned the pages. It spoke about a people in a valley. And they were black, and dispossessed, and denied. I skimmed through the pages, anxious to take it all in. I read :

'For this much all men know: despite compromise, war, struggle, the Negro is not free.'

192

The Negro is not free. . . . I remembered those 'Reserved For Europeans Only' signs; I remembered no white boys ever carried at the market or ran from the police; I remembered my long walks in the white sections of the city, and the lavatories, and the park benches, and the tea-rooms; I remembered Elsberg; I remembered Jim's Passes; I remembered 'The Burning Meat'; I remembered Harry at Diepkloof; I remembered Aunt Mattie going to jail; I remembered spittle on my face. . . . The Negro is not free.

But why had I not thought of it myself? Now, having read the words, I knew that I had known this all along. But until now I had had no words to voice that knowledge. Du Bois's words had the impact of a revelation.

Elsewhere, I read:

'I have seen a land right merry with the sun, where children sing, and rolling hills lie like passioned women wanton with harvest. And there in the King's Highway sat and sits a figure veiled and bowed, by which the traveller's footsteps hasten as they go. On the tainted air broods fear. Three centuries' thought has been the raising and unveiling of that bowed human heart, and now behold a century new for the duty and the deed. The problem of the Twentieth Century is the problem of the colour-line.'

I read on and found a reiteration:

'The problem of the Twentieth Century is the problem of the colour-line—the relation of the darker to the lighter races of men in Asia and Africa, in America and the islands of the sea.'

For all the thousands of miles, for all the ocean, between the land and people of whom he wrote and my land, Du Bois might have been writing about my land and people. The mood and feeling he described was native to me. I recognized the people as those among whom I lived. The only difference was that there was no laughter in this book. Here, in our land, in the midst of our miseries, we had moments of laughter, moments of playing. Though like us in every other respect, the Negroes in *The Souls of Black Folk* seemed very solemn, without laughter. But for all that, Du Bois had given me a key to the understanding of my world. The Negro is not free. . . .

I replaced the book and reached for others. There was *Up From Slavery*; *Along This Way* by Weldon Johnson; a slim volume called *The Black Christ*; a fat volume called *The New Negro*. I turned the pages of *The New Negro*. These poems and stories were written by Negroes! Something burst deep inside me. The world could never again belong to white people only! Never again!

I took *The New Negro* to a chair. I turned the pages.

FROM THE DARK TOWER

'We shall not always plant while others reap. . . .'

'Are you the young man who's been looking for me?'

For a while I stared foolishly at the neat little man who stood over my chair.

'My name's Rathebe.'

'Yessir!' I shut the book and jumped up.

'Well, young man?'

'I'm looking for Mr. Dabula, please.'

'Your name?'

'Peter Abrahams.'

'What's it about?'

'A job. I met a gentleman who said he'd phone.'

'That's right. Mr. Dabula's expecting you. Go up the stairs and it's the first door on your right.'

I replaced the book and followed Rathebe out of the room. He entered the door marked 'Secretary'. I climbed up the stairs. The voice of the man called Hlubi reached me from the big hall. He was practising without Robeson now.

Were you there when they crucified my Lord?
Were you there when they nailed him on the cross?

I knocked on the door.

'Come in!'

I went into a small office. A young man sat at a desk. In front of him was a typewriter with a sheet half-filled with writing. The young man was small and chubby: not much taller than myself but well filled out. He had a round face, smooth and dark brown. His forehead was large, large enough to give the impression that his hair receded. His hair, a shade less uncontrollably kinked than mine, was cut short and very well groomed. He gave the impression of quiet freshness. He studied me with brown eyes that suggested gentleness. Indeed, this gentleness of the eyes seemed a thing common to all the men I had seen at the Bantu Men's Social Centre that afternoon. Almost, it was as if I had met a new kind of black person.

'Mr. Dabula?'

'Yes. What can I do for you?'

'I met a gentleman who said. . . .'

'Ah! You're the young man from the market. . . .' His eyes ran over my neat and proper dress. 'I expected. . . .'

I grinned and helped him out:

'I had a proper scrub. Nearly didn't know myself.'

'Sit down. . . . You've really been a market boy?'

'Yes.'

His face creased into a smile.

'Well now, about the job.' He explained:

This was the office of the black section of the Boy Scout Movement. In South Africa even this international organization for co-operation, manliness, and understanding, was run on segregation lines. The white scouts had one organization, the blacks another, and the Coloureds yet another. As in all other spheres, there was no intermingling between black and white. The black scouts were called Pathfinders. And this little office was their headquarters.

He outlined my tasks as office boy. I would have to file letters and keep the files in order. I would have to deal with the orders for scout badges, whistles, lanyards, hats and belts: make them up into parcels, make out the invoices, and post the parcels. My wage would be ten shillings a week.

'What's your writing like?'

I did a specimen for him.

'Atrocious,' he grinned. 'All right. Start in the morning.'

I went down to the library and my newly discovered *New Negroes*.

> *We shall not always plant while others reap*
> *The golden increment of bursting fruit,*
> *Not always countenance, abject and mute,*
> *That lesser men should hold their brothers cheap;*
> *Not everlastingly while others sleep*
> *Shall we beguile their limbs with mellow flute,*
> *Not always bend to some more subtle brute;*
> *We were not made eternally to weep.*

A man called Countee Cullen said that to me. And this man loved John Keats in a way I understood.

A man called Langston Hughes said:

> *I'm looking for a house*
> *In the world*
> *Where the white shadows*
> *Will not fall.*

Then he checked me with:

> *There is no such house,*
> *Dark brother,*
> *No such house*
> *At all.*

There were many others. Stirling Brown wrote with the authority of a man who had had a long talk with history. Claude McKay stirred me to aggressive pride:

Oh, Kinsmen! We must meet the common foe;
Though far outnumbered let us still be brave,
And for their thousand blows deal one death-blow!
What though before us lies the open grave?
Like men we'll face the murderous, cowardly pack,
Pressed to the wall, dying, but fighting back!

I could go out and spit in a white man's face! . . . Fortunately, the mood passed long before I met a white man.

Georgia Douglas Johnson stirred me to pride in the darkness of my mother and sister; and Jean Toomer

Carolling softly souls of slavery,
What they were, and what they are to me,
Carolling softly souls of slavery,

stirred me to the verge of tears.

In the months that followed, I spent nearly all my spare time in the library of the Bantu Men's Social Centre. I read every one of the books on the shelf marked: American Negro literature. I became a nationalist, a colour nationalist through the writings of men and women who lived a world away from me. To them I owe a great debt for crystallizing my vague yearnings to write and for showing me the long dream was attainable.

My mother came from Vrededorp that night and we had a little family party. I told them about my job and about my discovery of American Negro literature. I tried to tell them what it meant to me. But they were not really interested. America and Harlem were at the other end of the world. And in Coloured terminology Negroes were black people whom both whites and Coloureds called Natives in their polite moments. I gave up my attempts, sat back, and listened. They talked happily about the little rounds of their days. I realized, quite suddenly, that I was rapidly moving out of this Coloured world of mine, out of the reach of even my dear mother and sister. I saw them with the objective eyes of a stranger. My mother touched my arm.

'You're growing up fast, Lee. . . .'

I looked into her eyes. Her lips curved in understanding. She had caught my thought. *She* was still with me.

[vi]

A world of activity opened to me. I joined the Pathfinders, attended their meetings, and read all the literature on Scouting. I learned the very useful things each scout knew.

In three weeks I had saved up enough to buy a ten-shilling postal order. *The Bantu World* carried a weekly advertisement of a correspondence school. The rate was ten shillings a month. I took their 'General Education' course. Also in *The Bantu World* I saw an illustrated offer of ten beautifully bound volumes entitled *Practical Knowledge for All* which could be had on easy terms. I sent off for these.

Often, I brought my lessons to the library of the Bantu Men's Social Centre. The atmosphere there was more conducive to learning than at home. Also, there were usually others studying. Some, like myself, had correspondence courses. Others, the more advanced, studied independently. And if I got stuck I could always find someone to help me out.

Sometimes, of an evening, I listened to the debates of the Social Centre's Debating Society. Sometimes I went into the big hall and watched men rehearsing their songs and dances. Almost every evening, after the day's work, my boss, Peter Dabula, went into Rathebe's office downstairs. Others would be there and they would sit talking. I wormed my way into these sessions and became a silent, unobtrusive listener.

Rathebe talked fascinatingly about his travels. He had been to England and America. And we never tired of hearing him tell of his experiences. In England he had lived in the homes of white people, had sat at table with them! England had no colour bar. A man could go where he pleased when he pleased. A man was just a man. Of course, people had looked. He was different. But there was no colour bar. And he had met Negroes living in England. They had made it their home. Why, the great Paul Robeson lived there!

But Harlem! Harlem. . . . The city of Negroes. A city within a city: not a suburb, not a location, not a slum area, a city. . . . We hung on his words; words spoken in an easy, subdued manner, stirred our hearts and minds, and led us on to wild dreams.

So many questions stirred in me; so many things I wanted to know, but I dared not ask in case they turned me out. They had forgotten my presence. Best leave it like that.

Once, one of Rathebe's listeners was moved to exclaiming: 'Freedom!'

Rathebe's words gave us some slight yardstick with which to attempt an understanding of the meaning of freedom. And, to a man, his audience dreamed of one day leaving this land. They all expressed a desire to go to America. America held the promise. America was the land of hope and opportunity.

My mind was divided. The call of America's limitless opportunities was strong. The call of Harlem, Negro colleges, and the 'New Negro' writers, was compelling. But Charles Lamb, Elia, John Keats, Shelley, and the glorious host they led, made a counter call. And my mind's eye saw a peaceful land that offered peace to a poet.

> *Ye who have yearn'd*
> *With too much passion, will here stay and pity,*
> *For the mere sake of truth; as 'tis a ditty*
> *Not of these days, but long ago 'twas told*
> *By a cavern wind unto a forest old;*
> *And then the forest told it in a dream*
> *To a sleeping lake, whose cool and level gleam*
> *A poet caught as he was journeying*

To Phoebus' shrine; and in it he did fling
His weary limbs, bathing an hour's space,
And after, straight in that inspired place
He sang the story up into the air,
Giving it universal freedom.

So as the others expressed their dreams of getting to America, I tried to take stock of the two forces that pulled me, first this way, then that. And it seemed that America had more to offer me as a black man. If the American Negro was not free, he was, at least, free to give voice to his unfreedom. And there was promise for me in the very fact that so many of them had risen to high eminence.

Yet England, holding out no offer, not even the comfort of being among my own kind, could counter that call because men now dead had once crossed its heaths and walked its lanes, quietly, unhurriedly, and had sung, with such beauty that their songs had pierced the heart of a black boy, a world away, and in another time.

I decided. I would go to England one day. Perhaps I would go to America afterwards. But I would go to England first. I would go there because the dead men who called were, for me, more alive than the most vitally living. In my heart I knew my going there would be in the nature of a pilgrimage.

But Harlem! A Negro city! Imagine Countee Cullen walking down a street and meeting Langston Hughes! And then imagine Paul Robeson joining them! And Du Bois! And Stirling Brown. . . . Go on! Chuck in Pushkin too! And then let them talk! Imagine. . . .

One day I discovered there were early morning gym classes at the Social Centre. I got up earlier and joined these before starting my day's work. I was easily the skinniest runt in the class and became body conscious. I began to read the 'Are you a man or a mouse?' ads. in *The Bantu World*. I came across an offer by a body-builder to make a 'he-man' out of me if only I would give him a seven-day trial. I wrote to the given South African address. I told the man I wanted to be turned into a 'he-man' by his specially planned course. The snag was that I could not at present stretch my money to meet his course. I explained my budget.

2s. 6d. a week was set aside for my correspondence course;

2s. 6d. a week to pay off the price of the ten volumes;

2s. 6d. went to Maggie for my keep;

2s. 6d. for clothing which I needed badly, and pocket-money.

But I promised to set 2s. 6d. aside to pay for my 'he-man' body as soon as I had finished paying for the books. I had no reply from the advertiser.

I wrote to another body-building expert, Mr. George F. Jowitt. He replied explaining in a kindly letter that he could not build up my body on credit and that all I really needed I could do by myself. He suggested a lot of fresh air and exercise.

To aid the fresh air and exercise, I later borrowed ten shillings from my savings for clothes and spent it on a large-size bottle of 'Vikelp' tablets. These were advertised as made up of precious, life-giving minerals from the bed of the seas. They were guaranteed to put 'pounds of solid, healthy flesh' on my body. I spent a large number of pennies weighing myself. In three months I actually put on two pounds in weight!

Periodically, there were dances at the Centre. Usually on Saturday nights. Young men brought their wives or girl friends. I attended some of these but never worked up the courage to ask a young woman to dance. Instead, I took lessons from Maggie at home. Even these, however, did not give me the needed confidence to approach a strange young woman. Even my new long trousers, moral supports in everything else, could not support me to the point of asking to dance with a young woman.

But my life was full and Vrededorp, the market, the tin-smithy, all seemed to belong to another lifetime, in another world.

Peter Dabula responded to my lust for learning and helped me learn to type. Because everyone at the Social Centre spoke English, it became a habit with me. I thought in English. It took the place of Afrikaans as my first language. My range of words expanded, and with it, the range of my thoughts. All my days and half my nights were crammed with learning, working, watching, listening, and the long, long dreams of youth.

[vii]

Winter gave way to spring.

I fell in love that spring.

When I got home one evening, I found Maggie and her friend, Rachel, on the veranda. From other verandas other women also looked out. They flung words at each other across the street about the standard of the neighbourhood being lowered.

A new family was moving into a house in the little alley-way that connected our dead-end street to the next. These loudly spoken remarks were for the benefit of that family. I watched the new family and the pile of junk they stacked on the pavement from the dray-cart.

The women were right. This was a slice of the slummiest, filthiest, Vrededorp and Malay Camp moving into our 'select' area. The beds were of the wooden variety we had called 'bugs' heaven' in Vrededorp. They had cracks and nooks in which armies of bugs lived. From there, at nights, the bugs came out and feasted on human blood. In our Vrededorp days Aunt Mattie had turned out the house once every fortnight and we had attacked the enemy with in-numerable kettles of boiling water and Jeyes Fluid. But somehow, we had never succeeded in making the army any smaller. We killed millions of swollen bugs at each turn-out, only to meet millions more the next time.

And the people were slumland's children: the old woman, hard and ageless, whose rasping voice carried to us as she interspersed her instructions with curses; the tough, brutal-looking young man who carried all the heavier things; the two fat, squat, ribald younger women who spoke at the top of their voices; the litter of dirty children of all shapes and sizes; all this was slumland suddenly catapulted into aspiring City and Suburban.

And we, the aspiring, were ashamed to see ourselves as we had once been. We resented being reminded of our origins. Having escaped the slums, we dreaded slipping back, and we resented savagely the turning of our new homes into a new slum area. All this resentment was flung at the new arrivals. Had they left their junk, dressed in their best and moved in with even one suite of new furniture bought on the instalment plan, the women would have turned out with cups of tea. For then the new arrivals would have declared their repudiation of the slums and would have been, like us, the aspiring. But they had brought the slums with them, defiantly. So the voices of the women were bitter against them. And they, sensing hostility, became aggressively louder and more vulgar.

By the time darkness fell they had moved nearly all their things in. And though it was a warm spring night, they lit a fire. The houses, here, all had grates. But theirs was the paraffin-tin fire of Vrededorp. They had no veranda as their house was smaller than the others. But there was a little clearing in front of the house.

I went in when Chris arrived from work. We had our meal. I did my chores and my lessons. Maggie talked indignantly of the new arrivals. She and Chris went off to neighbours to talk over this new problem. The whole street was united against the strangers. I went out to look at them. About me men and women stood, watching the strangers.

Their fire was glowing red and smokeless. And they sat

round it eating their evening meal. Their laughter rang up and down the street. And in the background, more controlled, more respectable, were the angry, protesting voices of the aspiring; among them, my sister's.

The tough young man went into the house and came out with a guitar. How many are there, I wondered. I counted them. Four grown-ups: three women and one man. Four children. Two boys and two girls. I had not seen the bigger girl earlier. About my size. Something about her stirred my interest. The man plucked at the guitar strings. The old woman pushed a white clay pipe firmly into her mouth and lit it. One of the women began singing. Soon, the others joined in. Only the girl did not join in. She sat with her head lowered, looking into the burning fire. I knew what it was. She felt and was hurt by the hostility of the aspiring. I felt ashamed for my sister suddenly. I wanted to tell the girl that Maggie was really a warm, kind-hearted person. . . .

I walked up the street and turned left, up the sloping land, away from the city and people and houses, in the direction of the towering mine dumps.

I climbed the rising land till I stood on a green hill. Ahead, on the other side of the land dipping away into a valley, were the mine dumps. They towered white against the moon-lit sky.

I turned and looked at the city. A sea of twinkling, multi-coloured lights leapt to the eye. They threw up the outlines of buildings. They made the wide streets shine. They spelt out advertisements. I could map the city by its lights.

That was the heart of it. There, where it was almost as light as day. I could see cars and trams clearly. And the outlines of people moving. White people. To the left, and a little towards me, was Malay Camp, an inky black spot in the sea of light. Couldn't see anything there. Dark folk move in darkness: white folk move in light. Well, Malay Camp wouldn't be a slum if it were as light as the city. Slum is darkness. Dark folk live in darkness.

Beyond Malay Camp, a little to the left again, was white Fordsburg. White: lights. Black: darkness. A strip of darkness ran through black Fordsburg and became a big black blob. Vrededorp. And to the left of it, that world of light was Mayfair. And the patch of light to the right of it was Upper, white, Vrededorp.

To the right of me, beyond the heart of the city, lights moved away in waves. Those were the white suburbs: there was Hospital Hill; beyond it, out of sight, was Parktown and the other suburbs of light. Light is white: dark is black.

And from the beautiful city a soft, eternal hum drifted up to me. And all else was silent.

The fat yellow moon hung low over the city. A cluster of bright, dancing stars looked down on the city. One exploded and streaked across the city leaving a tail of light in its wake. . . . Dear God! Has earth a fairer land? Can there be one as fair? And if there can, can I feel for it as for this? And can my heart ever ache for the people of another with the purity it does for the people of this? The whites here sing a love song to the land, from within. Would they have me sing it from without? Dear God, wherever you are, whatever you are, look down in pity on my unwisdom, on the unwisdom of man, and help me love this land as it *should* be loved. This land has made me, shaped my beating heart and wayward dreams. Dear God. . . .

I stayed there for a while, a little self-conscious and ashamed at the intensity of my emotions. New feelings, elusive and uncontrollable, played on my heart and mind. A need different from all the other needs I had ever known, moved me to longing. And I did not know what I longed for.

I left the green hill and went home.

From quite a way off, I saw the girl standing under the lamp at the corner of our street. I walked faster. As I neared, one of the boys joined her. They talked for a while, then the boy went away.

I could see her clearly now. She leaned against the lamp-post, looking at a book by the lamp light. She wore a cheap cotton dress that revealed her slim young body. Her long, kinky hair was pulled back straight and tied in a bun at the nape of her neck. Smooth brown skin stretched tight over a round face.

I neared the lamp-post. The longing left me. A new courage led me on. I stopped beside her under the lamp-light.

'Hello,' I said.

She looked up from her book. I smiled.

'My name's Peter. I live here. I saw you move in.'

'Hello.'

'What's your name?'

'Anne.'

'I like it.'

Her shy smile revealed a gap where a front tooth was missing.

'You don't mind my talking to you?'

'No.'

'I'm glad.'

I looked at her. She looked at me. I could think of nothing more to say. She closed her book and leaned her head against the post. I put out one hand and balanced myself against the post.

Time and the world stood still while a great and aching happiness crept into me and spread through my body. Many years, many ages later, one of the boys approached us.

'Gran wants you, Anne.'

'I'm coming.'

'She said now!'

'Go on. I'm coming.'

He turned and went back.

'I must go,' she said.

'Yes.'

Neither of us moved for a long while.

'Anne!'

'That's gran,' she smiled.

'She sounds angry.'

'She isn't really. . . . But I must go now.'

'Yes.'

Unwillingly, we moved down the street together. We moved as slowly as we could, making one step last a long time. But at last we had to part. We were near the fire. All her family turned to look. This disturbed me though Anne did not seem to mind her family seeing us together. She put out her hand. I took it.

'Good night.'

'Good night. . . . Anne. . . . Anne. . . .'

'Yes?'

'Please come for a walk to-morrow night. . . .'

Her lips curved in a quiet smile.

'All right. I'll ask gran.'

'Perhaps she'll refuse.'

'She won't. I know gran.'

Suddenly, gran's rasping voice cut at us.

'How long do I have to wait while you stand holding hands!'

I released Anne's hand hurriedly.

'Good night.'

'Good night.'

I slunk away from the watching eyes around the fire.

At home, Maggie had friends in for a game of cards.

'Hello, Lee. . . . Want to join? Take my place while I make tea.'

'No!'

I went through to my section of the kitchen and flung myself on my bed.

'I'll be damned,' Chris said. 'He usually pesters us to play.'

I lay in a wakeful dream far into the night. And Anne was the heart of the dream.

I stood under the street lamp. In my pocket was a large

bar of chocolate, and in my hand was a quart bottle of ginger beer. Our first night out would be a party.

There she was! . . . No. The girl who came to me was shorter and quite squat, not slender and long-limbed like Anne.

'Hello. You, Peter? I'm Loo. Really Anne's my aunt but I can't call her auntie because I'm twelve and she's only fifteen.'

'Isn't she coming?'

'Oh yes! She's ready. Gran wants you to come and get her.'

'Why?'

'Gran says she has a home and there's no need for you to meet on street corners. Really, gran wants to look you over. She's funny. Says she doesn't want me all over again.'

'Why?'

'Because I have no father and my mother wouldn't tell on the man who made me. . . .Come on!'

I followed her down and into the house. They were all there, waiting to look me over. I endured their silent scrutiny for a painful half-minute. Then Anne came out of the other room and came to my side. She took my hand in hers and tried to still my trembling.

'This is Peter, Gran. . . .'

She named her relatives for me. They said things to me. But I was too dazed to understand. The only comfort in the world was Anne's hand in mine. I clung to it while voices droned about me. At last, Anne pulled me to the door. The ordeal was over.

We walked up the street and turned the corner. Anne slipped her arm through mine. She chuckled softly.

'They liked you so much and you were so frightened.'

'Did they?'

'You heard what gran said.'

'No.'

'But you said "yes".'

'What did she say?'

'Don't you remember anything?'

'No.'

'Not even the promise you made?'

'No. What did I promise?'

'I'll tell you later if you want me to.'

'I can't think or understand when I'm frightened.'

'You did shake so. I'm sorry. But gran understands. It's because you're not used to big families.'

'Did they see me shaking?'

'Yes. That's why I took the bottle from you. Gran thought you would drop it. Better now?'

'Yes.'

We were silent after that. We walked through the streets, past people and houses. We walked till there were no more people, till the houses were behind us, and only we walked in that place. We climbed to the top of the green hill. We looked across the valley to the mine dumps that lay white in the moonlight. Then we turned and looked at the lights of the city, and at the islands of darkness in that lighted city.

I said:

'This is my place. You're the first person I brought here.'

'I'm glad,' she said.

'It is because I love you,' I said.

'And I love you,' she said.

We went down on the green grass. We sat holding hands, leaning against each other. Above us, in a cloudless sky, was the big moon, the Milky Way, and the Southern Cross. At last I turned my eyes from the city and looked at the girl beside me. She was beautiful, the most beautiful girl I had ever seen. And she was beside me. And her hand was in mine. And she loved me. And I loved her. I remembered lines from a poem written by one of the 'New Negroes'. I said it for her:

> *I love you for your brownness,*
> *And the rounded darkness of your breast,*
> *I love you for the breaking sadness in your voice,*
> *And shadows where your wayward eyelids rest.*

'I can't understand all,' she said.

I made a literal, line for line, translation into Afrikaans.

'I like it,' she said.

The poem had mentioned breasts. I reached for her left breast. She stiffened, then relaxed immediately.

'Why did you do that?'

'I'm sorry,' she whispered. 'I forgot what you said.'

'What did I say?'

'Really want me to tell you?'

'Yes.'

'Gran asked if you've ever had another girl. You said no. Only when you were little, at school.'

'Yes, that was Ellen.'

'Yes. You told us her name. Then gran asked if you'd ever slept with a girl. That was when you shook terribly. But you said no. Gran said it would make it easier for us.'

'Why?'

'Don't you know about these things?'

'No.'

'Didn't anybody, your mother, ever tell you?'

'No.'

'Oh, we know all about it. But then girls must so that they know what they are doing.'

'But why did gran say it was easier for us?'

'Because you are not as keen to do it as those who have.'

'Is that true?'

'Gran says it is and she knows a lot.'

'And you've never done it?'

'No. Boys tried to make me but I didn't love them.'

'Will you do it with me?'

'If you want to.'

'Any time?'

'Any time you want to.'

'Now?'

She hung her head and sighed.

'Yes, if you want to.'

'Do you want to?'

'No. . . . But I'll let you if you want to. I'm your girl.'

'I don't want to.'

'I'm glad.'

She relaxed and raised her head. 'I'm so glad,' she repeated.

She leaned more trustingly against me. I put my arm about her shoulder. I took out the bar of chocolate and put it on her lap. She undid it and put a square of chocolate into my mouth. A load seemed to have lifted from us.

'Is that all your gran said?'

'She said she would trust us both. She said you were free to come and go as you pleased and take me where you liked. She said if we felt we must sleep with each other we should tell her and she would try to help us so that we shouldn't get a baby. It was then you promised. . . .'

Something emerged from the fog of funk in which I had faced her family.

'Yes! I remember. I promised I would marry you and we wouldn't have a baby till then. And I will!'

'We'll have to wait a long time,' Anne said. 'And men sometimes get tired.'

'I won't get tired of you. You're beautiful!'

I opened the bottle of ginger beer. We drank.

'Peter. . . .'

'Yes?'

'I don't want to sleep with you and have a baby because we are too young. But I've seen boys leave their girls because they got tired of waiting. If you ever get tired, don't go and sleep with other girls. Come and I'll let you. Gran will help.'

'I'll never get tired!'

'I want you always.'

'I want you always, Anne.'

We had finished with sex.

I lay on my back, my head pillowed on Anne's lap. I told

her of my work, my studies, my dreams. The moon travelled east. The world went to bed. We ate all the chocolate, drank all the ginger beer, talked till we tired of talking, and then, hand in hand, we went happily down into the city.

The passing days only enhanced our rapture. I lost my shyness with Anne's people. An odd understanding grew between gran and me. Anne and I walked every night. But though I did not work at them with the same passionate fervour, I did not neglect my lessons. Indeed, I gave my love lessons in English. I wanted her to read the things I read, to enter fully into my private world. We had stormy scenes when she could not grasp some simple literary point. Once, she left me in tears because I had railed at her for reading a passage badly.

Occasionally, we went down to Malay Camp on a Saturday night to see a film. Occasionally we went into the heart of the city because Anne liked looking at the pretty dresses in the shop windows.

Once, on a Saturday night, she stopped at a window that displayed pretty dresses. Two young white women looked at the same window. Anne grabbed my arm.

'Peter! That one there! Oh . . . isn't it lovely. That's the one I want when we are rich!' Her eyes were bright, her lips parted.

The two young women turned their heads. They studied Anne and her shabby dress. They looked at the beautiful dress she admired. They burst out laughing. Till that moment, Anne had been unaware of them. She looked quickly at them.

The joy went out of her eyes. Her dark skin looked parched and pale suddenly. She shivered and hurried down the street, head downcast. I followed her. The laughter of the young women followed us.

I caught up with her near Park Station. Her arm trembled to my touch. There was restraint between us. I led her into the station and the 'non-European' tea room. She went to a corner table. I got two cups of tea and followed her.

The place was crowded with Coloured and black people. By the standards of 'The Burning Meat' it was wonderfully clean and comfortable. Only a few flies made sport of the cakes on the counter. And there was more room. By the standards of some of the white places we had passed it was drab and shoddy.

We sat drinking our tea in silence, not looking at each other. Presently the shadow would pass. We would push it as far down as we can. And, in a little while perhaps, we would look at each other. We would touch hands and smile. And, by stages, we would go back to being young and happy and in love.

A sudden hush came over the tea room. Three white policemen walked in. All eyes turned to them.

'Natives, get your passes ready!' one of them snapped.

'Let's go,' Anne said.

I looked at a young black boy who sat at the table with his girl. They were both quietly and neatly dressed. Their clothes were better than ours. They looked like two young people who came from better homes than ours. In all likelihood they were both better educated than we were. Their behaviour was that of refined people.

The black boy took out his wallet and began searching for his passes. His girl lowered her head and stared at the table-top.

I got up and followed Anne out, past the policemen at the door. We were Coloured and therefore free of the purely physical impact of this humiliation.

We hurried home without speaking. We parted at her door without our customary kiss. She looked at me on the point of parting.

'Peter. . . .'

'Yes?'

'You say we're as good as *they* are. . . .'

'Yes.'

'Do you *really* believe that?'

I didn't really know.

'Yes, Anne.'

'Then why do these things happen?'

I could not answer that. I did not know how. But her eyes told me she had found answer in my silence.

'Good night. . . .'

'Good night, my Anne. . . .'

[viii]

I had worked in the Pathfinder office for about three months. During that time I had filed numerous letters headed:

DIOCESAN TRAINING COLLEGE,
GRACE DIEU,
PIETERSBURG.

These were signed: S. P. Woodfield.

I learned from Peter Dabula that Canon Woodfield was the principal of the college as well as being assistant chief scout and operative head of the Pathfinder movement. I was always very careful about his invoices and the letters Dabula permitted me to type that went to him.

One day, as spring was slipping into summer, Canon Woodfield turned up at the office. He was an impressive little man; short and stockily built. There was an air of authority about him that flowed from more than the mere fact that he was white. His coming threw Peter Dabula into a whirl of nervous activity. The twinkle in his eyes suggested that he enjoyed the stir his unexpected coming caused.

I did not think of Canon Woodfield again till some weeks later. One morning, Peter Dabula told me that at a meeting the night before, the committee had decided they could not keep me on at the office. Orders had been small of late, and the movement could no longer afford an office boy.

My plans and dreams crumbled.

'What'll you do?' Dabula asked.

'Don't know.'

'What about your course?'

'I'll try and find another job to pay for it.'

'Or go back to the market?'

'Perhaps.'

'It won't be the same you know: you've changed.'

'I'll find something.'

'Ever thought of going to college?'

'College . . .?'

'Yes: like the Diocesan Training College?'

'But how will I pay?'

'Work your way. Boys did it when I was at college.'

'Really! Can *I* do it?'

'Why not write to Canon Woodfield? He can only refuse you.'

I wrote to Canon Woodfield that night. . . .

A few nights later I returned from work to find a letter, addressed to me, lying on the sitting-room table. The post-mark was Pietersburg. I tore it open. . . .

'MAG! MAG!'

'Oh God! What's the matter, Lee. . . .' She rushed in, worried.

I flung my arms about her and whirled about the room with her.

'He'll take me! He'll take me!'

'Stop it, Lee! What are you talking about?'

I stopped dancing. Maggie went to a chair and sat panting.

'Now tell me what it's all about.'

'I'm going to college!'

'What for? Going to be a teacher?'

That was the only thing to go to college for.

'No.'

'Then why? And where'll you find the money for books and things?'

'Here. . . .' I gave her the letter.

She looked up after a while, a bit dazed.

'But this is far away, in Pietersburg. Where's that?'

'Up in the north.'

'And you really want to go?'

'Yes.'

'But why don't you go to the Normal College at Vrededorp?'

Her eyes filled with tears. They spilled over her lids and ran down her face.

'Please don't cry, Maggie. This is what I really want.'

'Oh, Lee. . . .'

I went to her then. Suddenly, I was the elder, the stronger. I put my arm about her. She leaned her head against my chest. I ran my fingers through her long wavy hair.

'I'll come back, Mag.'

'All these books and all this learning of yours sometimes worries me. What'll you do with it? And will you be happy?

I hurried to Upper Vrededorp later to tell my mother. She was resting in her little room before giving the whites their evening meal.

'Hello, Lee.'

How was I to tell her? How would she take it? I had not expected Maggie to cry. Would my mother cry too?

'How are you, Ma?'

She laughed.

'It must be something important. I'm quite all right. Now tell me.'

'I'm going away, Ma. I'm going to a college in Pietersburg. They are willing to take me as a worker scholar.'

I watched her anxiously.

'What work will you do?'

216

'Father Woodfield's letter says I can work in the college office.'

'Then it won't be too hard.'

'No. . . . Is it all right, Ma?'

'Has Mag been upset?'

'She cried.'

'It's her soft heart. Don't let it worry you. I'll talk to her.'

'And you, Ma?'

'I'm happy for you, my child. Very happy.'

'Then you really don't mind my going?'

'A mother always minds. But don't you think about that. You go and I'll pray to God to look after you.'

Later, after the washing up, we went to black Vrededorp to see my brother as I was unlikely to see him again before leaving. We found Enna and her mother and the two little boys. The room was a little more tidy than it had been on my previous visits. But Harry was not there. For a while, my mother talked to Enna and her mother, played with her two little grandsons, then we left. Enna did not know where Harry was or when he would return. She thought he was out gambling.

As we walked away from Vrededorp, my mother said heavily:

'It is a bad place. I'm glad you are going out of it.'

I told Anne the news later that night.

We climbed our hill and sat looking down at the lights of the city. We did not have much to say to each other. The little we had, we said on the way back.

'It will be lonely, Peter.'

'I will come back.'

'It will be as lonely as it was before we met.'

'I will come back, Anne. I love you.'

'No, it will be worse because I will remember you.'

'We can write.'

'I can't. I'm not educated like you.'

'You must!'

'I'll try. But it'll be so lonely. You may find an educated girl like yourself and never come back to me.'

'I'll come back to you.'

'How long will you be away?'

'I must stay on and work in one holiday so it'll be a year.'

'A year's a long time. . . .'

'I'll come back.'

'If you don't. . . .'

'I will!'

'Please! If you don't, will you remember me?'

'Always. . . . But I'll come back. You'll see.'

'I'll remember you always and always. Oh Peter. . . .'

Ask me to stay and I'll stay, Anne. I'll stay for you. For you. Just say it. . . .

'Do you want me to stay, Anne?'

She did not answer.

We passed a street lamp. Its light touched her eyes and made her tear-drops glisten like precious stones.

With Canon Woodfield's letter had been a list of required things: blankets, towels, soap, clothes. There was also a voucher permitting me to get my rail ticket at a reduced rate. I had just over a week before the new term began.

Chris presented me with a strong leather suitcase. Maggie and my mother cleaned and pressed all my clothes. These just about met the clothes requirement of the list. I wrote to the correspondence school explaining the new position and asked to end my course with them. Their reply filled me with panic. I had either to complete the course or pay for it or else they would take me to law. I sent the letter to Canon Woodfield. He wrote back reassuringly. He would deal with it. I had better see that I arrived on time for start of term.

[ix]

The night of departure. The platform clock showed two minutes before nine.

'Better get in,' Maggie said.

I turned to my mother. Behind her, in the background, Anne stood alone. I had moved between her and Maggie and my mother while we were waiting. Now, I wanted all three of them to be together. I looked from my mother to Anne. She understood. She turned and held out her hand to Anne.

'Come, my child, it's time for him to go.'

Anne drew near uncertainly.

' 'Bye, Mag. Thanks for the sandwiches and money. Say 'bye to Chris for me.'

Maggie flung her arms about me.

I turned to Anne.

' 'Bye, Anne. . . .'

I couldn't kiss her in front of all these people, in front of Maggie and my mother.

'Kiss her, you gawp!' Maggie cried in tearful laughter.

We kissed.

'I'll come back.'

'Good-bye, Peter.'

I turned to my mother. The whistle blew. I clung to her.

'Take care of yourself, my child. Write. . . .'

I got in. The train began to move. I leaned out to them. Now, at the last moment, I saw my mother wipe her eyes. . .

Good-bye, my loves, good-bye.

The train gathered speed.

III

De-bo-rah—
The stars are weeping,
De-bo-rah—
The night is sleeping,
Wait for me,
I'll surely be,
Under your window to-night. . . .

The light baritone drifted gaily up to me. That was
Reuben, nicknamed Bing after the great Mr. Crosby.

I sat in the moonlight, under the old marula tree that
marked the highest point of the land. The week of 'treating'
—of the old students initiating the new by light-hearted
bullying, ducking, parading and other general tortures—was
over. I had ceased being a 'greenhorn', a 'thing', a 'dumb
newy', at the mock baptism ceremony the night before. I
was a student now, a person, the equal of all the others.
Those who had called me 'monkey face' yesterday called me
'Peter' to-day and sought my friendship. The tradition of
'treating' had been satisfied and set aside till next term when
I would take a hand in 'treating' the new students. Now, I
had my first moment of peace. Sitting under the old marula,
I took stock of the place. The night was warm. The moon
was bright.

Grace Dieu. The Grace of God.

It was a shallow, wide-bottomed green valley. A quiet, peaceful valley, miles away from the nearest farmstead, and eighteen miles from the town of Pietersburg: a valley in which low white buildings nestled. Far down to the left, off the sandy track that led to the big road and the outside world, stood the church: the finest building in the valley. About it trees grew. To the right of the church, and almost hidden by the shading trees, were the homes of the Fathers of the Church who were also our teachers. There were three white fathers: Father Woodfield, the principal; Father Jones, Father Adams. There was one white lay teacher, Mr. Jansen, an Afrikaner. I never found out where the handful of black teachers lived. To the right of the homes of the white teachers, and making one corner for the central quad of the valley, stood the college office. In line with the office, but moving upward to where I was, stood the large students' communal dining-room. Adjacent to it, after an interval of space, the long, low class-rooms began. Beyond the class-rooms, and completing the quadrangle, were the dormitories. In the centre of the quadrangle was the belfry.

A river, nearly always dry but cut deep in the earth, bordered our valley on the right. Across it was a bridge. On the other side of the bridge, in what must once have been part of our valley, was another quadrangle of low white buildings. That was the part of the college where the girls lived under the protection of the Sisters of Mercy of the Church of England.

And all about, beyond these two groups of low white buildings, the virgin veld, green and austere, and infinitely beautiful, swept away in all directions, rising and falling. And the air, here, was charged with a quiet peace that caressed tenderly. No deep hum came from the earth. No lights shone as in the city. Instead, there was the interminable song of the cricket; the private little light of the glow-worm in love. In the bright light of the big moon, and with the tolling Angelus, this was indeed the Grace of God. And there was Grace in the peace it brought to my heart and mind.

I took easily to my new routine of study and work. It was easy to learn in that peaceful place. And the work in the office was not exacting. From light and airy class-rooms I went to a neat little office. Arithmetic and maths still gave me headaches. I mastered all the other subjects easily. I swept and dusted the office, did occasional typing, and worked hardest on the stencilled monthly college magazine Father Woodfield edited.

The food was adequate but only just. But the fees were very small and I was one of a host of non-paying scholars. Food could not be improved without increasing fees. And the parents of most students could just afford the fees.

Between work and study and sleep, I learned to play. There was tennis and football. We also had athletic events. I learned to turn the earth and make things grow from it.

On my afternoons in the office, Father Woodfield sometimes talked about his home in England, his days at Oxford, and the English countryside. Fathers Woodfield, Jones and Adams, were the first white men whose colour I forgot. After a very short while they were just men, men of God, men without colour. The Afrikaner, Mr. Jansen, was a big, gentle-natured man with a tentative manner. He soon broke down the reserve all non-whites have towards Boers. He played football and tennis with us. In the end, I forgot even his colour and we had long sessions on Afrikaans poetry and prose. Through him I discovered the rich body of Afrikaner literature and the beauty of the language itself. I wrote some Afrikaans verses which we discussed.

Tall, thin, serious Father Adams was the literary expert. I did an essay that pleased him one day. At the end of class he invited me to his rooms to look at his books and borrow any I might like to. I went that evening after supper. We talked books, writing, and writers till five minutes before lights-out. That night began a new series of literary studies for me. At last I could talk about my reading, check my understanding of it.

Father Adams was a purist about both spoken and written English. He set an exacting standard in these private lessons. Whenever I used big words or made clumsy and almost meaningless sentences, he sent me to the Bible:

'The Bible says "And Jesus wept". I suppose that would be too simple for you. Read the Bible if you want to see how good English should be written!'

I read the Bible and saw.

Our days began and ended in the church. We attended chapel before breakfast each morning. After that the Sisters marched a column of girls across the bridge to school. The day ended with the Sisters marching the column of girls back across the bridge after the evening service. And between morning and evening we had the Angelus. Throughout the day, they interrupted us at work or study or play. We left whatever we did and turned our faces to the tolling bells. We crossed ourselves and responded:

> *Hail Mary, full of grace,*
> *The Lord is with thee;*
> *Blessed art thou among women,*
> *And blessed is the fruit of thy womb, Jesus.*
> *Holy Mary, mother of God,*
> *Pray for us sinners*
> *Now and at the hour of our death. Amen.*

After the echoes of the last toll we crossed ourselves again and went back to our duties or our play.

On Sundays we had more services than during the week. Those who were full members of the Church went to early morning Mass. Then there was the ten o'clock service. There was a catechism class for those preparing for confirmation. I attended this. And there was a Sunday school for the youngest students. We also had an afternoon service.

Sometimes both white and black people came in from the surrounding country for Mass or the afternoon service. The white visitors sat in the front row. Males on one side of the aisle, females on the other.

Religion, and the symbolism of religion were all about us, real and compelling.

With others, Father Woodfield confirmed me one beautiful autumn morning. Later, I received my first Communion at his hands.

I was a full member now of the fellowship of the Christ who offered life and offered it more abundantly, who taught:

Love thy neighbour as thyself.

Alone that night, I went into the empty chapel. I went on my knees. . . . Dear God, Dear Jesus, help me. Please help me. . . . Then I went up to the old marula tree and looked down into the valley that had been named The Grace of God.

Vrededorp, the market, the dark places and those past hurts were forgotten. There was peace here, and I was happy. I was among people who were as brothers one unto another, and there were books and the land was beautiful. Almost, I was in another land. A land free of hurt, insult, colour and poverty.

[iii]

I had four special friends. Dan Koza and Reuben—Bing—Makubele, were from Johannesburg. Both were bigger boys than myself. But we were all from the big town and that was the common bond. The third was a 'first generation' Coloured boy, the offspring of a present-day mixed liaison. His black and white parents had not set up house together and he had not been born in a big town where the Coloured community could have assimilated him. He was much fairer than myself, fair enough to be a highveld Boer. His hair was straight. But he had grown up in a black rural area as a black boy with a white skin. This had created tensions in him which the college, and contact with boys from the cities was gradually easing. He was growing less aggressive, less eager to fight whenever he thought anybody was disparaging him.

These three were intensely interested in a young man in America who was making a name for himself as a prize-fighter. They got copies of a magazine called *The Ring*. They stuck photographs of this young man on the walls near their beds. They never tired of talking about him. They knew the details of every fight he had been in, the time in which he had beaten his opponent. To them, he was the most important man in the world, the greatest hero of our time.

One morning I found my friends in moods of black tragedy. They could not eat their breakfasts. Later, Bing skipped classes and went to bed sick. I tried to find out what it was all about.

'What's wrong?'

'I'm sick, man.'

'Why?'

'The Black Uhlan smashed the Brown Bomber last night.'

'You mean in boxing?'

'What else. . . .'

'But if a black man smashed a brown man why should you be sick?'

'Go' way, Peter. You're dumb.'

All through that day, and the next, and the next, the gloom hung over my friends. In the end, I went to their pile of *Rings* to find out that the Black Uhlan was a white man from Germany. Their misery made sense then.

That moment of misery was only matched and outdone by a moment of joy that came a very long time afterwards when they woke the sleepers of a whole dormitory in the small hours because the Bomber had crushed the Uhlan. I woke to find Reuben dancing with his little radio in his arms.

The fourth, and most intimate of my friends, was a strapping, long-limbed boy called Jonathan. He came from a nearby native village. We had struck up a friendship when he had first come as a day scholar, making the long trek between college and his village daily. His excellent work in class had earned him a place as a boarder. As a worker-scholar, he looked after Father Jones's rooms and did his laundry.

Jonathan had never been to a big town. He had never been on a train. The little dorp of Pietersburg was his closest contact with the ways and world of white men.

Often, at the end of the day, we went on long, rambling walks across the veld. Sometimes we went through the wire fence that was the college bounds. Sometimes we set traps for *Springhaas*. The land, here, abounded in them. And sometimes we caught one. Then, for a few days, there would be enough meat to make our thick *pap* more palatable. But most often, we would fling ourselves on a strip of soft grass and lie talking.

Jonathan had the most innocent eyes I had ever seen. His eyes, his smooth black, open, countryman's face, and his rippling muscles, had led many of the boys from the towns to regard him as simple. I found a sharp, clear-thinking brain behind the simple-seeming face, and a warm, compassionate interest in the city-world he did not know. He even laughed kindly at the city boys' condescending attitude to him.

'They do not know the country. They do not know how much a man learns from it.'

Usually, he led me on to talking about life in the city. Once, after I had told him how I had run from the market police, he shook his head.

'And you were not ashamed to run like a dog before a white man?'

I tried to explain. Jonathan only understood the shame of it.

'Others do this too? Black people?'

I told him about the passes and the pick-up vans around Vrededorp and Malay Camp.

'And grown black men do this? Even when they've done no wrong?'

'Yes.'

'I do not understand. These white people are Christians. They believe like we do. They go to church. I do not understand.'

'You will if you go to the city.'

'I will go to the city.'

I wrote home. The answers told me all was well. I sent a few of my poems to *The Bantu World*. They were published. The Zulu poet, Dhlomo, wrote me a letter of encouragement. Some months later, I sent another batch. A new editor had taken Dhlomo's place. From him I got a note. In the note was a postal order for five shillings. The note said:

'Dear Peter,

They will all praise. Few will think that a poet must eat. This is an investment so that you will speak for us one day. Call on me whenever you need. Look me up when you get back.

Yours,

FEZILE B. TEKA.'

I had turned my first literary penny. I wrote a bubbling letter of thanks to Mr. Teka. He replied briefly:

'I have faith in your future.'

I wrote a long letter to Anne. A month later, I received a tear-stained, incoherent reply. I wrote again. I received no reply.

The seasons passed. The year came to an end. School ended. Students went home to spend Christmas with their

families. Father Woodfield was travelling to Johannesburg
and gave me a lift.

[iv]

The first thing I noticed was that strangers lived where
Anne had lived. It dulled the joy of home-coming. I knocked
on Maggie's door.

'Who's there?'

I knocked again. I heard footsteps. The door opened.

'Hello, Mag.'

'Lee!'

We flung our arms about each other and danced with joy.

'How are you, Lee? When did you arrive? Why didn't you
write? Did they feed you well? You've grown, Lee. You're a
big man now. You're thinner? Why are you so black?' Her
words tumbled fast. 'Have you eaten? Are you hungry? I've
a chop for you. Come in, darling! Come in!'

She hustled me into the kitchen. While she fried the chop,
she kept flinging questions at me. She gave me no time to
answer. Then, quite suddenly, her words dried up.

'Why are you looking at me like that, Lee?'

'It's nice to see you, Mag. How's Ma?'

She stared at me for a while.

'You've changed,' she said slowly, frowning.

'I've grown,' I said.

'It's more than that.'

She was more subdued after that. She sat opposite me and
watched me eat. There was a curiously intense quality about
the way she watched me. It was as if she would force something out of me with her eyes.

'Matter, Mag? I'm the same me.'

She said nothing. Her eyes said: No, you're not. And
because she had made me aware of it, I realized I had
changed. I had a new, seeing coldness that had nothing to
do with coldness of feeling.

In the late afternoon, we set out together for Upper Vrede-dorp and my mother's place of work. Maggie was dressed in her best and had made herself look very pretty. She came from her bedroom smiling. I saw the anxiety behind her smile.

'All right to go out with my educated brother?'

'You're beautiful, Mag.'

We walked to the tram terminus in the heart of the city, near the City Hall. The white conductor stared at me as I followed Maggie on the tram. She saw it. Her eyes blazed.

'It's all right. He's my brother. He's Coloured.'

'Enough of your lip,' the conductor snapped.

'Go on, Mag.'

We went upstairs and sat in one of the two back seats reserved for non-Europeans. Maggie shook with rage.

'Forget it,' I said. 'He's done nothing.'

The tram moved off. The conductor came up and took our fares.

'Don't know how to behave with educated people!' Maggie snapped.

The conductor stared at her then clattered down the stairs.

The tram turned a corner and rattled down the incline past the market. I looked at the corner where 'The Burning Meat' had stood. It was still there. Were the flies still in control? A crowd of market boys, scruffy and nondescript, gambled on the now empty parking square. The old man with his fatcakes and coffee was still there. Nothing had changed.

The tram rattled past Fordsburg, down towards the Vrede-dorp subway. It emerged on the other side. There was the stall on which I had led my gang on that first thieving raid. I could have been any one of those scruffy boys scrapping down there on the pavement. Nothing had changed here. There was Nineteenth Street, the street in which I was born.

The tram swept on. We got off at the top, where it turned

up to Newlands. Maggie and the conductor exchanged baleful looks. Then the tram rattled up the side of the cemetery. We crossed the wide street and went to my mother's place of work.

She was standing over a wash-tub in the yard. There was a huge bundle on the ground beside her. She looked small, very small and frail. She raised her head. Weary eyes looked out of a drawn face. Then the face changed.

'Lee. . . .'

I was caught up in waves of emotion and could see no more till the white woman came out of the house.

'My son, missus,' my mother explained. 'He's just come back from college, missus.'

'From college?'

'Yes, missus.'

'You must be very proud and happy.'

'Yes, missus.'

'Why not take the day off, Lina. I'll see to the food to-night. Leave the washing till to-morrow. You want to be with your son to-day.'

'Yes, missus. Thank you, missus. He's a good boy.'

'I can see that. He looks quiet and well behaved. I've just made a pot of coffee. Would you like some coffee and cookies, young man?'

I looked at the smiling, kindly, motherly face. She meant well. But she looked so rested, so strong and healthy, so comfortable. I looked at my mother. So frail and small and *so* weary looking.

'Have you lost your tongue, Lee? . . . He's shy, missus.'

I looked into the kindly, comfortable face.

'Thank you very much.'

The woman flushed and turned her eyes away from mine.

'Then it's there, Lina.' She turned and hurried into the house.

My mother shook the soapsuds from her pitted hands then wiped them. Her eyes touched my face.

'You want to be careful, Lee. They're not used to educated Coloureds.'

'I'll help you, Ma,' Maggie said.

'You go into the room,' my mother said to me.

We looked up the rest of the family that afternoon.

We found Harry in Fifteenth Street. He and his family lived in another tiny, untidy room, in the same yard as the rest of Enna's family. He was not completely sober. Enna was nagging him because her grandmother had paid their last rent. His two boys, both pot-bellied and with bowed legs, played in the dirty yard. Enna sat in the sun, and her mother combed her long tresses while she nagged.

I said:

'Hello, Harry.'

He said :

'Hello, my little gentleman brother. Hear you're a college man now. Don't be snooty about it. I sat in a dice school last night with two college men, and they're even worse than I am. Don't be snooty. You'll be like me yet.'

'See what he's come to!' Enna cried.

I played with the two boys while my mother and Maggie talked to Enna's family. My brother went into the room and flung himself on the dirty bed. . . .

We found Catherine and all her family at Albertville. Aunt Mattie was now too infirm to work and lived with them. Catherine's husband was out of work. He and his stepfather were putting up a new shed. Catherine's two fair little girls played in the sun. Though the younger of the two, when Catherine stood beside Maggie she looked years older.

Here, as in Vrededorp, they were really too concerned with their own problems to share my mother's and Maggie's joy at my home-coming.

On the way back at sunset, I asked about Anne.

'They moved about six months ago,' Maggie said.

'Do you know where to?'

'No.'

'Didn't Anne give you the address?'

'No. I told her to come and see me the night you left, but she never came.'

'Such a nice quiet girl,' my mother said. 'I liked her.'

That night, they talked worriedly about what I was to do with all my education. Whites did not like to employ nonwhites with too much education. And why didn't I want to be a teacher? Writing? Would that feed me? And what would I write about? And why did I want to tell the whites how bad things were among us? It would only bring more shame on us.

They were happy to have me back but behind their joy was an anxiety they could not quite keep from me. I had changed. What was to become of me? What could I do with all my learning?

I visited the office of *The Bantu World* next morning. Mr. Teka received me warmly. He was a young man with shrewd, kindly eyes and a very dry manner. He sent for tea and we talked. He asked about my college. We talked about books and poetry.

'We talk about you sometimes,' Teka said. 'We worry about your future. You know the Dhlomo brothers write in the vernacular. There are one or two others. The only place they can publish is the Lovedale Press. And they must be careful what they write. Well, we wonder about you. You write in English and already you are touching things that should not be mentioned. See what I mean?'

'Yes, I see.'

'Good. We say among ourselves: "He can become a teacher but even then he will have to be careful what he writes or else he will have to put it away." And someone else says: "If only he were in another land." And another says: "There is no future for him." See, your poems have reached us. And we think and talk about you; and we wonder and hope.' He leaned back and raised his eyes to the ceiling. 'We hope, my friend, we all hope. We know the road is hard but still we hope. Perhaps it is unfair, but we hope.'

A boy brought in the tea. Teka's mood changed. He talked about his home and childhood with amusing dryness. I gave him a batch of new poems. He made a little pile of three half-crowns and pushed them to me.

'It is not much but a man wants to help. . . .'

I spent days at the Bantu Men's Social Centre. Sometimes I borrowed a racket from one of the members and had a game on the Centre's court. Sometimes I attended their discussions and debates. The little office upstairs was closed. I rarely saw Dabula. I gathered he had found another job. Rathebe still ran the Centre with quiet efficiency. Mark Hlubi, the man who had tried to imitate Paul Robeson that day when I first arrived at the Centre, had won some kind of award and was going to England to study. This was the talking point at the Centre. Who had given him the scholarship? The Bantu Welfare Trust? No one I asked seemed sure. I put out feelers. The Welfare Trust was only for pure-blooded Africans. And although the Africans might accept me as one of themselves, the whites who administered the Trust did not. Those to whom I spoke thought it crazy, but there you are.

Sometimes of an evening, I wandered through slumland hoping to come across Anne or a member of her family. I went to Malay Camp, Jeppestown, Doornfontein, Fordsburg, Vrededorp, Sophiatown, and Albertville. But I found no sign of Anne and her people. Perhaps they had left the Rand. People often moved from town to town on the Golden Reef. Perhaps one member of the family had found a job in one of the neighbouring towns, and they had all gone there.

At last the holidays ended. I returned gladly to Pietersburg and the peace of Grace Dieu. Except for Maggie's home and the Bantu Men's Social Centre, I had felt out of place in

233

Johannesburg. I had been on the outside of things. The things I had wanted to do had been 'Reserved for Europeans Only'. There had been the concerts and theatres, the libraries and the parks, the bookshops and the clean, fresh-looking tea-rooms. All these I had wanted and found out of bounds. I had wanted Anne: a girl to take on long walks and talk to, quietly: the warm, living presence of a woman. But Anne had gone away and I found no other like her. I had gone to two Coloured 'Grand Hops'. But I was a stranger without a partner and I did not drink. That made contact difficult. I had had more fun at a dance at the Centre. But that had been the only one the Centre had given during holidays. I had been pushed off a moving bus once and endured the cold stares a crowd of Europeans had turned on a presuming non-European. I had been bundled off a pavement and walked away as though it had not happened for fear of being set upon by a group of young drunks. I had queued at the O.K. Bazaars, a big department store, while the young assistant pointedly ignored me as long as there was one white shopper in sight.

It was good to return to that peaceful valley after all this.

[v]

My friend, Jonathan, took me on a long walk that first night after assembly. The moon was big and high. The night was clear and warm. The silence of the veld, after the city, was very powerful. We went past the old marula tree and up to the boundary corner. The low white buildings, sprawling in the moonlight, were out of sight behind the rising land. We walked along the boundary fence to the other corner. I sat on a giant ant-hill under the moon. All about us, engulfing us, was the vast stillness of the land.

'I want to talk,' Jonathan said.

'Talk,' I said.

'It is about the city, your city. You know I went there.'

'You said you would go.'

'Yes. I went. You said I would understand. But there is a thing I do not understand.'

'What is it?'

He thought gravely for some time, then he said:

'I have told you about our village. I will take you there one day and you will see how it is. There is not much for a man there if he knows the ways of white men and the good things of the white man. The ways of the white man are better than our ways. I know that. There is more for a man in them. But this is the thing I do not understand. . . .'

Quietly, gravely, he talked about it.

A boy is satisfied with his village, and the life of his village, because he knows no other. That is his life. That is the life of his ancestors before him. And, for him, it is a good life. He herds his cattle and observes the rules and laws of the tribe. He is content.

And then the white man comes into his contentment. The white man shows him new things and new ways. And he is no longer content with the old ways. The white man says the key to this world is to become a Christian and to have knowledge and education. The boy looks at the things of this new world. He finds them good. The toilet where the chain is pulled and the waste matter is flushed away, is cleaner, healthier, and more desirable than the hole in the ground or the foul-smelling can that is cleared two or three times a week; clean running water from taps means healthier lives and the end of the many water diseases of the well, the river, or the un-clean spring; the journey by train is faster and more comfortable than the long trek on foot or by ox-wagon; roomy houses that let in air and light so that a man wakes fresh in the morning are superior to the dark, airless huts of old; electric lights instead of grease lamps and darkness; the superior medicine of the white man; oh, a whole world of

235

new things make the new world more desirable than the old.

And so he becomes a Christian and he goes to school. Knowledge brings new desires, new beliefs: the god of love in place of the pagan gods of war of old; the new view of the stranger, the foreigner, as a brother to be welcomed rather than an enemy to be destroyed or feared; long dreams of a new life; new ways of thinking and responding open to him. The vision of the humble Christ, the father of all men, of all races and colours, supplants the little gods of old. And so the boy turns his back on the old world of his ancestors, opens his arms wide, and reaches hungrily for the new, superior ways that offer a whole new world. And so, a new man, he goes to the city to see and get to know. All his future, now, will be linked with the city. Even if he is to spend the rest of his life in the country, he must go to the city because it is the symbol of this new world. . . .

Jonathan's quiet voice was silent for a while. He turned his dark face so that I saw only a stern profile.

'It is difficult,' he said.

'Yes,' I said.

'I went to the city,' he said. 'And I learned these things are not for me.'

'I told you,' I said.

'I did not believe. You know how the boys from the cities lie.'

'Yes.'

'They should have told me. I believed it was for me too. It was wrong for them not to tell us. . . .'

'Would it have changed anything?'

'I don't know. But it is better to know. . . . Did a white person ever spit in your face?'

He turned his face to me again. I looked into his eyes.

'Yes.'

'In mine too.'

Autumn gave way to the harsh highveld winter. Mornings were bleak: hard frost on the earth and sharp, penetrating coldness in the wind. Each morning a long line of boys ran briskly round the outer line of the football field. It was the best way of starting the day with some warmth. The class-rooms, so wonderfully cool in the hot summer, were terrible places in the winter. The hardier boys fought the cold with cold: they took icy showers first thing in the morning. They rubbed themselves till their dark skins glowed. They seemed refreshed and claimed they were warm. I tried it once. The icy water struck me and I was paralysed. I could not move my arm to stop the flow. My teeth chattered. I turned a bluish black. Jonathan came to the rescue. I could not walk so he flung me across his shoulder and carried me to the dormitory. He covered me with my two blankets, piled his own two on top, and borrowed four more. I came alive again in time to reach the dining-hall before late-comers were shut out. I was not of the hardier type. . . .

I was in the final phases of my second year at college. I was in my seventeenth year of life. I had decisions to make. My work at the college office had revealed how many applications from students, both paying and non-paying, had to be turned down because there was no room and because the class-rooms were full.

Of a total population of roughly eight million non-Europeans, about 500,000 were at school, about 6·5 per cent. Of these only 2·4 per cent received post-primary education of any kind. On the children of the two million Europeans the State spent something like ten million pounds: on those of the eight million non-Europeans about one million. The real burden of non-European education was carried by the missionaries. Without the missionaries of all denominations, but mainly the Anglican missionaries, much less than the half a million students would have been at school that year. And certainly less than 2·4 per cent, probably less than ·5 per cent would have received any post-primary education.

The college at Grace Dieu was a teachers' training college. I had no intention of taking up teaching. Was it right for me to take the place of someone who might become a teacher and help the missionaries in their fight against illiteracy?

'I don't know what I'm going to do,' I had told Canon Woodfield one day.

'There is a great need for teachers, Peter,' he had said.

His eyes had twinkled understandingly. I had turned to my work feeling a cheat. I was keeping a would-be teacher out and in doing so, I was robbing the thousands of others that teacher would have taught.

But it was not as simple and purely altruistic as that. This pattern of thought was partly the result of another and flowed out of a need.

In the months after his visit to the city, Jonathan and I had again and again brooded over the way the white man treated the black. We had worked it down to Christianity. The white man believed in God. He had brought God to us. God taught: 'Love thy neighbour as thyself.' Christ came that we might have life and have it more abundantly. The Church taught that we were all brothers in Christ, one with another. . . . And the whites, those who had spat on us and on others, were all Christians. The equation did not work out. Where was the error? In the religion? In the white people? In us? In God or in man? And how were we to work it out?

Here, in this peaceful valley, the equation worked out. The Fathers who taught us lived up to their teaching. They were good men and they poured their lives into good work. Belief was translated into reality. We were the witnesses.

But we would leave this peaceful valley and go out into the big world. And there, among the whites, it did not work out. It did not work out when whites came to our church. They

238

sat in the front row. What made it so very difficult for us was the fact that the equation did work out with the Fathers and indeed with the Sisters from across the little bridge. But we had proof that the rest of the white Christians of our land were not like the Fathers and the Sisters. If there were any fault that we could lay at the door of the good Fathers and Sisters, it was that they had taught us too well. They had made Christianity a living reality for us, a way of life, a creed to live by, to measure our relations with others by. And the tragedy lay in the measuring.

The equation did not work out. And in the harshness of our young idealism we demanded that it worked out as logically as a piece of mathematics. And it did not.

Where was the error: in man or God?

And so, under the pressure of my own and Jonathan's brooding, I thought of the would-be teacher whose place I was taking and thereby cheating thousands of others.

I wrote to Teka from time to time. He wrote and sent me copies of *The Bantu World*. My poetic efforts had spurred one or two other black boys on. Their poems were published. One of them wrote really brilliant verse. Teka thought he had the makings of a first-rate poet and his letters said this young man and I had to meet next time I got back. Then, one day, I received a note of acknowledgement to a letter of mine. It said that Mr. Teka had left *The Bantu World*. He had left no forwarding address. The tone and signature of the letter were those of a European. My last real contact with Johannesburg was gone.

It was customary for boys to be given periodic week-end leave to go out of bounds. Armed with a week-end pass, they usually went to the native location on the fringe of Pietersburg. Jonathan and I decided to have a week-end off.

Father Woodfield's eyes twinkled as we collected our passes that Friday evening. There was no real need for me to have a pass. I was Coloured. I had a sudden moment of fear as we stood in front of him. Would he say I did not need one? If he did it would be a barrier between me and Jonathan.

Father Woodfield looked from me to Jonathan. The twinkle in his eyes deepened and carried a smile to his lips. He wrote our names on the two printed slips and signed them.

'Thank you, Father,' Jonathan said.

'Thank you, Father,' I said.

'Behave yourselves and be back before "lights out" on Sunday.'

'Yes, Father. Thank you.'

We got a lift on the provision truck early next morning. Perched on the back of the truck, our feet dangling, we swept away in a whirl of choking dust. The truck bumped and bounded over the uneven dusty road. It was so old that its noisy rattle made talk impossible. Through a thick haze of dust, we watched the rolling land sweep away in all directions.

And again I was struck by the aloofness of the land. Just so would a proud, austere man stand on his dignity, relaxed yet aloof. Not stiff, nor bending, just a silent, firm, relaxed presence, commanding respect in just being. Is there a land with the compelling power of this African land? Can any other land be cold and austere and yet tender? How does one tell of such a land, of the feel and hold of it on the hearts and minds of its children?

I turned to Jonathan.

'It is wonderful!'

The rattling truck drowned my voice. His lips formed a word:

'What?'

I shouted louder: 'I love it!'

He shook his head. I waved my arms to take in the land. He shook his head again. I gave it up.

A watery, pre-Spring sun sat above the eastern hills when we got to the wide macadamized road. The dust settled. The rattling and violent shaking of our bodies eased. The truck pulled up. We jumped off and stretched aching legs. The driver took the cap off the boiling water tank. Steam blew out of the engine. He filled it with cold water.

A fine coating of dust covered us from head to foot, turned us into figures of grey dust. Our hair and eyebrows were coated with it. We spat dust, cleared our noses of dust, coughed dust, and blinked dust out of our eyes. We turned dust out of our pockets. We scratched our heads and raised dust clouds. We were possessed by great thirst but the motor needed all the water. So we continued on our journey bearing our thirst as best we could.

We passed a few farmsteads. We passed black folk on the road. They walked with the steady, unvarying pace that covered great distances. At last we could see the dorp's church spire far ahead. The truck slowed down as we neared a group of sand-hills some way off the road. We jumped off. We waved to the driver. He waved then accelerated.

We turned off the road and made for the sand-hills. On the other side of the hills, the sand was damp. We found the dampest spot. We dug with our hands and made a deep hole. While water filtered through, we stripped. We shook the dust out of our clothes then dressed again. The hole, now, was half-filled with clear water. We cupped our hands and drank. Then we washed the dust out of our hair and faces. We covered the hole so that others who passed here might find water that had been made clean by the earth. We continued our journey to the little dorp.

We reached Pietersburg a little before noon. It was very much like Elsburg, one of scores of little Boer dorps scattered up and down the land: a station, a church, a few rows of houses that make a few streets, a police station, a post office, and a few shops. A quiet place where life moves quietly, unhurriedly. And nearby, as in Elsburg, as in all the other little dorps, was a location of blacks who worked in the homes of the whites.

We went to the station first. The truck was there but the driver had gone. The truck would be there till late that afternoon. We jumped on the back of the truck and rested. That way we were safe. This was known as the college truck. We had passes to show we had a right to be on the truck. The police could not accuse us of anything. After our rest, we went to have a look at the town.

'We may meet some of the other boys,' Jonathan said. 'Then we can go to the location.'

'Yes,' I said.

'My friends will give us good food,' he said. 'You will like them. They are country people like me.'

'What shall we take to them?'

'Bread,' he said. 'They will like that.'

We walked to the heart of the little dorp.

'It is a nice place,' he said.

'It is,' I said.

'Maybe, one day, we will have little towns like this for ourselves. I prefer it to your big city. There is too much noise in your city and a man cannot think. In a place like this I would be content. Perhaps I would be the teacher at the little school. It would be nice.'

'I want to live on a farm,' I said. 'If I have the money one day, I will buy me a farm.'

'But you are of the city.'

'I would still like to get a farm.'

'And the city?'

'I will visit it. But I like to live in a quiet place.'

'You won't have time to write if you are a farmer. Our land is small but my father works all the time, and I, too, when I am at home.'

'Yes,' I said. 'But I will get someone to help.

'You will need many helpers if it is a big farm.'

'I want it to be very big.'

An open trap drawn by a prancing grey with a shining coat turned a corner and shot past us.

'A beautiful horse,' Jonathan sighed. 'A beautiful horse.'

I had been more interested in the cheerful young couple on the trap. They made a fine picture.

'And I will go around like that,' I said.

'With your wife?' Jonathan's eyes mocked affectionately.

'Why not!'

'You are such a dreamer,' he laughed. Then he grew serious. 'I wonder if a man who is not white can buy a farm.'

I did not know. We carried on in silence along the quiet street. This point of reality had spoiled the illusion. Far ahead, we saw the shops.

'I'll get the bread,' I said.

'I will pay half,' he said.

'I have more money than you.'

'I will pay half,' he said firmly.

We reached the shop.

'Come,' I said.

'I will wait,' he said.

I went in. There were two women, one man and the store-keeper. They all stared as I entered. The man behind the counter smiled at the others then moved slightly to my end of the counter.

'*Ja klonkie?*'

Better behave, Peter.

'A loaf of bread, please *baas*.'

'You're new here . . . ?'

'Not many of his kind around,' the other man said.

'They prefer the towns,' one of the women said.

They waited for me to tell them all about myself.

'I'm from the college, *baas*.'

'The kaffir college?'

'Yes, *baas*.'

'But you're Coloured, aren't you?'

'Yes, *baas*.'

243

'Then why are you at a kaffir college?'

Careful, Peter.

'Because my parents want it, *baas.*'

'Let him go,' the second woman said boredly.

The storekeeper reached under the counter. He put a loaf of bread on it and pushed it in my direction. I put my coin on the counter. He took it, counted out the change and put it beside the unwrapped loaf. I gathered bread and money and hurried to the door. As I reached the door I flung myself forward in a dash. Too late, I saw the looming figure of a giant of a man.

The big man's arms shot out and caught me.

'O-O-o-o-p-s!' he grunted gaily.

Then he saw my colour. My feet were off the ground. The laughter passed from his eyes. Disgust contorted his big tan face. He flung me away like one near the point of nausea through touching human waste. I hit the ground bodily. The bread and money went flying.

In a daze, I heard a woman's voice say something about 'church arrangements'. A booming voice, tinged with disgust, rumbled something about a 'black baboon'. I scrambled quickly to my feet. They might come out. Then Jonathan was beside me.

'Come!'

We gathered the bread and money and hurried down the street, back to the station. We did not look back. We got on the back on the truck. I sat shivering.

'Are you hurt?' Jonathan's voice was tight.

'No.' I felt awfully tired and numb.

I looked at Jonathan's face. It was bleak. He avoided looking at me.

'We will go back,' he said. 'I think it is better, heh?'

'Yes,' I said.

We got off the truck and took the road out of the little dorp, the road back to the college. We did not talk. There was nothing to talk about. In the late afternoon, we went off the road and sat on a green hill while we ate the loaf of bread. Then we set out again. My brain began to function once more.

. . . Perhaps the truck would pick us up on its way back. Yes, perhaps it would. The truck rattles. The truck rattles. Yes, damn, the truck rattles. It is no use. Why did he look so sick with disgust? The other wouldn't have mattered if he had not looked so sick with it. Am I really like ordure to him? Only the touch of that could make me feel and look as he did. Only that. Only that. Sick with disgust. Only that. Yesterday I phoned the station. The white man said good-day to me. And I said: 'Please reserve a first-class single coupé for Canon Woodfield.' And he said: 'I will do that. Thank you. Good-bye.' The disgust one feels when touching human waste. A first-class coupé and human waste. White and black. No! The truck will pick us up. You're only making it worse by being so tense, Jonathan. Relax. Let's try to forget it. Not the same as spittle. But that disgust. And the first-class coupé. No! . . .

Savagely, insistently, my mind forced the error of the equation into the peaceful valley called the *Grace of God*.

Late that night I knelt in the dark and empty chapel. I knelt in front of the black statue of my patron saint, St. Peter. I offered him the error Jonathan and I had found in the equation. Why was it so? God had made miracles for white folk, would He make one miracle for one black boy? Would He make it now, please. That bowl of water at your feet, Dear St. Peter. . . .

Jonathan moved from the shadows of a tree as I came out of the chapel. We moved slowly across the silent quad to our dormitory.

We lay awake far into the night, each aware that the other was awake. And our burning hearts ached as only the hearts of the young can.

245

A shadow now lay over our friendship. The weeks to the half-yearly holiday went heavily.

At last, end of term came. I was packing my case on that last night. At his bed next to mine, Jonathan was also packing.

'Peter. . . .'

'Yes?'

'Are you coming back?'

'No.'

'I thought not. I will miss you.'

'I will miss you, Jon.'

'Have you told Father Woodfield?'

'I can't. I will write to him.'

'Yes. It is difficult. But you must write. He likes you and it will upset him. . . . What will you do now?'

'I don't know.'

'Let us walk for the last time.'

In silence, under the early summer moon, we visited our old haunts.

In the morning, I took leave of my dear friend Jonathan and turned my face from that peaceful valley called the Grace of God.

BOOK THREE

I

[i]

I lay staring at the patch of moonlight on the wall . . . But afterwards? What were we to do afterwards? And was she sure? Really sure? . . .

She tapped lightly on the wall.

And what of the other two? My friends? Would they still be my friends afterwards?

I heard her move. I got out of bed and stood staring at the door. She tapped again, but only once. I went to the door and opened it. The house was very quiet. Two steps and I was at her door. I turned the handle quietly. The door moved without squeaking.

'Thought you'd never come,' she whispered.

The moonlight touched her face with cream and roses. Her hair was a dark halo about it. Her eyes were pools of bottomless depth.

'They might be awake,' I whispered.

'Stop worrying. You'll find out what they think to-morrow.'

'Do they know?'

'Better shut the door and come. . . . They'd have to be blind not to. Come.'

I hesitated and all my past was in my hesitation. She opened the bed. I went to her. . . .

'D'you really think they know?'

'You're stiff and cold. Relax. Of course, they know. Anyone would think love is unnatural. Forget your missionary inhibitions.'

'You love me? Really?'

'You're with me, aren't you?'

'But do you?'

'Of course. Oh my poor Peter, stop shivering.'

'Sure you want to?'

'I was seduced a long time ago, so stop worrying about that. There now, you're shocked. Shouldn't have told you. But it's true. You have a poet's romantic ideas about sex. But you'll learn.'

I lay beside her afterwards, completely relaxed but utterly depressed.

'All right?' she murmured.

'Yes.'

'Let's go to sleep.'

She nestled against me and closed her eyes. Cream and roses beside me: a woman's hair in my face—the scent of dry leaves and mystery. But it had all gone wrong. It had not been as it should have been. The beauty my mind had charged it with had not been in the act. My fault? I did not know about these things. But for all my ignorance, I had wanted it to be an act of dedication. It had worked out as liberation without dedication, freedom without beauty.

Beside me, she breathed evenly in sleep. I eased myself away and got out of bed. She stirred.

'Where you going?'

'To my room.'

'No.'

'I'll oversleep here.'

'Oh. . . .' she groaned. 'All right. . . .'

I knelt beside her and gathered the cream and roses to my bosom. The beauty will come. It had to come. The beauty must come.

'I love you, my dear, I love you.'

'Good night, dear,' she murmured, half-asleep.

248

I went back to my room and got into bed. I lay staring at the patch of moonlight on my wall. I was wide awake. My brain was too active for sleep.

Between this moment and that other when I had taken leave of my friend Jonathan, nearly two years had passed. I was nineteen now, and this was the year 1938.

On reaching Johannesburg, I had written to Father Woodfield and told him I was not returning to college next term. I had not the courage to offer him the error Jonathan and I had found in the equation so I had made some excuse about not intending to be a teacher. I had expected him to be done with me after such ingratitude. I had received a gentle letter from him. He was sorry I had decided not to return. Perhaps I would be happier at St. Peter's Secondary just outside Johannesburg. I could work for my matriculation there. It was near my home. He had written to the principal, Brother Roger, about me. He had also been in touch with Mr. J. D. Rheinalt Jones, Director of the South African Institute of Race Relations and Chief Scout for South Africa. Mr. Rheinalt Jones was willing to help. Both Mr. Rheinalt Jones and Brother Roger expected me to get in touch with them.

I had felt in a false position but unable to do anything about it. I had no way of coping with kindness. With a feeling of guilt and a sense of double-dealing, I submitted. I had seen Mr. Rheinalt Jones and gone to St. Peter's.

In Brother Roger, a tall, handsome man with the austere and hawk-like features of a Red Indian, I had met my first Christian socialist. Through him, the world of visual art and classical music had opened to me. He had introduced me to the English poetry of my day. I had grown familiar with the work of Auden, Day Lewis, Isherwood and Spender. He had presented me with William Plomer's beautiful little book *I Speak of Africa*. Through Brother Roger, I had made my first white friends, a young brother and sister, Sammy and Phyllis Lieberman.

In my holidays, I had gone to the beautiful University of

249

Johannesburg and there, in the offices of the Institute of Race Relations, I had worked. I had found young men and women there who seemed untouched by the racial disease of the land. Men like Julius Lewin. There, for the first time in my life, a white woman had served me a cup of tea. But there had been restraint: an unspoken, unexpressed, concern lest they go too far in their intimacy or lest I forget that outside these offices the racial laws were still in full flower.

At St. Peter's, a motherly woman teacher of English, Mrs. Lindsay, took over where Father Adams had left off and helped me on my journey into the golden realms of language and literature. With her, I first discovered the independent life possessed by a work of art and the strange loyalty art demands of those who would serve it.

At St. Peter's too, I had met a young couple. The woman had been with child and the man had had wrestling matches with the boys on the lawn. These had been the first white people to invite me to their home as a guest, the first white people who had sat at table with me. Gradually, over a period of time, they had nursed my friendship, had made me see that it was something they valued and desired. Then, in easy stages, they had offered an explanation of all the things that obsessed me: colour and the error Jonathan and I had found in the religious equation.

They had called their explanation Dialectical Materialism. They had called the creed by which they lived Marxism.

Marxism had the impact of a miraculous revelation. I had explored this new creed with delicate care. I had measured its adherents by their creed. A profound revolution had taken place in my heart and mind.

And I had tested the new creed called Marxism against the reality of my experience and the darkness of my land. And only by the Marxian theories of economics and imperialism had the racialism of the land made sense. Marxism had supplied an intelligent and reasonable explanation for the things that happened. Had it also the key to the solving of these problems?

My circle of white friends had extended. And only the Marxists had seemed wholly free of any taint of racialism in their dealings with me and other non-Europeans. But I had found subtle and dangerous complications as I had moved deeper into this Marxist world. I had found two major factions: Trotskyists and Stalinists. To each, the other was the greater enemy, greater even than the racialism of the land. I had listened to brilliant discourses about two men, one of whom preached 'permanent revolution' and the other 'revolution by stages'. And I had found a viciousness of abuse and vilification between the supporters of these two men.

Though Marxism had offered a reasonable explanation of the world in which I lived, the factional abuse and counter abuse disturbed me. And I had still to find, under the political creed, something that would take in human feeling, love and laughter, poetry and music, and the dear warmth of pure, motiveless friendship. Had Marxism any room for the compassionate humanity that pervaded the life and teaching of Christ?

Thus I had, in 1938, left school and gone into the world, groping after the meaning of life. Once, to know why would have been all. I had found out why. But in finding out, I had created a new need.

Could the creed of Marxism raise all men to the full measure of a dignified humanity?

Early in 1938 I had been 'discovered' by the European press. Oliver Walker of the *Daily Express* had written a feature article, 'Coloured Boy Poet'. He had used some of my less 'revolutionary' poems. The face of a skinny, soulful-looking young man had stared at the whites from their papers. I had gone after a clerk-and-messenger job shortly after the feature appeared. The white man had said:

'I know your face. You're the Coloured poet.'

251

'Yes, sir.'

'Well, we don't want you.'

So my friend Harold who had wrestled on the lawn at St. Peter's had taken me into his temporary trade. We had spent the nights repainting a block of city offices, and the days talking Marxism, attending meetings, and reading.

My mother and sister had grown worried about me. My new Marxist language had disturbed Maggie's religious mind profoundly. My mother had been silent. But I had sensed her unhappiness and fears for me. This new, challenging language of mine could only lead to trouble. Sooner or later my new attitude would lead to a head-on collision with the white law-makers. She had had a harrowing dread of that.

I turned away from the patch of moonlight on the wall. It had shifted and narrowed to a sharp point. I got out of bed and went to the window. A bright, reddish yellow light was creeping into the sky from the east. The weeks of painting offices had got me used to staying awake all night and sleeping by day. Anyway, it would soon be daylight. Next door, and in the other room, they were all sleeping. Lucky people. I went back to the bed. I got in and turned my back to the wall of light. What would Harold and Cath say if they found out about to-night? Cath and Jane are sisters. Jane says they know. Do they? And what would they say?

It had been saddening. It had left a heavy load of depression on my mind. It should have been different, an act of love and dedication, an act of beauty. It had been without beauty and she had not seen that. Spender echoed through my drowsing mind.

For I had expected always
Some brightness to hold in trust,
Some final innocence
To save from dust;

252

That, hanging solid,
Would dangle through all
Like the created poem
Or the dazzling crystal.

And it had been without beauty. I closed my eyes. . . .

'Peter! Wake up, Peter! Here's a cup of tea.'

I rolled on to my back. Jane, dressed and ready to go to work, stood over me with a steaming cup of tea. The early morning sun streamed into the room with dazzling brightness.

'Hello.'

' 'Morning sleepy woolly head. Drink this and then you can go off again. I'm a working woman.'

I took the tea.

'You all right?'

'Of course. Still worrying?' She ran her fingers through my woolly mop. 'Wish I had your curls.'

'Tell that to Coloured girls. They want theirs straight.'

'And we pay to curl ours. . . . I must go. See you to-night. Wish you could come and meet me. Oh damn! I'm sorry. This stupid set-up maddens me. I can't go anywhere with you. See you to-night.'

She went out. I tried to sleep again but could not. She was right. I would not be able to take her anywhere, not even on quiet walks. For us just to be seen together would bring disaster. It was bad enough when Harold and I travelled together. Still, better not think of that now. A lovely girl. Must have been my fault that last night had fallen flat. But she said she'd been seduced a long time ago. By whom? And had she been willing? A man wants to offer himself cleanly to the woman of his choice. He wants to say: Here, take all my heart and all the untouched purity of it. This is the best I have to offer. And he wants to hear her say: And here is mine, as purely untouched as yours and all for you. . . .

I heard Cath and Harold in the kitchen. I got up, went to the bathroom, and then dressed. I went to the kitchen. Cath was feeding the baby. Harold, in dressing-gown, prepared toast.

'Good morning,' I said.

' 'Morning, Peter,' they said.

The flaxen-haired, blue-eyed little girl opened her arms to me. I hugged her.

'Good night?' Harold said gruffly.

'Rather restless,' I said.

I intercepted a look between them. Jane was right. They knew.

After breakfast, Cath and the child went out. On the point of going, she touched my shoulder.

'I'm for you, Peter. You know that.'

Yes, they knew.

It came out into the open as Harold and I washed up.

'Peter. . . .'

'Yes?'

'Anything between you and Jane?'

'Yes. . . .'

'We've seen it brewing. Talk about it last night?'

'Yes.'

He embraced me with gruff affection then turned away.

'I want you to know we think you're good enough for anybody.'

'Thanks. Last night, Harold. . . .'

'You went the whole way.'

'Yes.'

'Serious?'

'I think so.'

'Jane's a nice kid, but there are problems. I don't mean about that. She knows how to cope. I mean political problems.'

'I'll be all right.'

'I know you will, Peter. . . . Funny thing about women.

Really, we shouldn't have this baby, but there you are. The ideal thing would be to do without them. For you more than me. You're not likely to find a woman as developed as yourself among your own people. That's why I say I couldn't marry a non-European myself. It isn't colour but the level of development. You're in the same situation. And for you it's a dilemma. In the present set-up your society is not likely to throw up many women who could be your intellectual companions as well as your bed companions. And there isn't much of an alternative, is there? Not in this country. But as I said, we're with you. You're good enough for anybody.'

Here at least, with these two friends of mine who were Marxists, the creed had measured up to reality. They had said colour was an artificial barrier. Now, though not deliberately, I had tested this belief and found them true to it. Was the Marxian creed then the true creed? If it could make people acknowledge my humanity so completely, without any reservations, why was it also charged with such strong factional hatreds?

Harold went out later to see about a job. This was a white suburb of Johannesburg so it was safest for me to stay indoors. There was a fine collection of books, most of Gollancz's Left Book Club editions. I had cigarettes, paper and pencil. I read and wrote.

For two weeks Jane and I spent evenings together. We read and talked and listened to records. During the day Harold went his way and I went mine, each hunting for jobs. At last he got a job as supervisor to a gang of native builders. He hated it but there was no money in the house other than the little Jane brought. My job hunt proved utterly hopeless.

On rare occasions Jane and I went to the homes of other comrades. She did not like these outings because we had to travel like strangers till we reached our destination. And these visits usually turned into serious political meetings. But

255

these, and the political meetings, were the only outings on which we could venture together. Harold and Cath looked on helplessly as our frustration grew. No theoretic analysis, however sound, could help us now. We grew irritable with each other, quarrelled, made up, and quarrelled again. We grew desperate. I told her to go out by herself and quarrelled with her for doing so. The end came as we sat alone one night.

'It's no good!' she cried suddenly. 'Perhaps I don't understand your poet's temperament. I want fun even if we can't go out together. You're always tense and anxious. It's getting on my nerves. I don't think it's any good, Peter. I'm sorry but it just isn't.'

'We can get away from here.'

'That's silly. We haven't a penny.'

'You're right. So. . . .'

'So I'm calling it off. There are mixed couples who manage in the Cape. Perhaps they're different from us.'

'We could go there and try.'

'It's no good.'

'Don't you love me any more?'

'That's another thing. Love's so important to you. It even interferes with your having fun. I just can't. I'm sorry.'

'All right, Jane.'

'I'm sorry.'

'Stop saying that!'

She left me and I sat alone. Really, I had been waiting for this, dreading it. There could be no other end. What I had expected on that first night had not come. But even if it had, the end would still have been this, still the same. This end had been inevitable long before the beginning. Spender had it.

> *What I had not foreseen*
> *Was the gradual day*
> *Weakening the will*
> *Leaking the brightness away,*

256

The lack of good to touch
The fading of body and soul
Like smoke before wind
Corrupt, unsubstantial.

I was glad the end had come, glad with a desperately aching heart.

When Harold came in later that night, I said:

'I'm going.'

'Going? Where?'

'I think I'll try and get down to the Cape. It may be easier to get a job there.'

'Jane?'

'Not only that.'

'But it is ended?'

'Yes. It is ended.'

'You sound almost cheerful. I'll write to the comrades in the Cape. They'll help.'

'No. . . . All right. But give me the letter. It may take time to get there.'

I loved my friends, Cath and Harold, but I had had enough of their particular brand of Marxism. I did not want to step into the same setting down in the Cape. I need not deliver the letter.

'We'll miss you, Peter.'

'I'll miss the three of you, Harold.'

'And Jane?'

'I don't know.'

'Don't swing from extreme softness to extreme hardness.'

I looked at him soberly. Marxism aside, this man and his wife had, by the nature of their friendship, helped me to the point where I could look beyond the whiteness of a white man's skin and see and comprehend his humanity. I knew if I told him this he would say it was because they were Marxists. But I had met other Marxists who had been unable

257

to do this. It had come out of their sense of humanity and their essential goodness as human beings.

'I want you to know how I feel about you and Cath. . . .' I choked on the words.

My friend nodded.

'We feel the same about you, laddie.'

[ii]

I went to Max Gordon's office the next morning. Gordon had built up a black trade union movement on the Rand. Blacks were not allowed in white unions. Black unions were not recognized by the State, the white unions, or the agencies of the employers. There had been black unions on the Rand before Gordon's time. The most famous of these had been Clement Kadalie's Industrial and Commercial Union. But these had been, for the most part, little more than movements of political protest, with little if any, genuine trade union content. Indeed, the members of these unions saw very little, if anything at all, for their subscriptions. The communists, too, had had a hand in Rand trade unionism among the blacks.

But it was not till Max Gordon appeared on the Rand that black trade unions were formed that really served the interests of their members and that were run on business-like trade union lines. Nominally, Gordon was a Trotskyist, but his determined refusal to turn his unions into part of the Left faction fight made him unpopular with the majority of his comrades. The African workers, on the other hand, trusted him. Gordon trained a number of African trade unionists. Among the most outstanding black unionists working with Gordon were Gana Makabeni, an ex-communist, Dan Koza who had been a fellow student of mine at Grace Dieu, and D. Gosani. That year, 1938, Gordon had formed a oint committee of native trade unions and was again trying to get recognition for his unions.

In person, Gordon was a small, cheerful, fresh-faced young man with a quiet, casual manner and a sunny, crooked grin that suddenly made him appear shy.

I went into the basement in Commissioner Street from where Gordon ran his unions. Part of the big room had been partitioned into little cubicles. Gordon and his assistants occupied a cubicle each. Rows of benches covered the rest of the room. And on the benches sat the black workers of the city, waiting to see their leaders and tell them of their problems. Others were unemployed and sat patiently waiting for Gordon's phone to ring. When it did, they looked up hopefully. And if Gordon came out of his little cubicle after a phone call, they grew tense.

I passed among the waiting workers and went into Gordon's cubicle. He was dealing with two men.

'Ah, Peter.'

'Hello, Max.'

'Sit down. There's material here for a story for you.'

He turned back to the two workers. I sat in a corner and listened. The phone rang. He picked it up.

'Yes? Yes. Yes. . . . I can do that. How many? Four dyers. I'll send them over straight away. Yes. You know our members are good. Oh, I say . . . Yes . . . No. . . . There is this question of a rise. You know the rest of the trade's accepted this threepenny rise? . . .

He put down the phone and sat beaming for a while. Tall Dan Koza came in.

'I say, Max. . . .'

'I've got it, Koza! The whole trade. We'll draft a new agreement.'

'Your threepence?'

'Yes! And improved conditions!'

The two trade unionists, the black and the white, laughed with the joyous gaiety of boys who had won a great prize.

'We'll get recognition yet, comrades!'

Then they went back to work.

And all through the morning, and well into the afternoon, I sat in my corner watching and listening. The picture was absorbing. Here, a new social and political consciousness was in the making. The black man of the past, the peasant, was being turned into a townsman, a modern man who was part and parcel of the highly industrialized world of the present.

On a different mental and emotional level, my friend Jonathan had gone through the same process. Christianity and the knowledge it brought had made the tribal past inadequate. So he had turned to the Christian present and future. These working men had found the tribal economy inadequate when the new taxes, the new offerings and new prices of the white men came. So they had turned to the city, which is the industrialized Christian present, for work.

Both the working man and my friend Jonathan had found the good things of this present

RESERVED FOR EUROPEANS ONLY.

We left the office late in the afternoon and walked to Gordon's flat. As we climbed the stairs to his modest home, he sighed tiredly and said:

'One day, a vigorous and strong native trade union movement will grow up. None of the government's prohibitions and restrictions and arrests will count for anything then. And that movement is going to play a key part in the political emancipation of all non-whites. So, for the present, I ask for a threepenny rise, for a recognized and proper lunch hour, and for decent and safe conditions of work. It's a small beginning, but it's a beginning. That's what was wrong with earlier efforts. They didn't know how to start.'

We entered the flat. Max went into the kitchen and prepared a bread-and-cheese-and-salad-and-coffee lunch. I cleared the table in his bed-sitting room.

'Zena rang my office and asked for you. Wants you to phone her.'

I stiffened.

'Tell you what about?'

'No. She only said it was important. Sounded funny. Anything wrong?'

'No.'

'Now you're sounding funny.'

He poked his head through the door and looked at me.

'You're a bad liar, so shut up.'

'What's her number?'

'It's on the pad.'

I found the number and rang. She answered the phone herself.

'Hello. Peter here.'

'I gave up hope of your calling. I rang Max yesterday because I didn't know how else to reach you. . . . I want to explain about yesterday morning. . . .'

'I understand, Zena.'

'Please. . . .'

'Honestly, I really do. There's no need to explain.'

'I must. . . . And you're making it terrible for me. . . .'

'But I tell you. . . .'

'Please listen to me, Peter. I must. Please. . . .'

'All right.'

'The man you saw me with yesterday morning is stinkingly rich and just as prejudiced. . . . He'd just been telling me how over-sexed all blacks are supposed to be. . . . How angry he got with white women who behaved. . . . Well, you know all about it. . . .

'Yes.'

'The point is, Peter, he can give me a job I want. A well-paying job. . . . And then, as we left the coffee-place we passed you. Do you see? . . .'

'Yes, I see.'

'He's a Jew, Peter, like me, and he's more prejudiced than any Boer I know. It makes me sick. And then I had to meet you and pass you as though I didn't know you. I've been feeling sick ever since.'

Behind me, Max put the food on the table. Then he returned to the kitchen. How could I ease the pain in this woman's voice?

'Zena, I know many more Jews who aren't prejudiced. And I know Coloureds who are prejudiced, and blacks.'

'But *I* had to pass you.'

'It could have happened to anyone.'

'But it happened to you and me. And I was the gutless one.'

'It's over. . . .'

Max brought in the coffee, sat down, and began to eat. I felt him looking at me and turned my back to him.

'Peter, please, will you come and see me. . . . Will you come to-night? Please. . . .'

'Yes.'

She gave me her address and rang off.

'A most illuminating conversation. All yesses, noes and I-sees.'

'You know, Max. This country does mess people up badly.' He looked at me in mock horror.

'How bloody profound!'

'Stop it!'

'Seriously. Are you in love?'

'No. I was. But that ended last night.'

'Zena?'

'Of course not, Jane.'

'What's the trouble with Zena? Colour?'

'Could be.'

'Thought it was about the only thing that could get her quite as upset. She has a good man, you know.' His eyes went impishly mocking.

I cheered up.

'Stop being foolish. I know and like her man. I'm seeing her tonight.'

In a flash, Gordon was in deadly earnest.

'One of those street scenes of no recognition, heh. . .

262

Don't be hard on her, Pete. She's a good woman. . . . Really, of course, real friendship between black and white is impossible in this country. You know that.'

I had not thought about it. But, thinking of it then, I realized he was right. Real friendship, friendship that had the creative force of building up wider areas of understanding, was impossible between black and white in our country. The precondition, freedom of association, did not exist. Those whites who associated openly with blacks were foredoomed to social and economic disaster. It needed courage on the level of near-martyrdom for even a communist white to associate personally, on the level of friendship, with a black.

'Max!'

'Well?'

'I want to get out of here. I want to go down to the Cape. I'm feeling choked.'

'Good idea. It'll help for a while.'

'It might help for good.'

'Don't be a bloody fool. You know, and I know, that there's no room for you here. Who wants a writer? The whites? Sure if you'll be a performing monkey and tell them how happy you are with your lot. The blacks? They've no time for reading. Most of them can't. And those who can are concerned with improving their miserable lot, not with reading poetry. You could become a propagandist but you are too much of a bloody artist for that. You'll never be satisfied with being only a propagandist. You look at too many sides of a question. And it'll get worse as you develop. So what's left? Nothing. Nobody wants you, or, at least, even those who do don't know it. Who's going to buy what you write and give you a chance to eat?'

'All right. So black writers are unwanted.'

'I'm not saying they're unwanted. The facts say that. The facts say a man must eat or he dies. The facts say there is no future for you here. You've known it in your heart all along. Keep to your plan and get out of here. You may, as a writer, exert an influence on events from afar *if* you succeed. You can do damn all from here.

'I'll write to Goolam Gool in Cape Town. He's a doctor. He's got a big house. He's been to Europe. Don't see why he shouldn't help. At least you can have proper food for a few weeks. When do you go?'

'Stop pretending you're such a tough bastard!'

'Shut up and tell me when you're going.'

'When I can raise the fare.'

'Ha! That'll mean next year!'

'I think I'll make it in a day or two.'

'I'll write to Gool to-night.'

[iii]

Zena opened the door.

'Hello, Zena.'

'Peter. . . . Oh, Peter!'

'It's all right, my dear.'

I closed the door. We went into a small, soothing, green room. A small table was laid for two.

I had been wrong about one important thing. I had not thought about the other side of the penny. The racialism of our land did not only hurt those who were not white. Basically, it hurt all of us, black and white alike. I would have to remember that, always. This deep, overflowing hurt of Zena's was the other side of the penny. And, really, her hurt was greater than mine. Whatever it had done to me, and other blacks, racialism had never driven us to this brand of shame and guilt that verged on self-hate. The sensitive, un-prejudiced whites of our land walk a dangerous emotional tight-rope. And the non-whites rarely understand it.

We ate. Then we sat in the sheltered moonlit garden with a glass of beer each. We did not talk much but we got as near understanding each other as I have known white and non-white get in our land. We both knew the corroding influence of the laws of our land could destroy this understanding if we met daily. But I was leaving. Normal friendship was not possible, so it was best that I leave on this high note of understanding. And it was good to leave the strange and harsh city in which I was born with the knowledge that the white girl beside me had suffered as grievously from the colour-bar as I had done. The knowledge was sadly, but hopefully, comforting. The other side of the penny. . . .

'When do you leave?' she said at last.

'I'll try and raise the fare to-morrow. I'm selling some of my books and my typewriter.'

'Oh. . . . Now listen to me, please. . . . I've got that damned job. The wage is stupidly high. I'll have more money than I need. I've only a few pounds now, but please take them. I'd feel so much better about the job. Please. Keep your typewriter and write that book. Please say you'll take it! Dedicate that book to me and I'll be more than paid. Yes! . . .'

'You may wait a long while.'

'I'll wait for it. You'll take the money?'

'Yes. You'll get your book.'

'I know I will!'

'You and my mother!'

'She must be a fine person.'

When I left, her man thanked me silently for Zena's new cheerfulness. I felt good. . . . The other side of the penny. . . .

II

[i]

I reached Cape Town on a dull and misty morning. The journey down had taken a week. I had started it with three pounds in my pocket. I had got off the train twice. Once in the Orange Free State, and once on the borders of the Cape Province. I had spent four days moving from one village to the next. I had built up a picture of non-European life. But for slight differences of detail, the picture had been the same as in the Transvaal. Everywhere, I had found the great majority of the people living in poverty and hunger, in sickness and misery, in shanty homes and with uncertainty and fear for companion. As I had neared the Cape border, I had noticed the numerical increase of Coloureds over Africans.

When my three pounds were spent I had gone back to the railway line and continued my journey. Now I was in Cape Town.

I was tired, and terribly hungry. I had lived on cups of tea since I had left the last village a day and a half back. I had one and threepence in my pocket but I wanted to hold on to that till I was sure of the morrow. I booked my suitcase with 'Baggage' and went to look for a telephone. Gool. Gool. Dr. Goolam Gool. I found the number and phoned. The phone kept ringing. I held it for ten minutes but no one answered. My stomach rumbled with hunger. What now? I put down the receiver, pressed the wrong button, and lost my tickey. Only a shilling left now, and I had made no con-

266

tact and knew no one. Better nurse the shilling in case Gool does not appear.

I left the phone box and went out of the station. A fine, invisible sheet of misty wet permeated the atmosphere. My clothes felt slightly damp. All about me, Coloureds moved. There were two or three of them for every black or white person I saw. I watched a bus go by. It was filled with Coloureds. They sat everywhere, upstairs and down. The racial line was not as rigid here as in the Transvaal and Free State.

I crossed the parade-ground and walked in the direction of District Six, the big Coloured slum area. I passed the old fort that the first white settlers under Jan Van Riebeck had built. Table Mountain loomed over the town, as though in everybody's backyard. Its top was completely hidden in a white cloud—the traditional table-cloth.

District Six is on a steeply sloping hill. At the foot of the hill, on the edge of the District, I saw a nondescript café: neither clean nor dirty; the kind the poorer whites frequented in Johannesburg. My stomach rumbled again. I was slightly light-headed. . . . Better have a cup of tea. . . .

I waited till I saw a Coloured man go in. I followed him. A fat, cheerful, big-bellied Greek welcomed me with a large smile. The cheapest food on the menu was sausages and mashed potatoes at one and six a portion. I wondered if I dared ask for a half-portion. The Greek came to me.

'What'll it be?'

I stared blankly.

'Oh. . . . Waiting for someone?'

He seemed friendly and interested.

'Yes. Hope my friend knows I arrive to-day.'

'New here? . . . Where you from?'

'Johannesburg.'

'Long way. Been there myself once. Business too sharp. Cuppa tea while you wait?'

'Yes, please.'

267

He went away and came back with the tea.

'Why not ring your friend?'

'I did. No answer.'

'Don't worry. He'll come back. Stay here a while. Ring later on my phone. You know nobody else?'

An idea stirred in my brain.

'May I use your phone?'

'Sure thing. I'll get your number if you like.'

'Thanks. I want *The Cape Standard*.'

'I get it for you. Mr. Manuel comes here sometimes. Fine writer, Mr. Manuel. . . . Something to eat?'

'No.'

'Ah, go on! We can settle later.'

'I don't know Mr. Manuel.'

'I send it over and we settle later. All right?'

'Thank you, Mister. . . .'

'Fatty. Everyone call me Fatty. No Mister, heh.'

'Thanks, Fatty. I'm Peter.'

'Fine. I get the *Standard* and send the food. What you have?'

'Sausages and mash.'

'Best in town!'

A haggard young woman who might have been Greek, or pale Coloured, brought me the sausages and mashed potatoes. I was half-way through the meal when Fatty called me.

'Your call. I think it's Mr. Manuel.'

I took the phone. Fatty waved his arms at someone. The voice at the other end said:

'Hello? Hello?'

'My name is Peter Abrahams. I wonder. . . .'

'What name?'

'Peter Abrahams.'

'The poet?'

'Yes.'

'*Hello*, Mr. Abrahams. I'm Manuel, assistant editor. Why didn't you let us know you were coming. I could've. . . .'

268

'I've just arrived. I'm supposed to stay with Dr. Gool but I can't get him on the phone. I wonder if. . . .'

'Where are you?'

I turned to Fatty.

'Where am I?'

'I tell him.' He took the phone from me. 'This is Fatty, Mr. Manuel. You know my café . . . Yes . . . Yes . . . I'll make him very comfortable. . . . Good-bye.' Fatty put down the receiver and beamed at me. 'Mr. Manuel comes. . . . Yes, I was right. You learn to know people in my trade. When I see you, I say to myself: That one is different. It is in the way he looks at people and things. It is in the eyes. You learn these things in my trade. . . . The girl keeps your food warm. Now she brings it. . . . Mr. Manuel says you're a big writing man, a poet.'

'I'm broke.'

'What the hell! Money ain't everything.'

I felt cheerful suddenly. The prospects were much brighter now. Manuel would soon be here, and he would help. I grinned.

'You'll never get rich if you think like that.'

'What the hell again! I do my business; I make a little; I have my friends and I eat a lot: I'm fat and happy. I laugh a lot. My name is Fatty. Money ain't everything.'

'It is when you're broke.'

'You think it is, but it never is. One day I will tell you of the Greek poet who lived in my village when I was a boy. He sang a song about the happiness that you cannot buy. . . . Here's your food. Now you eat. One day I will tell you of that poet. . . .'

I went back to my table and finished my meal. Manuel arrived soon afterwards.

He was a big, copper-brown young man whose present bulk gave warning that he would be as fat as, if not fatter than, Fatty in a few years' time. He stood a head higher than the tall Greek.

'I've heard so much about you, Mr. Abrahams. I'm glad to meet you. Welcome to Cape Town.'

'You'll never know how glad I am to meet you, Mr. Manuel!'

So this was the man who, under the pen-name 'Gemel', had turned out the finest pieces of journalism yet done by any Coloured South African.

We talked about writing, and about the only two Coloured newspapers in the country. He made notes for a profile of me. We had tea and cakes. He paid Fatty for all I had eaten. As we left, Fatty touched my arm:

'Come back, my friend. Come even when you are broke. You can always pay another time. Money ain't everything. And I want to tell you of that poet in my village.'

'I'll come back, Fatty.'

Manuel took me to a photographer. The ghastly result of that visit appeared on the front page of the *Standard* on the Saturday, two days later.

I phoned Gool at the photographer's. A suave, cultivated voice answered immediately.

'Dr. Gool?'

'Y-e-s.'

'Peter Abrahams here.'

'Ah, yes. Gordon wrote me. Where are you?'

'Near the Parade.'

'I'll pick you up in about fifteen minutes. Afraid you'll have to go with me on my afternoon rounds. Your bags?'

'One. At the station.'

'Get it and I'll meet you outside the station. 'Bye.'

I turned to Manuel.

'What's he like?'

'He's the leader of the young intellectuals and of the left-wing in the Liberation League. . . . You'll find out all about that.'

Manuel walked with me to the station, paid for my suitcase and then slipped three half-crowns into my hand.

'Sorry it's not more. You deserve more for all your stuff we've used. But they don't believe in paying writers, or me.'

When Gool's car appeared Manuel left me abruptly.

'You know where to reach me. Good luck, Peter.'

'Thanks, George.'

The man who was to be my host got out of his car. He was tall and graceful: a light brown, but more Arabic and Malay and Persian than Negro had gone into the brownness. His features were sharply defined. He seemed assuredly relaxed and aloof. He wore his fine clothes with the casualness of those born to wealth. Forget his light brown skin and he could be any successful doctor or business man anywhere in the land. I thought: This man has never gone hungry, has never known the stark misery of want and poverty. I grew worried. I had not expected this when I had accepted Max Gordon's offer. I picked up my case and moved hesitantly to him.

'A-h! Abrahams!' he beamed. 'Welcome!'

The welcome in his voice was genuine. He pushed my case into the back.

'Sorry you have to go the rounds with me. But it'll show you the poverty in which the masses live. A writer needs to know that. Cigarette?'

I took a menthol-cooled cigarette.

'I'm most grateful for your taking me in like this, Doctor. . . .'

'Say no more; our comrades are always welcome. How's Gordon doing with his unions? . . .

The car purred and moved off. A white pedestrian hurried out of the way. . . .

[ii]

I lay on my back and listened to the sound of the surf. The warm sun beat down on me. I kept my eyes closed. To the left, on a green hillock overhanging the sea, Goolam Gool

271

played with his wife. Not much more than a year earlier, his wife had been a young woman in *purdah*, behind the Moslem veil. Now, she was playing in the sun in a bathing costume. But, more important to her, she was a revolutionary Marxist, rapidly becoming tough and skilled in the vicious art of Marxian Trotskyist invective. Behind them, in a sweet green hollow, Gool's sister, Jane, and her boy friend lay quietly talking. And all about me was beauty and the eternal voice of the unending sea. Without opening my eyes, I could see the dazzling blue sky, far away—so far away that it was nothing but an eternity of space. And there, almost just behind me, almost so that I could reach up and touch its cloud-kissed top, was Table Mountain. Cape Town had no point from which it could not be seen. What a thing to have in your backyard! And everywhere, in the nooks and crannies of the sloping land, grey-white houses lay, half-hidden by luxuriant trees. On, the sun! And the sea! And the green! And the gold! Oh paradise! This must have been the Garden of Eden that announced the beginning of time! The beauty of this land brings an ache to the heart of a man. A man wants to say thank you for such beauty. A man *needs* to offer reverence and homage to the force that makes the green leaf sprout, to the force that makes his own heart ache.

Gool's sudden laughter reached me above the sound of the sea. Gool. . . . Yes. . . .

It was over two months since that day he had picked me up at the station. He had taken me to a lovely little house in a suburb of Cape Town called Wynburg, a 'mixed' area. Coloureds and whites lived side by side.

For me, the transition had been remarkable. I had gone into what was, in the Transvaal, a comfortable 'European' home. I had eaten regularly. My diet had been balanced. I had eaten, for the first time, well prepared green vegetables with each meal. The day had started with a tall glass of fruit juice. The sallowness had gone from my skin. My body had begun to fill out. My eyes had strengthened surprisingly. I had discarded the steel-framed glasses Canon Woodfield had got for me at *Grace Dieu*.

At week-ends, we had driven out to the sea. It had always been the same four people, with me as the odd one. The sun and sea and air had worked on me.

Some evenings, Goolam and I had driven into Cape Town and visited the home of his brother. The elder Gool possessed all the qualities of an Eastern epicurean. He loved good food, good music, and his home was filled with things of beauty. I met a number of white artists and non-political intellectuals at his home. I was fascinated by the grace and sophistication this man had gathered about him. I had not believed it possible for a Coloured man in our land to be as far removed from the ugly realities of life there. But then I had also believed, before coming to the Cape, that no Coloured doctor or lawyer existed in our country and that no Coloureds lived on an economic level that compared favourably with that of the majority of whites. And then I had met the Gools.

But the Gools, and the family with which they were linked by marriage, the Abdurahmans, were singular exceptions in the general scheme of Coloured poverty. With the handful of Indian merchants in Natal, and the three or four African families like the Jabavus and Sogas, they formed the very small group of wealthy non-Europeans. Indeed, of the ten million non-whites of the country, no more than a dozen families knew the meaning of economic security and genuine freedom from want.

Once, I had met Edward Roux at one of the gatherings of the elder Gool. He was tall and gaunt and there was something in his face that said the man had suffered much. I had not been able to say a word to him. For Roux had long been a hero to all non-whites who questioned the scheme of things.

Roux had sacrificed a brilliant academic career to work for African freedom. The wrath of white authority had broken on him. He had become a communist, had been involved in nearly all the labour and political struggles of the blacks. He

273

had taught blacks to read and write, had organized night schools, and worked out a basic English for black workers. Then there had been a change in the communist line. Roux had not agreed with the new line. He had been broken. His fine record had been swept aside in the campaign to 'discredit' him among the blacks. But in this the communist party had failed. They had, however, succeeded in driving him into the social and economic wilderness.

I had wanted to talk to Roux that night at the elder Gool's. But I had been driven to silence by the quiet sincerity and marks of suffering on the man. Instead, I had again marvelled unhappily at the ruthlessness with which the comrades seemed determined to herald in the New Future. I wanted to believe in that New Future that promised the equality and security of all men. If only they had room for pity, compassion, and mercy. . . . If only they allowed for the human heart. . . .

In the Transvaal I had met only one Coloured man who was interested in politics. He had been a communist. The rest, the teachers, artisans, casual labourers, were too busy trying to keep alive to bother about their Coloured lot. Or if they bothered, they did so in silence and in private. In the Cape, political interest was intense. The Coloureds had, subject to qualifications, the right to vote. Unlike their Transvaal and Free State brothers, they could affect local issues. Their attitude could even determine the results of a few parliamentary elections. The most popular Coloured leader in the Cape, Cissie Gool, estranged wife of the elder Gool, sat in the Cape Town city council. Her father, Dr. Abdurahman, had had a seat in the provincial council. Father and daughter were in opposite political camps: the father represented the conservative leadership of old Coloured families; the daughter was the champion of the miserably poor, and the communists supported her. Her organization, the National Liberation League, was thrustful and young. Coloureds from all walks of life flocked to it. At their meetings and parades they sang their anthem:

Dark folk arise
The long, long night is over;
Faint in the east,
Behold the dawn appear:
Out of your evil dream of toil and sorrow,
Arise ye dark folk
For the dawn is here!

And her father's group, the African Peoples' Organization, once the most famous Coloured body in the Cape, was little more than a name. It had never been popular with the mass of the ordinary Coloured people. But they had followed its lead at election times because there had been no other lead. Now, all were for the Liberation League.

Teachers and professional men made up the inner council of the League. And Goolam Gool was the leader of the left wing inside the council of the League. He had behind him a group of young teachers who were the most brilliant young intellectuals in the Cape, skilled in debate and public speaking. Goolam Gool's left wing was a potent minority inside the League. Gool took his line from one of the two Trotskyist factions in Cape Town. And Cissie Gool was suspect because of her relations with some communists though she was not a communist herself. So the old Trotskyist opposition harried what they regarded as the old Stalinist betrayal. This Trotsky versus Stalin scrap at times assumed more importance than the interests of the 'masses' who looked to the League for leadership.

Early in my stay with Gool I had been introduced to this 'inner struggle' for power. It had soon grown clear that Gool expected me to join on his side in the factional fight. His sister spoke with more frankness about my becoming a 'stooge' to be launched against the 'Stalinist stooges'.

Things had come to a head a little later. A Coloured cul-

275

tural body, The New Era Fellowship, had invited me to lecture on the prospects for the growth of non-European literature in South Africa. Some communists turned up for the lecture. At the end of my little piece, Gool phrased a question so that only one answer could be given. I refused to accept the premise of the question. After him, a Coloured communist, John Gomas, phrased another in like manner. I agreed with what he was leading up to. I answered the question and so said the things he, the communist, wanted me to say. Gool's face had flushed when I had not accepted the premise of his question as correct. Now I had answered the communist. The Stalinists had scored over the Trotskyists! The rights and wrongs of the question were unimportant beside this fact. Really, what I had been trying to say was unimportant except where it endorsed one line or the other. Yet both Gool and Gomas were bitterly opposed to racialism, and both were sincere and honest in their strivings for non-European emancipation. And each was all that was untruthworthy to the other. Labels had conquered the men. . . .

Again Gool's laughing voice cut into my thoughts. And the sea was about me, and the sky above. The sun had travelled far to the west. I opened my eyes and sat up. The trees were starting to cast long shadows. Night, as yet unseen, was racing on. Though Gool had said nothing after that meeting, I knew it had finally convinced him that I was no good. The break could not be long now. And I would be glad when it came.

I walked down to the roaring sea.

Gool had taken me in. He had housed me and fed me. When I had mentioned finding a job he had dismissed it laughingly, had over-ridden me with his easy charm. But a man cannot live on the kindness of another for ever. And there had been something clean and acceptable about his kindness. I wanted to tell him of my gratitude. But I knew the shadow of left-wing political intolerance would be over our parting. I did not mind that. What I minded was that this political intolerance would stop the genuine gratitude I wanted to convey to him before I left. And I wanted to say to him: Of all the Coloureds I've met you are, most completely, most naturally, free of the slightest hint of prejudice, upwards, to the whites, or downwards, to the blacks. And that is important.

But I left him, two days later, with only time for a hurried 'Thank you very much for everything.'

[iii]

On my own again, I drifted back to District Six and Fatty's. I had no money so I slept in the office of the Liberation League. I rarely spent a night there alone. There were others who had nowhere else to go. Fatty fed me one meal a day on the cuff. Finding a job seemed impossible. The few that were advertised had numberless applicants. And the whites were not inclined, in any case, to give jobs to 'a well-known Coloured agitator'. I went down to the docks. But there, too, Cape Town's Coloured 'skollies' waited in their numbers for one ship that might need one more stoker. And these men were giants beside me. No captain was likely to look at me while they were about. Oh, damn their rippling muscles! Damn the hair on their chests!

Cape Town docks were out. I would have to try another tack. I went to the Passport Office.

'What do I do to get a Passport, please.'

'Going to study?'

'No.'

'What're you going for?'

'Just going.'

The man's face hardened.

'Any money?'

'My fare.' I lied.

'Any more?'

'Fifty.'

'You'd have to leave the fifty as a deposit. How would you live?'

'What deposit?'

'In case you can't pay to get back.'

'I see.'

'Well, how would you live?'

'I have relatives,' I lied again.

'In England?'

'Yes.'

'How old are you?'

'Twenty.'

'Got a letter from your parents?'

'No.'

'They know you want a passport?'

'Yes.'

'You'll have to bring a letter from them, from your father.'

'He's dead. Will my mother do?'

'Yes . . . What's your name?'

He wrote it on a slip of paper.

I went back to the office of the League and wrote to my mother. While I awaited her reply, I typed a thesis of some three hundred foolscap pages for a Chinese student. He gave me a pound and a parcel of groceries for this job.

My mother's letter of consent arrived a few days later. Would she see me again before I went away? She wanted to look at my face just once more. England was so far away. I must take care of myself and behave myself when I got to the world of white people.

I went back to the Passport Office with the letter. I still had ten shillings left of the pound I had earned from the Chinaman. I had cleared up my account with Fatty.

The man who had spoken to me the first time, faced me. I took the letter out of my pocket.

He read the letter then looked at me. His eyes were cold and remote. They looked at a thing, not a person. I forced myself to speak though I knew it was hopeless.

'You said I needed a letter of consent.'

'I can't give you a passport.'

'But you said. . . . I have the money. I can get it and show it to you.'

'You can't have a passport!'

'But why?'

He lost his temper.

'I said you can't have a passport!'

I took my mother's letter and slunk out. No use wasting any more time there. And there was no authority I could appeal to. I went back to District Six.

This year, 1938, was the year the South African Government made its first moves to deprive the Cape Coloureds of their right to vote on the same roll as the whites. Hertzog was Prime Minister and Smuts was his deputy. In 1936 the Hertzog Government had removed the blacks of the Cape from the voters' roll. The two major organizations of the black people, The African National Congress and the All African Convention, had protested to no effect. One or two of the more far-sighted of their leaders had called on the Coloureds for joint action and had warned that the Coloured vote would go after the African vote. A miserably small handful of Coloureds, chief among them Goolam Gool, had shown interest and tried to work with the Africans. The rest had been indifferent. The Africans in the Cape had lost their right to vote on an equal footing with the whites. Now the turn of the Coloureds had come.

The National Liberation League formed a non-European United Front to fight the Hertzog Bill. The United Front wooed the African organizations. In spite of the earlier Coloured indifference, the two big African bodies gave moral support. Perhaps this was largely due to the part Gool had

279

played in their struggle. And quite a surprising number of lesser African organizations came into the United Front.

A day of national protest to wind up with a march on the Houses of Parliament was planned. I flung myself into the work of preparation.

At last the day arrived. Delegates poured into Cape Town from all corners of the Province, and from further afield. The streets of District Six seethed. The office of the Liberation League was crowded. Throughout the day a conference was held. Documents were drawn up listing the harsh disabilities under which non-Europeans lived. Delegates made fiery speeches.

That evening, a monster meeting was held on the parade-ground. The huge ground was packed with dark faces. The atmosphere of tension spread from the Coloured area to the areas of the whites. Police and soldiers were brought out in force. They were armed and made a ring about the monster meeting. Beginning with Cissie Gool, speaker after speaker stirred the vast throng to a new realization of the misery of their lives in such a fair and pleasant land.... Look at this land on which the warm sun shines. Look at the vineyards and the orchards; look at the wheat-fields and corn-fields; look at the vegetable gardens. Who work in them? You, the dark people of this land. Who get the rewards of your labours? They do, the white people. Nowhere else on earth do white people do as little real work and live as well as they do here. Do you know why? It is because they have slaves to do the work for them. You sow and they reap. You sweat and they have beautiful homes. You hunger and they are well fed. Remember your own homes; and with that in mind, remember the homes in which you work. For your one room, how many rooms have they? Remember the meals you eat. For your dry bread and coffee, what do you put on their tables? And remember the places where their children play. And your children? Why, the slum streets are good enough for your children. Turn and look at what they have. And then look at what you have. They have all and you have nothing. Is it because they work harder than you? You know the answer to that. You know who does the real work. They say you are not civilized. They say you don't understand machines. And they have a law called The Civilized Labour Policy with which they want to make sure that you never understand machines.

They say you're not educated. They tax you, pay you starvation wages, and spend so little on your education that it becomes impossible for you to educate your children. They speak of democracy. General Smuts has quite a way with words about freedom. But when you say: I am a man too, what about this democracy and freedom for me? the Smutses talk about 'parallel development' and about 'developing along your own lines'. They lie. And you know they lie. And they know they lie. They do not believe in democracy. It is all a mountain of hypocrisy. They believe in slavery. Their Pass Laws, their Colour Bar Laws, their Civilized Labour Policy, their taxation without representation, the low wages they give you, the miserable conditions in which they keep you: these are the chains of your slavery. But all their soldiers and all their police cannot keep you there for ever. Let us tell them that. Let us tell them we have had enough! Let us fight to be free! Dark folk, arise!

And a voice cried:

'TO PARLIAMENT! LET THEM KNOW HOW WE FEEL!'

The procession formed. The toughs of District Six flanked their leaders. I strayed out of the tight little group. A huge giant grabbed me and lifted me bodily. He pushed his fierce face close to mine.

'Damn you! Stay there! You're a damn leader now!'

My laughter angered him so much, I thought he was going to swipe me into kingdom come.

The procession moved. Directly in the path it took, soldiers stood, their arms at the ready. There was a moment of ugly tension, then the soldiers broke and gave way. The procession turned into Parliament Street. I heard the tinkle of glass as huge shop windows were knocked in. Most of the windows had iron grilles to protect them, but all those that did not have such protection were smashed that night. A cordon of police that barred the way was swept aside. Angry slogans rent the air:

WE WANT FREEDOM!
DECENT HOMES!
WORK!
DOWN WITH SEGREGATION!
FREEDOM!

We neared the Houses of Parliament. A body of members had come out to the steps of the House to see what was going on. They soon retreated to their chamber because of the angry, howling, crowd. One tipsy Member tried to address the crowd from behind the protection of the high iron bars. This infuriated the crowd. They flung whatever came to hand. A handful of 'skollies' tried to shin up the bars. The tipsy Member fled.

The procession swept on past Parliament. There were no white people on the streets that night. . . .

Back at the League office, I heard stories of clashes between the police and groups of marchers who had continued to roam the town at the end of the official demonstration. When most of the demonstrators had dispersed, police vans swooped through District Six arresting and attacking whoever they saw on the streets. In the early hours of the morning they raided the office of the League. With others, I got away through a window and over a roof. . . .

The monster demonstration was a seven-day sensation throughout the country. A number of Coloureds and police had been injured in the clashes. A number were in hospital. Some of the injuries had been serious. A number of arrests had been made. The papers were full of the affair. Some

282

papers revived talk about the 'Black Peril'. There were a number of court cases. Questions were asked in Parliament. The proposed Bill was postponed. For many days police vans haunted District Six. Whites did not come near it. Coloureds did not venture far from it. In the end, excitement died down. The League seemed to have exhausted itself in that one giant effort.

Though an active participant, I had been shaken by these events. I had seen a terrifying quality in mob-anger. At best, mob justice would be savagely brutal and blind. Had the whites seen the portent in that night? Could they visualize that night, expanded to take in the whole country and with all the dark folk gone blind with anger? For it seemed to me, after that night, that unless the whites did something to stay it, a day would come when non-European anger will burst throughout the land, and angry black voices and angry black hands will be raised against the white citizens of our land. And it seemed so unwise and stupid, so against their own interests, for the whites to push the blacks so hard toward that horrible and ugly day. For it *would* be a horrible and ugly day for us all. . . .

One day I found a message at the League office. My sister was in Cape Town and had looked for me. I hurried to the address she had left. I found Mag in an overcrowded little slumhouse in District Six. She fought back tears while she told me her story. Chris had lost his good job. Things were bad on the Rand. He had suggested that they tried the Cape where it might be better. They'd been here a while, nearly a month. He'd gone out looking for a job every day. But Cape Town was full of skilled Coloured cabinet-makers. This was the home of a relative of Chris's. They had a small room. She remembered her beautiful house and fine furniture and the tears finally flowed. She had eked out a living for them by hawking fruit and vegetables. She touched my hand.

'They all seem to know you here, Lee. They say you're a

leader and friends with rich people like the Gools. Can you help?'

'Have you any money, Mag?'

'A little.'

'Enough for two single tickets back?'

'I think so.'

'Well, get those two tickets. Get them and go straight back home. I don't think Chris will get a job here. There are fifty men standing by for every job there is. Sure there's less colour bar here, but there are also less chances of making a living. Life is hard for the poor here, harder than in Johannesburg in some ways. Go back, my love. Go where ma can help and advise you. If you spend your fares now, it may take you years to make it up again. And you'll be very unhappy here.'

'But can't you help with all your important friends?'

'Darling, I haven't a penny and I haven't a home.'

'But when you wrote about going to England.'

'I know: you thought I had money. Well, I haven't.'

'And nowhere to sleep. Oh Lee. . . .'

'Don't worry about me. I'm a man and alone.'

'But will you ever get away?'

'I'll get away. What about you? Will you go?'

'Chris will be difficult.'

'You insist.'

'He likes it here. But I think you're right. We'll go back and start again. I can get a job there. I don't like this place.'

'It's all right, but hard.'

'Yes! We'll go back!'

I recognized decision. Nothing Chris said would change her now.

'Better make it as soon as possible, Mag.'

'But what about you, Lee?'

'I think I'll try and get to Natal. A seaman told me it's easier from there. There are not so many Coloured giants there. The Indians are more my size.'

'Got your passport?'

'No.'

'Then how'll you get away?'

'I'll get away. But don't worry about me. Look after yourself and get home, Mag.'

We remembered old times. Soon I was cheered by Mag's laughter. She was a woman born for laughter, my plump, smooth-skinned, dimpled sister. I carried her laughter away with me. She would be all right. She would go back to where she could cope. I thought of my quiet, introspective mother. Really, my mother had performed a miracle in giving us a sense of family without the support of a husband.

A stranger stopped me on the stairs to the League office.

'Aren't you Mr. Abrahams. . . .'

'Yes.'

'My name's Roderiques. I've just been in there trying to get your people to give me some help. They say they can't. Perhaps you'll persuade them. . . .'

'What's wrong?'

'Can we talk somewhere?'

I led him to Fatty's. He cheered up as we entered the café.

'Hello, Fatty.'

'Ah! It's good to see you, my friend. I see your poem in the *Standard*. I like that one. . . . Two teas?'

'Please.'

We sat in a corner. Roderiques looked at me out of clear green eyes. He was small, with reddish kinky hair and a fair, freckled face. His mouth protruded. He smiled anxiously.

'Look, man, I've not eaten since last night. . . . I'm sorry. . . . But I'm sick with hunger. . . .'

I laughed. It had to be me.

'I haven't a penny, but I can get you a meal.'

'I'll pay you back. I swear. . . .'

Fatty brought the tea.

'Could we have something to eat, Fatty—on the cuff?'

'My cuff is good for you. . . . As usual?'

'Yes, please.'

In a little while Fatty brought two plates of sausages and mash. We ate in silence. Roderiques pushed his plate away.

'You know the Cape Flats?'

'I've seen them,' I said.

'Well, the place I'm talking about has about fifty families. The men mostly work on the docks as casual labourers. Well, they have no school and they are too poor to send their children to Cape Town. Their leader is a good man. He's a dock labourer but he's also a preacher. He asked me to start a school. It is about the school that I want help.'

'What kind of help?'

'I need everything. I've got the children and a tin church and that is all. I haven't one book, one slate, or one blackboard. Can you persuade your people to give me some money, about a hundred pounds, and some books?'

'I know they won't do it. It's a waste of time to ask them.' I made up my mind. This Roderiques did not look the pioneering kind. There was something faintly unwholesome about him. But I would go and see and give a hand. And I thought I knew where I might be able to get help. 'But I can give you another kind of help,' I said.

'Any help will do. . . . What?'

'I can come along and help you with the school for a while.'

'Of course, I'd like that. But how will we teach them?'

'Let me come with you now and see the place. To-morrow I'll get in touch with someone who'll help with books.'

'And money?'

'No. But with everything we need.'

'Really think they will?'

'I'm sure they will if they can. . . . How much is the return fare? I'll borrow it from Fatty.'

'Don't worry. I have a season.'

'I haven't.'

'Oh, you'll use my season. We'll meet at the other end.'

The sun was down when I got off the train. Roderiques waited for me.

'How'd you do it?'

He smiled with secretive cunning but gave no answer.

We walked away from the small station and soon entered the desolate world of the Cape Flats.

[iv]

Entering the Cape Flats was stepping into a new Dark Age.

The earth, here, is barren of all but the hardiest shrub. It is a dirty white, sandy earth. The sea had once been here. In its retreat it had left a white, unyielding sand, grown dirty with time. Almost, it had left a desert. And in this desert strip, on the fringe of a beautiful garden city, men had made their homes. They had taken pieces of corrugated iron and tied them together with bits of string, wire and rope. They had piled sacking on top of this. The 'fortunate' had made floors; the unfortunate had the sandy earth for floor. Into these hovels men had taken their women. . . . They had called these places home. They had lain with their women. And their women had brought forth children. And the children grew, stunted as the shrubs on this desert strip.

The people gathered in their tin church to hear the result of Roderiques's mission. A tall, haggard man with greater authority and assurance than the rest, but with the same parched skin and bloodshot eyes, moved among them as we entered. I found it hard to believe that these dried-up creatures were human, till I looked into their eyes and heard their voices. But they were such humans as I had not seen in all my wanderings through the land!

The preacher came to us. The people stood up. The oil lamp cast shadows that made phantom forms of them.

'This is Mr. Abrahams from the League.' Roderiques's voice was hushed and sanctimonious. Automatically he

287

pressed his palms together as a Jesuit brother might do in chapel.

The old man took my hand. He spoke normally:

'I have heard your name, Mr. Abrahams. You are one of our leaders. It is a great honour. . . .'

Roderiques cut in on the quiet voice of authority.

'They would not help. Then I met Mr. Abrahams and. . . .'

'Report it to all of us, Mr. Roderiques. That is what we are all here for.'

Roderiques seemed put out but nodded. He moved slowly, measuredly, to the preacher's platform. He went on one knee in front of the little cross, crossed himself, and then stood up. He went through an elaborate little ceremony of bowing and crossing himself, his lips moving all the while. At last it was over. He mounted the platform. He raised his hands as in the act of benediction. An odd fellow, I thought. I turned my eyes to the old preacher at my side. He had read my thought and nodded.

Roderiques spoke in a 'special' voice, as though preaching a sermon. When he had done, he held out his hand to me.

'Mr. Abrahams will tell you his plan to help.'

I looked at the preacher. He nodded. I said:

'I haven't much of a plan. I want to find out what you need, and to-morrow I'll go into Cape Town to get it. I can't get money but I think I can get books and slates and all the other things a school needs. And I should like to stay here for a while and help with the school. That is all.'

The preacher said:

'I speak for all my people when I say we are honoured to have you here, Mr. Abrahams. We will never be able to repay you but God, in His mercy will. I read the paper from Cape Town and I have preached to my people about you and those like you. Now God has sent you here. Let us be thankful. . . .'

He prayed. Then the gathering ended. We stood at the door of the little church. People filed out, said hushed 'good nights' and walked away into the darkness. When all but the three of us had gone, the preacher took my arm.

'I will take Mr. Abrahams with me, Mr. Roderiques. Sister Adams has food for you but not enough for two.'

'I will come with you,' Roderiques said.

'There is no need for it. And do not worry. You are head of the school and Mr. Abrahams knows it. I will return him to you.'

The old man guided me past the houses and over a number of fine sand-hills. Suddenly, the moon burst through the clouds. It lightened the dark earth a little. We walked in silence till we neared another cluster of houses.

'There is only a little soup and dry bread, my son. But you have known hunger so there is no need to apologize.'

He led me into his home. It was a little larger than most of the others I had seen. A deal of effort had gone into making it a home. A young woman, the preacher's daughter, stood over the soup in the kitchen that was also the dining-room, and a bedroom.

'We have a guest, my child.'

The girl could not have been my age, but already her face was lined, and there were hollows under her eyes. She put potato soup and bread in front of us. The preacher said grace; then we ate.

Afterwards, he sat back, took out his pipe and began the long preparation for a pleasant smoke. I looked about the room. It was as dried and parched and barren as all this place, as the people of this place. Everything had faded to a dirty grey. And there were sand grains everywhere. A stove in one corner, a bed in another, a home-made kitchen cupboard for crocks, a table, and two benches, were all the furniture of the room. Pictures from magazines of another world were pasted on the wall.

Two sandy grey children, a boy and a girl, came in noisily. The elder girl hushed them and gave them their soup.

'My grandchildren,' the old man said. 'Their mother's

289

somewhere in Cape Town. Some of my children are bad, and they haven't a mother to control them. . . .' He lit his pipe. 'Now you want to know about me, Mr Abrahams. . . .'

'No, I don't. Please.'

His face creased in a gentle smile.

'Then I will tell you about Mr. Roderiques. . . . He's a Roman—or perhaps I should say he was. But he still has the habits of a Roman. No, that is not fair to the Romans. But let us come to the matter. He was trained in a Roman school for priests when I first met him. It was at the docks. . . . You know I'm just an ordinary labourer there?'

'I know.'

'Well, he was on a journey in his long black dress. I think it was to the Portuguese land. He saw me there and he spoke to me. I don't know why, but he spoke to me. He said he was going to be one of those people who worked among heathens. There's a word for them.'

'Missionaries.'

'I thought he did not look strong. Not just in body: I mean the will. I know the Romans, especially the leaders, are not foolish. So I wondered how they had made such a mistake as to think this young man could win souls. But I said to him, half in play, "I am the preacher of my people. But although we are not heathens, and although we are not Romans, we would welcome some of you to teach us and our children to read and write." He tried to make me a Roman on the spot! Said that was the only true church. He said I would not have to work as a labourer if I were a Roman preacher. I told him we were all children of the same God if we were Christians. It did not matter whether we were Romans or not. "You tell them to send us teachers," I said. "And if they make our children Romans, I will not object, as long as they teach them." I believe that knowledge is the key to a better life, my son. Anyhow, his boat came. I told him where we lived. He put it in a piece of paper and then he went. I did not expect to see the young man again.

'But he turned up here a little while ago, without his Roman dress. He was hungry and homeless. So I fed him. He told me something had gone wrong and he had to leave the Roman school. He said he had no people. He said he would start a school here if we would feed him and give him shelter. I knew there had to be good reason for the Romans to turn a person out. But I also knew he was a weak young man, too weak to do any real evil. I did not think he could harm my people if a few of us kept watch. And our need for a school is great. . . . That is the story of Mr. Roderiques. It is right that you should know it. You have understanding, my son. Do you think he can harm our children? I don't.'

'I don't think so either, Father.'

'Then you will still help us?'

'All I can.'

'If you have trouble. . . .'

'Please don't worry. . . . Tell me though, are the Cape Flats like this everywhere?'

'Not everywhere. There are places that are better, much better, further along the coast. Some are as good as District Six: some better.

'Any worse than this?'

An odd smile crossed his face without touching his eyes.

'I've seen two places worse than this. Can you believe it? Man is so strong, he can live where nothing else can live. It makes you wonder. . . .'

When I got back Roderiques had gone to bed. He had a bit of candle stuck to the wall above his head. By its light, he read Judge Rutherford.

'Yours is the other room,' he said. 'Here.'

I took and lit the bit of candle he offered me. I went into the next room. As with Roderiques's room, there was nothing except a small iron bed in a corner. Half the room had wood flooring. I heated the wall and stuck my candle against it as Roderiques had done.

'Good meal?' Roderiques called.

'Bread and soup.'

I examined the bed. Two blankets covered a much-stained mattress. There was no pillow or sheets.

'What did you talk about?'

'Oh, nothing much. Politics mostly.'

I took off my jacket, folded it, and propped it up as a pillow. I sat on the bed. It creaked dangerously. A gust of wind came in through the nearest crack in the wall. It blew out the candle. I found matches and relit it.

'What d'you think of him?'

'I like him.'

'You want to be careful. He's not a fool. These people are cunning. Don't tell them too much about yourself.'

'He didn't try to pry.'

I took off my shoes.

'Talk about me?'

'Only said how glad they are to have you here.'

Should I take off my pants? No, better not. Mattress not too clean. I took off my shoes but stayed in my socks. I got under the blankets. The bed shivered and groaned as though it would collapse.

'I sometimes wonder if they are grateful. . . . Want anything to read?'

'No thanks. Good night.'

'Thought you might like to talk. . . .'

'I'm rather tired.'

'All right. Good night.'

I blew out the candle. The many cracks and holes in the ceiling and walls showed up clearly. In the corner immediately above my bed was a round hole, as large as the head of a man. I looked through it and saw part of the sky and a cluster of stars.

'Roderiques. . . .'

'Yes?'

'Where are the lavatories here?'

'You walk away from the houses and dig a hole. But some of the people have built some.'

'Thanks.'

In the morning, Roderiques took me to the home of Sister Adams. He explained that she would give us our meals and look after our laundry. The Adams family had the best house and were the most 'well-to-do' in the community. The husband had a job in a factory near Cape Town and owned a bicycle.

Husband and wife received us cheerfully. Their three young children gaped shyly at me. Mother and father could not be much over thirty, and they, and their children, though patched and parched, looked better clothed and fed than the rest of their neighbours.

Sister Adams fed us bread fried in dripping and black coffee. She fussed about us while we ate.

After breakfast we walked to the little church where a growing crowd of youngsters awaited us.

'There are more than I've had before,' Roderiques said.

'The preacher said he was sending some from nearby houses.'

'He should have told *me*.'

'My fault. He asked me to tell you last night. I forgot. If you lend me your season I'll go into Cape Town this morning.'

He gave me the ticket.

'Sure you'll get the things?'

'Yes. I think so.'

'We need some money, you know.'

'Can't do anything about that.'

'Why not try. . . .'

I thought it best to say nothing.

'In you go!' Roderiques cried.

The skinny, dried-up, ragged mass of children fought and scuffled their way into the little church.

Roderiques went through his elaborate little ceremony in front of the cross. Then he made the children kneel while he prayed in Latin. I had the feeling of looking on at a queerly distorted ritual, robbed of all substance. There was something ugly about this. It was a mockery of the Christian ceremony of prayer. When he began a little sermon, my mind revolted. I repressed an urge to stop him, and went out.

In Cape Town, I went to the office of the *Guardian*. The *Guardian* was South Africa's only 'popular' socialist paper. All the other papers of the left were 'official' organs of factions and parties. The *Guardian* was the only national weekly of the left that attempted an objective statement of the South African situation. But even it rarely saw anything good in any 'line' other than the communist party 'line'.

I had met Betty Radford who edited the *Guardian*. She and a young woman building up Coloured trade unions, Ray Alexander, had impressed me as the most human of the C.P. wing of the South African left. Ray Alexander was an avowed communist. Betty Radford claimed only to be a socialist.

I went into Betty Radford's office and told her about the school.

'How many children?' she asked.

'About fifty.'

'I think I can get what you want by this afternoon.'

I had expected such an answer. I had slowly worked my way to a view of the South African left. Whatever labels they had, there were two types of left-wingers: those who were hell-bent on revolution for its own sake and were, really, indifferent to the welfare of individuals or groups of people; and the others, the humanists, who saw an ugly world and wanted to make it better. And Betty Radford had struck me as belonging to the humanist left.

I told her how to get to the little village then went back.

Betty Radford drove into the little place in the late afternoon. All the women, and some of the men had watched me teach their children the game of rounders. They gathered

294

about the small car and watched the finely dressed white woman get out. They made way for me and were silent while I welcomed my white friend.

'You've found a place for work all right,' Betty said.

The back of her car was stacked with school material. The children formed relay teams and carried the books, pencils, slates, chalks, rulers and paper into the church. We stacked the material at the back. Roderiques tugged at my sleeve.

'Introduce us.'

I introduced him. He whispered:

'Tell her we need money.'

I shook my head. As the pile in the back of the car grew less, I notice Roderiques steeling himself to mention money. I began a long and foolish speech of thanks that lasted till Betty Radford drove away.

Work began in earnest next morning. Once Roderiques felt assured that I had no desire to usurp his position as head of the school we got along well. I managed, in time, to make him shorten his morning services. On the few occasions when we had differences the old preacher mediated with great skill and wisdom.

The children learned eagerly. A month after Betty Radford had brought the material, we started a night-school for the grown-ups.

Development was uneven, and we were soon faced with the problem of classes. Also, people started sending children from neighbouring villages. Roderiques took the whole school for the morning prayers and Bible lesson. Then we split them into three classes: beginners, those who knew their alphabet and were starting to build words, and those who had begun to put one word behind another and make sentences with sense. I coped with the beginners, Roderiques with those who had begun to build words; and we shared the lessons for the more advanced. We split the night-school into two classes.

I was soon so immersed in the work of teaching that I forgot my plans to leave the country.

So the months passed. Autumn gave way to winter. Life on the Flats became terrible. We had not enough to eat and we were always cold. I put on all the clothes I had to go to bed. Still, I lay shivering for the best part of the night. When the winter was at its worse Roderiques pulled up half the flooring of his room and burned it. For a few weeks we had a fire every night. Then the wood ran out. We now both only had flooring where our beds stood. The community brought us bits of fuel whenever they could. But the majority of them were in a worse plight than we were. Children came to school so cold that they could not grip their pencils. They were too listless and hungry to exercise some warmth into their bodies. In common with the majority of the villagers, I began to cough.

A man arrived from Namaqualand that winter. He came among us and made our misery seem paradise. He was a walking skeleton. He had walked all the way from Southwest Africa to this place to seek for help. He stood in our little church and told us calmly that his people were dying of starvation, that they had eaten all the snakes and lizards they could find and that there were now none left to dig up and eat. And my miserable community managed to collect a few shillings together for the starving people of Namaqualand. Our old preacher took him preaching through the Flats to try to raise help. Roderiques went with them. For some days I managed the school alone. The memory of the man from Namaqualand and his quiet statement about death and starvation kept me awake for two nights. On the third night I slipped paper into my battered typewriter and wrote. I called what I had written 'Cape Flats Limited'. Then I went to sleep.

On the day the preacher and Roderiques returned I went into Cape Town with the piece I had written. I took it to Betty Radford.

She looked at my face and exclaimed:

'Good heavens! You're sick!'

'Will you please read this?'

'Here,' she wrote on a piece of paper. 'Go and see my husband. Now.'

'Will you please read that thing.'

'If you'll go and see my husband now.'

'All right.'

'I'll phone him. Go straight there. Have you the bus fare?'

'No.'

'Here.' She gave me a ten-shilling note. 'Now you go over.'

I read the address on the piece of paper then went to the door.

'You will read it?'

'Yes. Go on.'

Her husband's surgery was in the white section. I could not just walk into the waiting-room and sit down among his white patients, if there were any. Best knock on the door and see. I knocked. A young woman opened the door.

'Mr. Abrahams?'

'Yes.'

'The doctor's waiting for you.'

A big, cheerful man welcomed me. The young woman left us. He gave me a cigarette and made me feel at ease.

'Betty's worried about your health, and I can see why. I think it would be a good idea to give you a thorough examination.'

I stripped to the waist and stretched out on the table. He examined me carefully.

'Tell me about the school. Do you eat enough?'

While he worked he plied me with questions. At last the examination was over.

'Now I'll check your blood.'

'I've not messed about with women.'

'Copulation isn't the only way you get these things. . . .

When did you last have a woman? Don't be shy. I'm a doctor.'

'In Johannesburg. Nearly a year ago.'

'Remember that's not the only way you get these things.'

'How else?'

'You get some of these things by contact: beds, food, filth, and not having enough of things. We don't know all the causes yet. One more thing. I want you to go over to a friend of mine. He'll X-ray your lungs. When can you go?'

'Now.'

He phoned.

'Yes. He's free. Go over now. Here's the address. Come back here in three days' time.'

From the X-ray place I went back to the Cape Flats.

I returned to the doctor's surgery three days later. The news was good. My lungs were all right. My blood was negative. The doctor said:

'Medically you're all right. But you need proper food. That place isn't doing you any good. Can't you teach in some more healthy place?'

'I'm leaving it,' I said. 'I only helped them to start.'

'Perhaps that would be best. . . . Oh, Betty's printing your article. Best thing you've done. Better than your poetry. It might start something.'

Back on the Flats, I went to the home of the old preacher that night. Now that I had decided to leave I might as well go the next morning. I would try and work my way to Durban.

'I've come to tell you that I'm leaving in the morning.'

'Leaving? . . . For good?'

'Yes.'

We sat in silence for a long time. The young woman gave us coffee. At last the old man sighed and looked at me.

'I knew you would go some day, but not so suddenly. I thought we would have a little time. I thought it might be good to send you away with something to show our gratitude. Why do you go so suddenly?'

'My doctor advised it. My health isn't too good.'

'Yes. . . . I've noticed your coughing. Perhaps it is better that you go. You might do more elsewhere.'

'I'm sorry, Father.'

'So am I, my son. You've become like a real son to me. And how can I tell you of the thanks in my heart?'

'There is no need.'

'There is always need to say thank you. It is good for the sayer. . . . Where will you go, my son?'

'I don't know. . . . I'll try and work my way to Durban and get on a ship there.'

'And then?'

'I want to get to England.'

'And what will you do there?'

'I want to write books and tell them about life in this country.'

'Will you tell them about us? About this little place?'

'Yes, Father. I will try to tell everything; the bad as well as the good.'

The old man got up and went into the other room. He came back with a black gabardine overcoat. It had a rubber lining, and over that, a silk lining.

'I have noticed how thin your overcoat is. It keeps out the rain but there's no warmth in it. They say winter is cold in England. Take this and I'll take yours.'

'But I can't, Father!'

'You'll do as I say, young man! . . . I want you to wear it and to remember me by it. Remember that an old man is always praying for you. And tell them about us. They must be good people over there. Tell them about us.'

'I will, Father.'

'Remember the story you made up for the children at Christmas? Well, the children, and many of us grown-ups still remember it. If you make stories like that for the white people of England, they will listen and you can tell them about us.'

'I will try.'

'Come now, my son. We will go to the church. All our people will want to pray for you and wish you well on your journey. Put on your new coat.'

We walked across the sand to the little church. The tinny bell rang out. The people came from their shacks to wish me well on my journey. Strange Roderiques wept his farewell to me.

Early next morning, I walked across the sandy earth to the station for the last time. And the children watched me go. I would have to make up for leaving *them*.

III

I got off the train at the furthest point to which my ticket allowed me to travel. It was about a hundred miles north of Cape Town. I gave up my ticket and went out of the station. I walked through the little dorp till I struck the main high-way to the north. This was part of Rhodes's dream of linking the Cape with Cairo. I rested for a while, then picked up my case and set off for the north.

I did not bother to wave at the shining cars that shot by. Their occupants were white.

I grew hot and took off my three-ply overcoat. About me, the land stretched, vast and unending. I looked back. Far behind, in a mist of distance, Table Mountain towered over the city I could not now see. I was nowhere, and a long, long way from everywhere. Better keep moving, brother; the road is long; better keep moving, brother. A weak, red-rimmed sun kept pace with me, or so it seemed.

I had walked for what seemed hours when a lorry slowed down near me. A Coloured man was driving.

'Hello, there!' he called.

'Hello!'

'Which way?'

'Making for Natal.'

'Jesus! . . . I turn off about ten miles up. Get in.'

I flung my case on the back and got in beside him. The lorry sped along.

'Hell of a trip to make,' the man said.

'Yes. Must get there though. And they say this is the best way.'

'Yes. Long way round but the best. No lifts on the coast roads.'

He dropped me off ten miles further along the road and veered off to a wine-growing farm far off the road. I stuffed the two bunches of carrots he had given me into my case.

Towards sunset I reached a little siding. I sought out the Coloured section and knocked on the first door I came to. Yes, they would be glad to put me up for the night. Was half a crown too much? No, not while I had the money. Well, really, things hadn't been too bad of late and I might need the half a crown later if my journey was very long. A member of their family might be on the road one day. . . . Was I going far? Durban. An awful long way off, wasn't it? It might be an idea to try and get to a big railway station where Coloured stewards might help. We poor had to stick together in these times.

I left with a little parcel of sandwiches the next morning.

Thus, I made my long journey through the land: up to the northern borders of the Cape Province; into the Free State, and then down into Natal. Sometimes I got lifts. Sometimes only cars with whites in them were on the roads. Occasionally I had to spend a night in the open. But mostly the dark people fed me and housed me. Often, they provided me with a little food to carry me on to the next stage of the journey. They rarely asked for money. On one farm a kindly old Boer grandma spread a feast before me in her kitchen while her farmer son argued politics and race with me. He was a Stellenbosch University man.

In another place I came across a tense situation. The ugly problem of 'miscegenation' had reared its head. A Coloured boy and a white girl were or had been in love. It had been discovered. The Coloured community said the whites were now trying to make the girl say the boy had raped her. They wondered how long she would hold out. The boy? He had gone into hiding. I sensed that they knew where the boy was. But I was a stranger, and they would not tell me.

I left the valley of tension and moved down into the beautiful Natal grassland. Here, my scanty knowledge of Zulu stood me in good stead as I exchanged Coloured hospitality for African hospitality.

I paused at villages where life seemed not to have changed since before the coming of the whites. I stopped at others where the men had gone off to the cities and only the women and children and old men were there. Sometimes I arrived during a feast of drinking and talking and much laughter. And always, they welcomed the stranger and shared what they had with him. It was only the better-off among both Coloured and African who occasionally turned me away.

And so I reached Durban on a scorching day in June, 1939.

[ii]

I found a small room with an Indian family. I paid them ten shillings for the first week. That left me with only coppers in my pocket. But I had arrived. The journey had taken me nearly three months, but I had arrived.

I still had some bread in my case. It had gone hard. But that could be remedied with milk. I went across the street and got a pint of milk. The Indian woman lent me a bowl. I soaked the bread then ate. Then I went to bed. I slept all through that day, all through that night, and all through the next day. I got up on the second night. I had some more bread with milk gone sour, then I went out to see Durban.

Just as Cape Town was essentially a Coloured town, so Durban was essentially an Indian town. In place of Coloured quarters like District Six and the Cape Flats, there were Indian quarters, equally slummy and equally mean. For Natal was the home of just over a quarter of a million Indians, the descendants of those who had been brought from India as indentured labour in the early history of the country. They had been brought to work on the sugar plantations in the days before the Africans had been reduced to their present acceptance of white rule. And in time, the Indians had become as much a part of the country as the Africans or Coloureds or whites. Like all the others, their sweat and strength had gone into the making of this beautiful dark land.

I knew no one in Durban, but the Indians also had their nationalist movement and I was familiar with the efforts of the younger men, so I made my way to their headquarters, the Liberal Study Group. They had been in contact with the United Front in the Cape.

They welcomed me as one of their own. Soon, I was as involved in their efforts as I had been in those of the United Front in the Cape. The Liberal Study Group published a stencilled monthly bulletin. I was soon up to my neck in editorial work on this. For this work the study group helped me with my rent.

But I had not forgotten my main purpose in coming to Durban. I visited the docks often and built up an extensive system of contacts.

Thus June and July passed. The meetings of the Liberal Study Group aroused the interests of the police. One day in August I was called down to the police station. The white sergeant who had attended many of our meetings questioned me.

'Now Abrahams, you're no fool. I don't know why you mess around with these Coolies. None of your other Coloureds do.'

'They're South Africans just like you and me, sergeant.'

'Don't be silly, Abrahams. Do you see any Coloured riding about in big cars like they do?'

'I've also seen the poor among them. And you have the same number of Coloureds with cars in the Cape. Anyway, what do you want?'

'You're a bright fellow, Abrahams. We can make things right for you.'

'What do you want to know?'

'Who's behind this?'

'Behind what?'

'These meetings and this Bulletin of yours. You're a lot of youngsters, you can't think this up by yourselves. Who's behind it?'

'We're doing this by ourselves.'

'You're not! There are some clever white communists who write your articles. Who's "Jim Fish"?'

Even if it meant going to jail, I could not help laughing.

'Well . . .?'

'I am, sergeant. I wrote that article about passes.'

'Who told you about it? You never carried one.'

'I was born here, sergeant. I know what goes on in this land.'

'I don't understand you, Abrahams. Here you are, the country's given you a good education. You could make something good out of it for yourself. Instead you mess around with these foreign communists. What's wrong with you?'

'I don't think there's anything wrong.'

'You're against your own country. Are you a communist?'

'It so happens that I'm not, but I don't see that it's any of your business whether I am or not. Your business is to see that I don't break the law, not to examine my thoughts.'

'This is your last chance, Abrahams. Why did you write that thing about the passes. Who told you to do it?'

'I wrote it because it is the truth. No one can tell me what to write, not you or the communists.'

'Where do you think all this will get you?'

'Do you know the meaning of the word freedom, sergeant?'

'I tried to be friendly. I've warned you. You've had your chance. You may go.'

In September of that year, war broke on the world. The government and country were thrown into a crisis. Pirow, the Union Minister of Defence, had just returned from Germany where he had been an honoured guest of Hitler's. Smuts and Hertzog split. The Prime Minister was for neutrality and showed his pro-Hitler sympathies. Smuts, the Deputy Prime Minister, was for war on the side of Britain and France. The split between the two leaders divided the whites of the country into two camps.

One day, in the period of uneasy crisis, I heard there was a ship needing a whole crew. I rushed down to the docks. There was a queue at the shipping office. I joined it behind a hulking Coloured man.

The clerk glanced at the man then made him sign the articles. It was my turn. The clerk looked me over and snorted.

'And what do you think *you* can do?'

He passed on to the next person. The Coloured giant bent over me and whispered:

'Any money?'

'Two pounds,' I whispered.

'Not enough.'

'How much do you want?'

'Five.'

'And can you get me on for that?'

'Yes.'

'I'll give you the rest to-morrow morning.'

'All right. Give me the two. But I'll break your neck if you don't give me the rest.'

'Don't worry. You'll get it.'

'I'm not worrying. It's your neck.'

I didn't like the sound of this. This brute *could* break my neck with no effort. I gave him the two pounds. The clerk moved back up the line. The giant said:

'Aren't you going to sign my buddy, sir? He's the best trimmer I ever shipped with. Had a lay-off for a while but

306

he's damn good. Don't be fooled by his size, sir. You know how these Bushman types are.'

I expanded my chest as far as it would go. I held my breath till I heard drumming in my ears.

'All right,' the clerk said doubtfully. 'Sign here and get your police clearance.'

I signed and sighed. The moment had arrived. This was the turning point. Dear God, the moment had arrived!

We left the shipping office. The giant brute called:

'Three pounds to-morrow, or God help you!'

I hurried to the police. I thought: God help me in any case with that unholy-looking crew.

At the police station I explained my business.

'Name?' the policeman said without looking up.

'Peter Abrahams.'

The man stopped writing. He raised his head and stared at me. My heart began to pound, my body to tremble. He picked up the phone and called the political sergeant. Then he turned to me.

'Know where the sergeant's office is?'

'Yes.'

'He wants to see you.'

I leaned against a wall for a long time outside. When I felt a little more under control, I went to the sergeant's office.

'What's this about your getting on a ship, Abrahams?'

'I want a change, sergeant.'

'But why on a ship?'

'I don't know. I just thought a change would be good and I'll be earning my keep.'

'You're an odd one. Wish I knew what went on in that brown head of yours.'

I thought it best to remain silent. The sergeant said:

'Well, I can't decide this by myself. Wait here while I go and see my chief.'

I sat in the office for a long while. At last he came back.

'We are going to let you go, Abrahams. The chief thinks it

will be better to have one less of you on our hands. Here, take this back to the officer and he'll give you your clearance. Good fishing, Abrahams.'

'Thank you, sergeant!'

I got my clearance and went out. I felt drained of all strength so I sat for a long time on a bench in the yard of the charge office. It was true! I was free at last, free to go. And down there, at the docks, a ship was waiting for me. I was free!

[iii]

I raised the last few shillings that made up the three pounds late that night. My neck was now safe. I was too worked up and too tired to feel hungry or be able to eat. I went to the office of the Study Group. It was locked up. That meant I had nowhere to sleep. I had given up my room a long time ago. I met an African friend and told him I needed a bed.

'What's the matter with you, man? There are compounds. You can hire a bed for fourpence. Come with me.'

He took me to a compound. It was like going to prison. High walls shut the place in. Black policemen guarded the entrance. My friend paid eight pence at the little office. In exchange, he received two blue slips. These entitled us to beds for the night. An old black man led us through a maze of connected rooms. Each room was a dormitory filled with beds. They went in three tiers. There were enough beds to sleep well over a thousand men. Many of the men had already come in. Some lay on their beds. Others sat talking to their neighbours. Yet others sat doing little jobs on their clothes. Here and there, men chewed pencils and frowned with painful concentration as they tried to let those at home know about this place. The warm, sickly smell of many bodies in a confined space, hung over the rooms.

This was home from home for the peasant who had been driven to the city in search of money to pay his taxes: here the young boys ended who had come to the city in search of the wondrous things of the white man: here, on these beds, many black dreams were played out. This was the home of the rickshaw-boy and the casual labourer. A man has been uprooted and this took the place of his tribal home and the customs of his village. Here he spent long weeks or months or years of his life.

At last we reached the room where we had to sleep. The old man showed us two beds then went off. My friend was an educated man, a teacher, and I sensed his embarrassment at having taken me to this place. So I said:

'This will be heaven compared to some of the nights I spent on the road.'

But I was wrong. The bed came alive as soon as I got into it. Creatures attacked my body with a brazen boldness that left me helpless. I turned back the blankets to see. They marched like armies: armies of lice, armies of bugs.

Nearby, an old rickshaw-boy lay coughing his lungs out. His drawn face, glistening with sweat, and the bloody spittle about his lips told their story well. He could not last long. Perhaps to-night, or to-morrow night, or the night after.

But really, the bed was no good. I knew now that I could not sleep. I was tired but I would not sleep this night. This was the last night.

I got up. I went to my friend's bed.

'The animals?' he asked.

'No. I just can't sleep. I'm leaving in the morning.'

'Back north?'

'No. On a ship. Out of this country. To England. I'm going down to the beach now.'

' 'Bye, old man. Don't forget us.'

'I won't.'

I left the compound. I walked through the empty streets of the moon-kissed town, down to the sea.

The big yellow moon hung low over the sea. The sea, though calm, seemed raised in an effort to meet the moon. I stripped and walked into the cool water. I kept walking till the water rose to my chest, my armpits, shoulders, my neck, my chin. Then I flung myself forward and kicked out. I looked back. The beach was a long way off. I swam on. My arms began to ache. They grew sluggish. Turn back! Turn back! I swung about desperately. I was terribly tired. Easy does it. Easy does it. I went down once. Don't lose your head. Don't fight. Keep your head and live. Easy does it.

At last, my toes touched earth. Joy shot through me. I crawled on to dry earth and flopped down. After a long while, I rolled on to my back and looked up at the stars. They were very bright and very far away.

With my eyes on the stars, I took stock and searched for the meaning of life in terms of the life I had known in this land for nearly twenty-one years.

All my life had been dominated by a sign, often invisible but no less real for that, which said:

RESERVED FOR EUROPEANS ONLY.

Because of that sign I had been born into the filth and squalor of the slums and had spent nearly all my childhood and youth there; because of it a whole generation, many generations, had been born, had grown up and died amid the filth and squalor of the slums. I had the marks of rickets on my body; but I was only one of many, not unique. I had had to go to work before I went to school. Many had never gone to school. Free compulsory education was 'Reserved for Europeans only'. All that was finest and best in life was 'Reserved for Europeans only'. The world, to-day, belonged to the 'Europeans'.

And in my contacts with them, the Europeans had made it clear that they were the overlords, that the earth and all its wealth belonged to them. They had spoken the language of physical strength, the language of force. And I had submitted to their superior strength. But submission can be a subtle thing. A man can submit to-day in order to resist to-morrow.

My submission had been such. And because I had not been free to show my real feeling, to voice my true thoughts, my submission had bred bitterness and anger. And there were nearly ten million others who had submitted with equal anger and bitterness. One day, the whites would have to reckon with these people. One day their sons and daughters would have to face the wrath of these embittered people. The two million whites cannot for ever be overlords of the ten million nonwhites. One day they may have to submit to the same judgement of force they have invoked in their dealings with us. . . .

For me, personally, life in South Africa had come to an end. I had been lucky in some of the whites I had met. Meeting them had made a straight 'all-blacks-are-good-all-whites-are-bad' attitude impossible. But I had reached a point where the gestures of even my friends among the whites were suspect, so I had to go or be for ever lost. I needed, not friends, not gestures, but my manhood. And the need was desperate.

Perhaps life had a meaning that transcended race and colour. If it had, I could not find it in South Africa. Also, there was the need to write, to tell freedom, and for this I needed to be personally free. . . .

When the first rays of the morning sun touched the sky in the east I got up and dressed. The long night was over. This was the moment of departure. I felt in my pocket. The three pounds were still there.

I walked briskly down to the docks. And all my dreams walked with me.